Mentoring for Social Inclusion

D0972999

What does mentoring really mean? What can be achieved through mentor relationships?

This timely book examines one of the fastest growing social movements of our time. As millions of people worldwide are drawn into the mentoring phenomenon, the need for this authoritative text becomes increasingly evident. It capably traces the history of mentoring, unravelling the many myths that surround it, with a combination of intellectual rigour, insight and lucid discussion.

The author draws upon detailed case studies, providing a unique and vivid account of mentoring from the perspective of the participants. These eye-opening narratives reveal the complex power dynamics of the mentor relationship, giving the reader the chance to:

- contextualize mentoring against the background of policy-driven schemes and social inequalities;
- look beyond popular myths of the self-sacrificing and devoted mentor, and understand the emotional cost of mentoring;
- appreciate young people's view of mentor relationships;
- recognize the benefits and the counterproductive outcomes mentoring can produce;
- reflect on different models of mentoring, and consider policies to support good practice.

The strength of this book lies in the author's ability to present complex material in a highly readable form. It offers a radical new theoretical analysis of mentoring, based on award-winning research, arguing that mentoring cannot be separated from the wider power relations that surround those involved. For anyone with a professional commitment or link to mentoring, including managers, practitioners and policy-makers, this is an essential, incomparable read.

Helen Colley is Senior Research Fellow at the Lifelong Learning Institute, University of Leeds, and a Fellow of the National Institute for Careers Education and Counselling.

Mentoring for Social Inclusion

A critical approach to nurturing mentor relationships

Helen Colley

 RoutledgeFalmer
Taylor & Francis Group

LONDON AND NEW YORK

First published 2003
by RoutledgeFalmer
11 New Fetter Lane, London EC4P 4EE

Simultaneously published in the USA and Canada
by RoutledgeFalmer
29 West 35th Street, New York, NY 10001

RoutledgeFalmer is an imprint of the Taylor & Francis Group

© 2003 Helen Colley

Typeset in Baskerville by
Keystroke, Jacaranda Lodge, Wolverhampton
Printed and bound in Great Britain by
Biddles Ltd, Guildford and King's Lynn

Cover design originated by Tara Cleveland Web Design and
Consulting, www.taracleveland.com

British Library Cataloguing in Publication Data
A catalogue record for this book is available from the British Library

Library of Congress Cataloging in Publication Data
A catalog entry for this book has been requested

ISBN 0–415–31110–1 (pbk)
       0–415–31109–8 (hbk)

**To the memory of
Mike Watts**

Contents

Tables

Preface

I first became interested in mentoring when I was working as a careers adviser in a comprehensive school at the centre of a very deprived housing estate in Salford. The school ran a scheme in conjunction with the local Business–Education Partnership to provide mentors from industry to pupils in their final year. I was able to observe some of these relationships as they developed, and a number of pupils brought their mentors with them when they had careers interviews with me.

One relationship in particular fascinated me. School staff were concerned that the mentor – a wealthy, middle-aged business man – was bullying the boy with whom he had been matched, and I grew anxious too. They often met in the careers library as I worked, and I could hear the older man badgering his mentee, criticizing in a negative way, and setting unreasonable targets for the boy's work. However, when I approached the lad to discuss these concerns, he was adamant that he wanted to keep this mentor, and refused to consider any replacement. When I asked how he coped with the demanding timetable his mentor set for him, he replied: 'Oh, I don't *do* that, I just *tell* him I do it. We get on fine. I don't want a new mentor.'

This glimpse of mentoring did not fit any of my vague ideas of how mentoring was supposed to work, and the mentor's behaviour went against the grain of my own person-centred approach to working with young people. Yet the boy seemed genuinely attached to the relationship, and resisted attempts by the school to replace his mentor. It did not make common sense, and the meaning of the situation tantalized me.

At the same time, I was also supporting a number of young people facing particular difficulties in their post-16 transitions from school. Some had disabilities, others faced severe social problems. All risked long-term social exclusion if their transitions were unsuccessful. I felt stressed, and sometimes distressed, by the demands of this work. I felt very committed to these clients, but I also worried that I committed too much. Often the intensive time I had to spend with them meant that I had to work late back at the careers office, catching up on routine tasks that still had to be done.

I know that my situation was not unusual. Across the country, thousands of professionals involved in youth support and guidance experience the same pressures, stresses, dilemmas and overwork. All too often, the extra efforts needed to combat social exclusion impose a heavy personal cost on those front-line workers, including an emotional toll. At the same time, policy-makers and the media are swift to lay the blame at these workers' feet when anything goes wrong, or when the process of social inclusion does not appear to move fast enough.

Since mentoring has recently become one of the most popular means of trying to achieve social inclusion, huge numbers of both professionals and volunteers are being drawn into this work. Sometimes they are designated as mentors, in other cases mentoring is a less visible aspect of their role as, for example, personal advisers. Tens of thousands of students are volunteering as mentors, on top of their demanding degree courses and part-time employment to support themselves and pay their university fees. Yet, as I began to study mentoring, I was shocked to realize how little evidence there is for this practice, and how flimsy its theoretical base. My own professional training in guidance allowed me to develop my practice through understanding of a range of theoretical models, and through insights into the social and economic context of careers work. I knew the same was true for youth workers in their field. Mentoring seemed to lack such anchors, the more so since many volunteer mentors have almost no education or training in preparation for the role. Yet everywhere, the stories told about mentoring were always happy ones. It was an intervention which, apparently, could not go wrong.

As I progressed my research on mentor relationships, spending hours talking with mentors and mentees, it quickly became evident that the reality was often less than happy. I felt for mentors in their anxiety, confusion, frustration and guilt, as their relationships failed to progress along pre-ordained lines. I was able to see both sides of the battles that sometimes went on between mentor and mentee, or between them and the staff who ran the scheme. I heard from most of the young people how much they valued their mentor's support, but also heard their bitterness at how 'the system' treated them. With great sadness, I witnessed how the benefits they had gained were sometimes undermined by their re-exclusion from that system.

I have written this book to bear witness to the complexity of real-life mentor relationships, and to the fact that they are not always happy. I have tried to explain the roots of the unhappiness I observed in a number of cases, pointing to the unrealistic expectations that policy-makers have of mentoring for social inclusion, and to the age-old assumption that carers – most often women – should nurture others in a self-sacrificing way. I have also tried to show how happier outcomes can be achieved, or at least made more possible.

In doing so, I offer a new theoretical analysis of mentoring, one which applies sociological ideas, rather than an individual, psychological approach. I believe deeply that it is worth the effort of all those involved with mentoring to engage with these ideas. I also believe there is much here that would help young people get a better deal from mentoring, if their supporters can help them access the stories I have told and the conclusions I have reached. The mentoring movement as a whole needs to think 'outside the box', and the analysis presented here aims to provoke some radical rethinking.

During the course of my research, I have presented the ideas in this book to many audiences. Without exception, these stories of mentor relationships have tapped a deep vein of recognition, and this authenticity indicates their value as case study materials for a range of courses dealing with mentoring and with social inclusion. My findings have resonated not only with professional youth support workers and volunteer mentors, but also with mentors in a range of other contexts. They have also found a response among teachers and parents of socially excluded youngsters, who are concerned about the way mentoring is currently being pursued.

A 'critical friend' who has read the book commented that 'this will be really empowering for practitioners'. That is an ambition I have tried my hardest to realize. I do hope that policy-makers will read it and take note of it too. Their actions could do a great deal to improve mentoring in practice. Finally, as I was inspired by previous studies on mentoring, I hope this book provides inspiration for further research – there is much that we still need to find out about how mentor relationships work.

Acknowledgements

I would like to express my thanks to all those who made this book possible. The Manchester Metropolitan University (MMU) funded a Ph.D. bursary for the research project on which it is based. I owe an enormous debt to Jane Artess, Mary Issitt and Phil Hodkinson for their exemplary supervision of my doctorate. They combined vigorous support and rigorous challenge in equal measure. Ian Stronach and Peter Gilroy also contributed invaluable insights. My examiners, Meg Maguire, Dave Hustler and Janet Batsleer, provided a testing and stimulating viva that has helped to refine the presentation of my ideas here. More recently, Phil Hodkinson's sympathetic management of my role at the University of Leeds, and his advice and encouragement in the substantial task of recasting my Ph.D. thesis, have been vital in enabling me to write this book, and I am deeply grateful for his continued support.

Other colleagues have been generous with their time and efforts as critical friends, especially Kathryn Ecclestone at Newcastle, Glenn Rikowski at Northampton, Elizabeth Atkinson at Sunderland and Geraldine Crawford at Connexions Trafford. Janis Jarvis at MMU provided much valued peer support. I owe particular thanks to some fellow researchers in the field of mentoring – Kate Philip at Aberdeen, Heather Piper at MMU and Andy Roberts at Birmingham College of Food, Tourism and Creative Studies – who have provided inspiration, encouragement and debate. Geoff Ford of the National Institute for Careers Education and Counselling (NICEC) deserves special mention, as his enthusiastic response to my critique of his work has been a wonderful example of academic collegiality. He and Tony Watts, also of NICEC, provided invaluable suggestions and feedback for the newly written final chapter.

I am very grateful to Alison Foyle, Senior Editor at RoutledgeFalmer, for her time and effort in supporting the book in so many ways from start to finish. Thanks also to: Joyce Osuji and Diane Rushton, who transcribed the interview tapes with great accuracy; Mon Miah, who calmly rescued me and my work on several occasions when I managed to crash my computer and my nerves at the same time; Joan Arthur, who traced the original Pepsi advertisement used in Chapter 2; Janet Barton at the Lifelong Learning Institute, University of Leeds, for expert administrative support and endless patience; and to Tara Cleveland Web

Design and Consulting at http://www.taracleveland.com for originating such a beautiful cover design.

I hope all the family, friends and colleagues who have supported me, and tolerated my unsociable seclusion while writing this book, can forgive me for thanking them collectively. I must, however, mention two names. Without the foresight and persistent chivvying of the late Mike Watts, a former colleague and manager at Careers Partnership in Greater Manchester, I would not have returned to study or been in a position to move into research in the first place. Mike was dedicated to helping young people and to the principles of social justice, and his passing is a sad loss to the field of youth support and guidance. I hope he would have liked this book.

I also record here my heartfelt thanks to my husband, Mike Colley. Not only did he encourage me to take up the research studentship, and take care of me beyond the call of duty as I wrote this book. He has also provided constant inspiration through his own creative endeavours. I could not have had a more perfect companion for the journey.

Finally, I can only thank anonymously the managers, staff, volunteer mentors and young mentees involved at New Beginnings for their participation in the research. I am particularly grateful to the young people, who were so generous in allowing yet another unfamiliar adult to pry into their lives. Their determination to engage constructively with the mentoring process while resisting its unwelcome pressures is a lesson to us all.

Some of the material in this book has already been published as journal articles, notably in Chapters 1, 2 and 7. My thanks are due to Taylor & Francis at http://tandf.co.uk for their kind permission to reproduce material from the following:

Righting re-writings of the myth of Mentor: a critical perspective on career guidance mentoring, *British Journal of Guidance and Counselling*, 29, 2, 177–198 (2001).

A Rough Guide to the history of mentoring from a Marxist feminist perspective, *Journal of Education for Teaching*, 28, 3, 247–263 (2002).

Engagement mentoring for socially excluded youth: problematising an 'holistic' approach to creating employability through the transformation of *habitus*, *British Journal of Guidance and Counselling*, 31, 1, 77–98 (2003).

Engagement mentoring for 'disaffected' youth: a new model of mentoring for social inclusion, *British Educational Research Journal*, 29, 4 (2003).

Abbreviations

AHS	Annual Household Survey
CV	curriculum vitae
DfEE	Department for Education and Employment
DfES	Department for Education and Skills
EC	European Commission
EMA	education maintenance allowance
ESU	Employment Support Unit
FE	further education
GCSE	General Certificate of Secondary Education
HE	higher education
ICG	Institute of Career Guidance
IT	information technology
MAP	Mentoring Action Project
NMN	National Mentoring Network
NVQ	National Vocational Qualification
PCET	post-compulsory education and training
PDP	personal development plan
SEU	Social Exclusion Unit
TEC	Training and Enterprise Council
UoW	University of Wellshire
WASP	white Anglo-Saxon Protestant
WellTEC	Wellshire Training and Enterprise Council
YT	youth training

Introduction

mentor: an experienced and trusted adviser; an experienced person in an institution who trains and counsels new employees or students; origin – from the Greek *Mentor*, the name of the adviser of the young Telemachus in Homer's *Odyssey*.

(Concise Oxford English Dictionary)

The rise and rise of mentoring

Mentoring, as a planned activity, has undergone a spectacular expansion in North America, the UK and other countries over the past two decades. It has become an integral aspect of initial education and continuing professional development in business management, teaching, healthcare and many other fields. It has also become especially popular with policy-makers as an intervention with disadvantaged young people. Mentoring for social inclusion has drawn hundreds of thousands of professional practitioners and volunteers into mentor roles with such youngsters. The very word 'mentor' has acquired a mythical status, suggesting almost superhuman powers to transform the mentee in the face of all odds.

This movement has grown to such an extent that it can now be regarded as a social phenomenon in its own right (Freedman, 1999). Yet, on closer examination, we find a set of contradictions at the heart of mentoring. There is no clarity or consensus about its meaning. We know little about dyadic (one-to-one) mentor relationships or how they work. Existing research evidence scarcely justifies its use on such a massive scale. Furthermore, the movement has not yet developed a sound theoretical base to underpin policy or practice.

This book addresses these issues (leaving aside the less common practice of group mentoring). It does so through a critical approach that may be seen as highly controversial. This is not intended to decry the valuable help and support that many mentors provide, nor the benefits appreciated by mentees. On the contrary, I argue that we need to unravel the romantic myths that surround mentoring, see beyond its rhetoric and question its taken-for-granted assumptions if we are to make the most of mentor relationships. Part of this task relates to the story of mentoring itself. In the early section of the book, I explain why it has risen to such prominence at this particular moment in history, and review different schools of thought about mentoring to date. How has mentoring evolved, and under what influences? What stories are told about mentoring? What stories are left untold? And how, in turn, do these stories work to shape mentoring in practice?

Typical accounts of mentoring are focused at an individual level, and tend to erase the broader social, economic and political context in which mentor relationships are located. They obscure our view of power relations – associated with class, gender, race, disability, sexuality and other factors – and the role that mentoring may play in either reducing or reproducing inequalities. Given my own standpoint and interests, my analysis has focused on issues of class and gender. In particular, I critique two parallel problems in the practice of mentoring: on the one hand, the tightly prescribed outcomes that many mentoring programmes impose on mentees; on the other, the selfless 'labour of love' that mentors (so often female) are expected to perform. This analysis leads to a controversial redefinition of mentoring that will be relevant to any context.

Against this general background, much of the book discusses the specific practice of mentoring young people for social inclusion, particularly in the UK. I describe how one particular model, which I call 'engagement mentoring', has come to dominate. This model, which is tied to employment-related outcomes, has become pre-eminent thanks to a number of key factors related to:

- the impact of globalization on the economy, and resultant beliefs about the 'new world of work';
- government responses to social exclusion which have been focused on welfare-to-work policies;
- youth policies which assume linear school-to-work trajectories, despite the fragmented and uncertain nature of young people's transitions today.

In this context, mentoring has become a central ingredient of almost every UK policy initiative for social inclusion since the Labour Party was elected in 1997. Formal programmes of engagement mentoring have become the order of the day, sponsored by substantial government funding. This includes the wholesale transformation of career guidance services and youth services in England into the generic youth support and mentoring service, *Connexions*. But what do such programmes accomplish? Whose interests do they serve? What can they do to solve the concrete problems faced by socially excluded youth? And what might it be unrealistic to expect them to achieve?

The research presented in this book provides valuable new evidence in answer to these questions. It tells in vivid and unprecedented depth the unique stories of a small number of mentor relationships formed at New Beginnings, a local engagement mentoring scheme within post-compulsory education and training (PCET) provision. The mentees were 'disaffected' 16- and 17-year-olds recruited to a vocational preparation programme, and their volunteer mentors were university undergraduates. Their mentor relationships formed the focus of my doctoral research project at the Manchester Metropolitan University, completed in 2001.

Mentors and young people talk about how they made sense of mentoring, and where it fitted into the wider context of their lives. They described how they had been matched together, how their relationship had developed over time, and how they felt about it coming to a close. Their narratives reveal complex dynamics at play, driven by factors that were often external to the dyad itself. Young people's expectations of mentoring often clashed with those of the scheme, and with the policy objectives that shaped it. Mentors responded in different ways to these tensions, some choosing to support their mentee's agenda, while others doggedly tried to pursue the goals set by the scheme. At the same time, class distinctions, cultural distance, gender and disability all impacted on their relationships.

A key finding is that the power relations that affect mentor relationships are far more complex than has been recognized until now. The young people I met were not passive recipients of mentor support, but exercised their own agency and resistance, although with contradictory results. Mentors, generally regarded as the powerful member of the dyad, felt themselves subordinated through processes of surveillance and control. These stories thus bear little resemblance to the celebratory anecdotes of neat progression that dominate the contemporary mentoring movement. But they do enable us to ground broader questions of policy and theory in real-life experiences of mentoring, and to see that mentoring dyads are always located within the wider power structures of patriarchal capitalist society.

The value of case study research

> [Y]ou must immerse yourself in the particular to find in it the invariant. . . . A particular case that is well-constructed ceases to be particular.
>
> (Bourdieu and Wacquant, 1992: 77)

My research was conducted as a small-scale case study of one engagement mentoring scheme. Before describing the structure of the book, and offering the reader a map of its contents, I want to explain briefly why I chose to do the research in this way, and to answer some important questions: Are case studies merely descriptive? How can they be relevant beyond the inevitably small sample they involve? Can their findings be generalized beyond an individual investigation?

It is true that the vast majority of research on mentoring has adopted a quantitative approach, using large-scale questionnaires to diagnose processes and to measure outcomes. Such methods suit the current climate of educational policy, with its emphasis on finding out 'what works'. However, the scale of these surveys, the limited responses they allow, and their analysis of data into highly simplified and generalized categories, all make it impossible to understand how mentor relationships actually develop. Complexities and idiosyncrasies disappear amid averaged trends, and a limited view of what *tends* to happen substitutes for the rich possibilities of what *can* happen.

Case study research offers a number of advantages which offset its small scale against the depth of knowledge it can generate. Here, it provides rich data with multiple dimensions, reflecting a variety of perspectives on mentoring at an experiential level that is usually hidden from view. It encourages a holistic understanding of mentors' and mentees' experiences, in the context of their personal life histories and social situations. Individuals' stories also allow the reader to experience something of those mentor relationships for themselves, to make connections with their personal experiences, and to draw their own conclusions – perhaps in contrast to those I offer – about the realities of mentoring in practice. Moreover, when they are clearly contextualized and integrated into a theoretical framework, as they are in this book, their evidence becomes transferable to other instances, and this in turn allows advances in theoretical understanding. In my previous career as a guidance practitioner, I found this kind of research accessible, educational and inspiring, and I hope this book will engage readers in the same way.

The values of this research

> . . . to understand the larger historical scene in terms of its meaning for the inner life and the external career of a variety of individuals . . . to grasp history and biography and the relations between the two in society.
>
> (Wright-Mills, 1970: 11–12, cited in Ball *et al.*, 2000: 20)

Case studies do not just have value in terms of the knowledge they generate. In the critical interpretive approach I have adopted, they also express the researcher's values. I have discussed philosophical questions of methodology in detail elsewhere (see Colley, 2001c, d). However, it is important to signal briefly to the reader some of the deeply held values I brought to the research, so that you can make your own judgements about its worth as you follow the stories I tell.

No doubt my own background – an upbringing on a poor housing estate, disaffection from education, socialist and feminist activism, many years in unskilled jobs, then becoming a careers adviser in inner-city areas – has greatly influenced this work. I explicitly seek to challenge injustices I perceive in much mentoring practice to date. These values lead me to concur with Bourdieu (1989b) that critical researchers have a responsibility to expose relationships of power that are almost always, by their nature, hidden. Cultural explanations of social processes tend to focus on individual behaviour, so that social structures – class divisions, gender oppression, racism – disappear from view. However, as Anderson (1989) notes, critical investigations are also unsatisfactory if they focus on structures so much that individuals and their agency disappear from sight.

I wanted to keep both social structures and individual agency in view, because what interests me most is the *interplay* of the two – their dialectical relationship, in philosophical terms. This book therefore investigates mentoring on three levels that, for me, are inseparably intertwined. I build up a detailed picture of each mentor relationship at the micro-level of personal interaction. To understand them fully, they have to be clearly located in their setting at this scheme. This means interpreting individual interactions in relation to the meso-level of their institutional context and the factors that shaped that context. Some of these factors are local, such as the population and labour market in that geographical area. Others are national or international, such as the policy decisions that brought engagement mentoring schemes into being and influenced their design. Both these levels also need to be related to macro-level factors: overarching political forces, economic conditions, social structures and inequalities. I urge anyone using case stories from this book as teaching materials to ensure that students do not lose sight of these institutional and structural factors. The greatest danger in ignoring them would be to lay the blame for negative or damaging outcomes of mentoring at individuals' feet.

Writing and reading narratives

> Deciding how to present voices and lives is a continuous problem for qualitative writers. Because we use the voices and experiences of the people we study, both for their own sake and as evidence of our credibility, we are constantly making writerly decisions about who gets to say what and how often in the text, and who the narrator talks about, how and how often.
>
> (Richardson, 1990: 39, cited in Hodkinson *et al.*, 1996: 158)

The reader needs to bear three points in mind about the narratives of mentor relationships in this book, which are based primarily on interviews with those involved. First, they are not objective representations of 'what happened' in mentoring. Such perfect representations are impossible (Smith, 1993). As some of the stories illustrate very well, there were often different versions of what happened, from the young person, their mentor and the staff at the scheme. Each of their accounts is true, in the sense that it reflects the perceptions, intentions and beliefs of the speaker. In this respect, the differences between their stories are far more illuminating than the pursuit of some factual resolution.

This relates to a second important issue about the stories which participants told in the research interviews. We have to understand that these are themselves narrative constructions, a partial making sense of their experiences of mentoring at one moment in time. In the words of a country sheriff in an American film I have long forgotten: 'The evidence ain't the truth: it's just the bits we happen to know' – and the bits we happen to know are what respondents choose to tell us. Like all rememberings, they are 'interested', weighted with an underlying purpose of which the speaker may not even be aware. This has led some researchers to see interview data as untrustworthy, sanitized accounts produced to please the researcher (e.g. Delamont, 1999). However, all human narratives are to some extent both deceptive and self-deceptive, since we instinctively become defensive to protect ourselves from painful experiences (Hollway and Jefferson, 2000). This may be particularly true in those mentor relationships which ran into problems. The point is not the veracity of what mentors and mentees said, but the revealing nature of the stories they chose to tell. Once again, the focus of our understanding shifts from 'what' to 'how' and 'why'.

Third, I have then reconstructed these narratives, by selecting, interpreting and ordering small portions of lengthy interview transcripts. At this level too, narrative is interested, and my earlier comments serve to make some of my interests transparent. Some mentor relationships are told in greater detail than others, some are not told at all, although the evidence from them has informed the research as a whole. The biggest challenge I faced was to ensure that the young people's voices were not drowned out by the voices of others. The student volunteers who mentored them, and the scheme staff and managers, were all educated and articulate people who had had ample opportunities to develop their ideas about mentoring and about social exclusion. They gave lengthy replies to my questions, and the data was accordingly 'thick'. By contrast, the young people's responses were often brief, even monosyllabic at times, so their transcripts appeared 'thin'.

Conventional methods of analysing the data – coding and grouping it according to key categories – thus presented two main problems. Not only would this fragment the holistic view of mentor relationships that I wanted to convey, 'slicing' the data across a number of stories; it would also risk submerging the voices of the young people. There was so much more to code from other respondents, and the coding was much more easily done. The only way to balance their perspectives was to transform the data through a process of *creative synthesis* rather than traditional methods of analysis (Moustakas, 1990), to put the stories together rather than take their elements apart. These are *my* stories in a fundamental sense, so I refer to the accounts of individual mentor relationships as 'case stories' rather than 'case studies'. Following Wolcott, I may not always 'quite get it right', but I have always been concerned to 'go to considerable pains not to get it all wrong' (1994: 346). Having thus indicated the contours of this book, I move on to outline its structure and content.

Structure and content of the book

The book is organized into three parts, with the case stories from the research narrated between the policy analysis that sets them in context, and the theoretical analysis that flows from them. This structure serves two purposes. The first is to ensure that the reader does not view mentor relationships in a purely individualized way, but understands them in terms of their local and global settings. The second is to ground a new theoretical framework for mentoring in the data. This has the added virtue of allowing readers to interpret the case stories for themselves, rather than imposing a preconceived theorization.

Part I consists of two chapters describing the background to the mentoring movement. In Chapter 1 I present a social history of youth mentoring, and identify the recent emergence of a widespread model of planned 'engagement mentoring' for social inclusion. This model aims to re-engage young people with the formal labour market by altering their attitudes, values and behaviours. I locate the evolution of engagement mentoring in relation to major economic, social and political developments of the late twentieth century, particularly developments which impact on young people's transitions from school to work. (Given that the great majority of mentors drawn into this movement are female, the context of women's status in the labour market is an important issue too, but this is addressed in more detail in Chapter 7.)

In Chapter 2 I consider the difficulties so many authors and practitioners have in defining mentoring, and I unravel the rhetoric and myths that surround it. I argue that previous studies of mentoring have been flawed by their individualized focus on its power dynamics, and by their tendency to disembed the practice of mentoring from its broader context. Such studies not only divert attention from negative effects of mentoring upon the mentee, but also ignore the potential subordination of mentors – particularly women – to the power and control of dominant groupings. This analysis has implications for mentoring across its full range of contexts. The chapter closes by describing the background to my research, which I conducted primarily through repeated semi-structured individual interviews with mentors and mentees matched together in established relationships.

Part II presents the data from the empirical research at New Beginnings. This will be of inherent interest to all readers concerned about mentoring young people for social inclusion. However, it also raises issues about mentor relationships that may be relevant to many other settings. As well as offering rich descriptions of the scheme I studied and particular relationships formed within it, each of these chapters offers an initial interpretation of the data.

In Chapter 3 I describe the design of the New Beginnings scheme, and show how policy imperatives and funding requirements shaped it as a typical example of the engagement mentoring model. Scheme managers talk about its purpose and goals, and I describe the recruitment and induction processes for young people and student mentors. The following chapters present detailed case stories of individual mentor relationships.

Chapter 4 focuses predominantly on the young people. It reveals the resistance young people displayed towards aspects of the scheme, and the way they asserted their own agendas within their mentor relationships – to differing reactions by their mentors. They also show that young people gained important benefits from mentoring, although often these did not coincide with the outcomes expected by the scheme. Chapter 5 focuses on the students' experiences as mentors. It includes the contrasting stories of two students who were matched, at different times, with the same young person. These narratives reveal ways in which mentors perceived normative pressures within the scheme to adapt or conceal their own identities through the process of mentoring. Chapter 6 tells the detailed story of one lengthy relationship between two women. It shows how the dispositions of both mentor and mentee were shaped by a female stereotype of caring for others, and reveals a cycle of frustration and disappointment in which both young women became trapped. I question the way in which mentoring aspires above all to a relationship, while it reinforces oppressive gender roles that undermine genuine connection with others. The management of mentors' and mentees' feelings – emotional labour – emerges from this story as a key aspect of engagement mentoring.

The writing style shifts within this central section. Chapter 3 is presented according to the typical conventions of research reports, so that direct quotes from interview transcripts are separated out from the main text and indented. Omissions from the text are shown by ellipses (. . .) and for clarity, some words are inserted [*thus*]. Chapters 4–6 are written in a more continuous discursive style, and slight changes to the transcripts for the sake of clarity are not flagged. In this way, I hope that readers can absorb themselves more easily into the flow of the narratives.

Part III presents a new theoretical analysis of mentoring, and concludes with recommendations for policy and practice. Chapter 7 revisits some of the questions raised in Chapter 2 in the light of the case stories. I draw on feminist readings of Bourdieu, Foucault and Marxist theory to interrogate the interplay of structure and agency in the power dynamics of mentor relationships, and show that the complexity of these dynamics is commonly overlooked. I argue that engagement mentoring is constructed as a labour process, to alter mentees' dispositions in line with employer demands in the post-Fordist world of work. This labour process in turn demands a disposition of devotion on the part of mentors, and a commitment to undertake emotional labour, which is further defined and explained.

Chapter 8 raises a number of issues and recommendations for policy, practice and future research. I argue that engagement mentoring policy contains a counter-productive paradox: the more it seeks to ensure outcomes related to employment, the less successful it is likely to be for a significant number of young people. I analyse the implications for policy interventions seeking to promote social inclusion, and then apply these conclusions to make recommendations for practice. These practical recommendations are aimed at all those participating in mentoring on the ground – mentors, staff and young people. Finally, I outline a research agenda to test out further the ideas advanced in this book, and to gain more knowledge about mentor relationships. Let us begin by turning to the history of youth mentoring, and the emergence of engagement mentoring at centre stage.

Part I

The rise of the mentoring movement

Chapter 1

The emergence of engagement mentoring

Youth mentoring moves centre stage

Youth mentoring has expanded spectacularly over the past decade. By the early 1990s, tens of thousands of middle-class adults across North America were volunteering as mentors for poor urban youth through the programme *Big Brothers Big Sisters* – a mass movement which has come to represent a social and historical phenomenon in its own right (Freedman, 1999). By the mid-1990s, this movement had also begun to grow rapidly in the UK.

'Industrial' mentoring involved almost 17,000 pupils in hundreds of British schools, and encouraged thousands of companies to allow their business people to volunteer as mentors (Golden and Sims, 1997). From 1994 to 1998, the European Youthstart Initiative funded almost a hundred programmes of employment-related guidance, education and training for socially excluded young people in the UK, and the majority of these included mentoring. Within that Initiative, the Institute of Career Guidance (ICG) co-ordinated the Mentoring Action Project (MAP), the largest such programme in Britain to that date. Over a quarter of all statutory careers services in England and Wales took part in the MAP, which allocated mentors to 1,700 young people (Ford, 1999a). During the same period, the Dalston Youth Project, a voluntary sector scheme working with young black offenders in London's deprived East End, became nationally lauded as an exemplar of mentoring for socially excluded youth (see Benioff, 1997). As similar projects proliferated, the National Mentoring Network (NMN) was established in 1994 to promote both local mentoring schemes and the development of a national infrastructure.

Miller (2002) traces the international expansion of youth mentoring in a number of advanced capitalist countries (mainly, although not exclusively, Anglophone) during the past five years. In the US alone, *Big Brothers Big Sisters* now boasts a quarter of a million volunteers. With presidential backing from George W. Bush, it is currently engaged in a five-year campaign to recruit 1 million more mentors to work with 14 million young people 'at risk'. That model has been taken up in Canada and Australia, while Israel and Sweden have also seen the development of significant youth mentoring programmes. Undergraduate students have been a popular group for the recruitment of volunteer mentors (as in the New Beginnings scheme reported later in this book). The largest mentoring project in the US, *GEAR-UP*, is currently aiming to double the 750,000 undergraduate mentors it had in 2000, working with 16- to 19-year-olds at risk of disaffection. In Israel, 20 per cent of higher education (HE) students act as mentors to children in schools, and in Sweden a similar pattern is being followed. Although mentoring has not yet flourished to the same extent in other European countries, Miller suggests that there are more favourable cultural conditions and growing support for it in Ireland, Norway and the Netherlands.

Mentoring has also burgeoned massively in Britain since the New Labour government was elected in 1997. Labour's policy-makers have shown enthusiastic support for mentoring as an intervention to promote social inclusion. The Department for Education and Employment (DfEE) (now renamed the Department for Education and Skills (DfES)) immediately began to provide the NMN with a Mentoring Bursary which has been substantially increased year on year. Soon after, the House of Commons Select Committee on Disaffected Children stated that all programmes seeking to address disaffection should include mentoring (House of Commons Education and Employment Committee, 1998). It has since been promoted by four different government departments, with responsibility for: education, training and employment; youth justice; health promotion; black, Asian and other minority ethnic communities; and social exclusion. In education, mentoring has become a standard ingredient in the recipe of almost every major new policy initiative, including prevention of school truancy and drop-out from PCET, responses to the report on the Stephen Lawrence inquiry which highlighted institutional racism, proposals to develop 'gifted and talented' children, and the *Learning Gateway* initiative to support labour market transitions for young people who have not succeeded at school (DfEE, 1999a–d).

By the start of 2003, the number of affiliates to the NMN has grown from an initial 350 to over 1,500 and is still rising. It has also attracted sponsorship from the McDonald's fast food chain. One in three schools in Britain now offer mentoring to pupils, while one-third of NMN-affiliated programmes are in PCET contexts. Two major new government programmes represent the culmination of this trend: *Excellence in Cities*, aimed at improving the academic performance of children from disadvantaged communities in inner-city schools; and the *Connexions* service, a new national service which is replacing the former statutory careers services in England and incorporating youth services. *Connexions*' aim is to provide multi-agency support for young people aged 13 to 19 through their transitions from adolescence to adulthood and from school to PCET and employment (DfEE, 2000a).

Britain follows the international trend of seeking volunteer mentors from the undergraduate student population. The National Mentoring Pilot Project was launched in 2001, linking twenty-one Education Action Zones (in deprived inner-city areas) to seventeen HE institutions, providing 800 undergraduate students to mentor 2,500 young people. Undergraduates have also been recruited as mentors by *Excellence in Cities* and by mentoring programmes organized through *Millennium Volunteers* and other local initiatives. The major programmes use paid mentors as well as volunteers. *Excellence in Cities* and *Connexions* have already employed 2,400 learning mentors in schools since 2000, and this is set to rise to 3,000 over the next two years. In addition, *Connexions* is seeking to recruit 20,000 personal advisers to work with 16- to 19-year-olds.

In January 2001, Gordon Brown, Chancellor of the Exchequer, announced a further £5.3 million from the Treasury as part of a £13 million funding package to develop youth mentoring over the next three years. Subsequently, the Home Office has provided more than £1.4 million to establish seven regional 'Mentor Points' in major cities to co-ordinate the recruitment and training of mentors for many of these projects. In addition, *Connexions* has its own large-scale training programme now underway. While Freedman (1999) characterized the initial rise of the mentoring movement in the US as 'fervor without infrastructure', these recent investments suggest that an infrastructure is indeed being put in place. However, the scale of funding remains small when the number of participants is taken into account. NMN figures indicate that over a million mentors may now be active in the UK. The government funding package, if it were to be allocated in just one year, would provide only around £14 per head. Although the successful and often-cited Dalston Youth Project estimated costs of around £2,000 per year to train and support an effective mentor, it appears that mentoring is regarded by policy-makers as a low-cost intervention.

For the most part, this fervour has carried all before it in a surge of celebration. Mentoring seems to encapsulate a 'feel-good' factor, typified in scenes at the NMN Conference and similar occasions: joyously tearful presentations of bouquets from mentees to mentors; or playlets where young people represent their mentors as angels, replete with halo and wings. Yet there is an irony in such a practice being sponsored so heavily by a government overtly committed to evidence-based practice and to the pursuit of 'what works'. Reviews of research indicate that, despite its popularity, there is little evidence to support the use of mentoring on such a vast scale (Skinner and Fleming, 1999). While Ford's evaluation of the MAP (1999a) shows that young people often perceived highly positive outcomes, he notes that the mentors in this programme were qualified and experienced careers advisers and youth workers. Moreover, they operated with young people willing to re-engage with formal education and training systems rather than with those who were deeply alienated from them.

There is alternative evidence that mentoring may be counterproductive to policy intentions for interventions with socially excluded young people (Colley, 2000b; Fitz-Gibbon, 2000; Philip and Hendry, 1996), and that even where young people are enthusiastic about their experience of being mentored, their mentors may not share this view (Colley, 2001a). Moreover, as we shall see in Chapter 2, it is a practice that remains ill-defined, poorly conceptualized and weakly theorized, leading to confusion in policy and practice. Before detailing the model of engagement mentoring that has emerged in recent years, this chapter continues by explaining how interest in mentoring young people for social inclusion first developed.

Early interest in mentoring youth for social inclusion

One of the earliest spotlights on mentoring for young people 'at risk' of social exclusion came from Werner and Smith's extraordinary work *Vulnerable But Invincible* (1982). This reported a psychological study of young people from poor multi-ethnic communities in Hawaii throughout the first eighteen years of their lives. Their research identified twenty-one major risk factors which made young people vulnerable to maladaptive outcomes such as mental ill-health, criminal offending and long-term unemployment. These included chronic poverty, physical or learning disabilities, teenage pregnancy, serious accident or illness, and disruption of the family for various reasons. However, this vulnerability did not inevitably result in negative outcomes in a deterministic way. The researchers found that about two-thirds of the cohort studied, irrespective of the level of difficulties they faced, had the resilience to achieve successful, coping transitions to adulthood. This led Werner and Smith to emphasize the need to consider *protective* factors and positive attributes in young people, rather than the predominant focus on risk factors which, they argued, tended to pathologize disadvantage. Their findings identified one crucial and unexpected protective factor: resilient young people demonstrated an ability to seek out and gain support from informal mentors among their kin and community. Similar benefits from informal mentoring were observed elsewhere, for example, among teenage mothers in Latino communities in the US (Rhodes, 1994; Rhodes *et al.*, 1992). However, while these findings about the importance of mentoring in these contexts were seized upon and much referenced in the subsequent literature, some important caveats they had raised were ignored in the ensuing fervour.

Garmezy, in his foreword to *Vulnerable But Invincible*, warned against a 'false sense of security in erecting prevention models that are founded more on values than on facts' (Garmezy, 1982: xix). There are two main flaws in assuming that the benefits of such mentoring can be replicated in formally planned contexts. First, it is impossible to conclude from Werner and Smith's research whether the successful mentoring bonds created by some young people are a *cause* or an *effect* of their resilience. They may represent neither, but simply a researcher-constructed *correlation*. This issue is thrown into relief if we consider less resilient young people, who might find it difficult to bond with adults at all. In such cases, allocating them a mentor might be of little benefit, and would risk reinforcing rather than diminishing the young person's sense of isolation. The second danger is that planned mentoring schemes risk ignoring or even working against the community-based networks of significant adults that this and similar studies revealed. Value-judgements may dominate decisions about the social groups from which mentors will be sought. If there is a lack of understanding about the positive resources and adult support that are already available to young people, planned mentoring may well conflict with those informal networks.

Nevertheless, research agendas have continued to assume that investigations of young people's self-sought mentor relationships 'are likely to indicate fruitful ways of crafting policies and programs so they can be maximally effective for a more diverse population of young adolescents' (Scales and Gibbons, 1996: 385). Beginning in the US at the start of the 1990s, and in Britain at the mid-point of the decade, the proliferation of such programmes indicates that the transference of mentoring into planned settings has been widely accepted as unproblematic.

A series of evaluations of localized projects in the US (e.g. Blechman, 1992; Dondero, 1997; DuBois and Neville, 1997; Haensley and Parsons, 1993; McPartland and Nettles, 1991; O'Donnell et al., 1997; Ringwalt et al., 1996; Zippay, 1995) indicate how planned youth mentoring began to flourish there. These projects reveal a distinct trend in respect of the goals that mentor relationships were supposed to pursue. These goals include so-called 'soft outcomes', such as enhanced self-esteem, but funding requirements almost always focus on 'harder' targets: educational goals including school-related behaviour and academic progress; social goals, such as the reduction of criminal offending and substance abuse; and employment-related goals, such as entry to the labour market or train-ing programmes (McPartland and Nettles, 1991). As another project evaluation noted:

> The use of mentors in social services programs has become an increasingly common intervention, and *typically aims to increase education and job skills among at-risk youth.*
>
> (Zippay, 1995: 51, emphasis added)

Some of the reports of these schemes proffer uncritical and biased promotion of mentoring, appealing to policy-makers and institution managers to introduce prevention and/or intervention programmes with a strong mentoring element: 'Mentoring is an old idea that works. . . . Adult mentors serve as beacons of hope for young people adrift in an uncertain world', declares Dondero (1997: 881). Despite such optimism, they present extremely limited evidence of their claims for the benefits of mentoring.

Others avoid unsubstantiated claims of this kind, finding evidence of inconclusive and even negative outcomes of mentoring in relation to school achievement and/or antisocial behaviour (for a fuller review, see Dishion et al., 1999). One summer jobs programme for young African-American men reported worse outcomes in violence-related behaviours for those who had been mentored than for a non-mentored control group (Ringwalt et al., 1996). It is accordingly cautious about its conclusions. Similarly, McPartland and Nettles (1991) found that mentoring in Project RAISE appeared to produce no effects for student promotion rates and school test results, and only slight positive outcomes in relation to school attendance and grades for English coursework. While emphasizing the need for rigorous evaluation of future mentoring programmes given the lack of evidence to support such practice, they noted that this was not inhibiting its growing popularity:

> RAISE managers are using our evaluation of the project's first two years *to intensify and focus their efforts* for the future. They expect one-on-one mentoring to gradually become available for most student participants.
>
> (McPartland and Nettles, 1991: 584, emphasis added)

Big Brothers Big Sisters shares a similar approach to these localized projects. It links young people from single-parent households with unrelated mentors, claiming the sole aim is to provide these young people with an adult friend, rather than seeking to improve or eradicate specific educational or socio-economic problems (Grossman and Tierney, 1998: 405). Nevertheless, it too promotes the setting of goals for young people around improved educational performance, the development of life skills and access to the labour market (Freedman, 1995: 216).

However, Freedman (1995, 1999) suggests that broader policy considerations have driven both practice and research in this field. He argues that mentoring is popular with policy-makers because it resonates with a number of their concerns: the moralization of social exclusion; the drive of economic competitiveness which proclaims the need for 'upskilling' and the threat posed by an 'underclass'; the attraction of a cheap 'quick fix' to social problems; and its facile affinity with the individualistic philosophy of the 'American Dream'. This produces a 'heroic conception of social policy' (Freedman, 1999: 21), which exhorts the white American middle classes to undertake a 'crusade' towards socially excluded (often black and Latino) young people. It is interesting to note here that President Bush's support for the *Big Brothers Big Sisters* programme is linked to the use of the armed services as a pool for potential mentors (Miller, 2002). As youth mentoring has come, slightly later, to develop with similar fervour in Britain, the focus on employment-related goals has sharpened. This is particularly true in England, where there has been little funding for the looser model of befriending that has developed in Scotland (Forrest, 2002). Let us look at the emergence of engagement mentoring that has resulted.

The emergence of engagement mentoring

Skinner and Fleming (1999) argue that three broad models of youth mentoring have emerged in Britain. First, since 1993, Business–Education Partnerships have contributed to the formation of a model of 'industrial mentoring' in schools (Golden and Sims, 1997). Mentors are recruited from local businesses, and mentoring aims to encourage and raise the self-confidence of pupils, often prioritizing those who are predicted as 'borderline' for achieving Grade C GCSE passes. (This grade is regarded as the primary benchmark of achievement for the purposes of school league tables, entry to further education and training programmes, and employers' recruitment and selection.) During the period of economic upturn which characterized the latter half of the 1990s, many firms have been willing to encourage employees and managers to volunteer as industrial mentors. Benefits to the companies are expected, both in the mentors' development of communication and other mentoring skills that may be useful in their work roles, as well as in demonstrating corporate support for the local community.

The model aims to achieve four key goals:

> Firstly, through enhancing students' awareness of the world of work, mentoring contributes to the delivery of the work-related curriculum. . . . Secondly, [it] may have a positive impact on schools' examination results. Thirdly, by focusing on the development of the individual, [it] can contribute to the delivery of students' Personal and Social Education. . . . Mentoring may also make an indirect contribution to the development of local economies by helping to increase young people's motivation and confidence to take advantage of training and employment opportunities.
>
> (Golden and Sims, 1997: 26)

The outcomes identified for mentoring here are aimed at tailoring school-leavers' aspirations to the demand-side of the local labour market, and raising schools' performance in league tables. Despite some similarities with the employment-related goals of engagement mentoring, the target group differs significantly. Golden and Sims argue that a 'good scheme will avoid targeting complete non-attenders as mentees' (1997: 28). Schools are reluctant to waste busy mentors' time, or to allocate them to young people whose attendance might be unreliable, or whose behaviour might prove unacceptable. Such schemes therefore tend to exclude the most disadvantaged young people.

A second model is that of 'positive action' or 'community mentoring', aimed at supporting young people from oppressed groups. These often target young men from black and Asian communities. Some schemes have targeted young women, to encourage them to pursue careers in science and engineering. Female youth workers have used mentoring to challenge aspects of young women's oppression (Philip, 1997). The latter approach emphasizes young people's autonomy and their voluntary participation, the negotiated and trusting nature of mentor relationships, and efforts by youth workers to minimize their own authority, status and power. Often this model aims to present positive role models for success, from within the community or oppressed group wherever possible. It is also more likely to offer support and advocacy for young people in overcoming obstacles such as institutional discrimination and structural inequalities. In some cases (see e.g. Forbes, 2000; Majors *et al.*, 2000; Usman, 2000), black and Asian mentoring projects have sought to change other people's beliefs, values, attitudes and behaviour towards young people from oppressed groups, as well as institutional cultures. As a result, they have sometimes been refused access by schools and colleges which did not welcome such a challenging approach.

The third model of mentoring is an intervention responding to disaffection and social exclusion. Such projects identify targeted groups of young people 'at risk' of disengaging, or already disengaged from formal systems of education, training and employment. They then seek explicitly to re-engage young people with these systems in preparation for entry to the labour market. It is for this reason that I have dubbed this model 'engagement mentoring'. It is this model of mentoring which characterized New Beginnings, the site of my research described in the central chapters of this book.

Engagement mentoring emerged in 1994 to 1995 during the rule of the previous Conservative government. However, as we have seen, it was not developed at that time as an aspect of central government policies. All the schemes were funded through sources other than core funding from the DfEE or other departments. Some were funded through local, discretionary sources, but a considerable number arose through funding opportunities provided by the European Commission (EC) Youthstart Initiative, although these origins are not acknowledged in later policy initiatives.

Many professionals committed to helping disadvantaged young people had been frustrated by Conservative government policies. In the world of career guidance, for example, the privatization of careers services in 1994 had gone hand in hand with funding targets that severely restricted practitioners' ability to work with disadvantaged clients needing intensive levels of support (Ford, 1999a). 'Blanket' interviewing of the majority of pupils in their final year of compulsory schooling was the order of the day. Consequently, youngsters categorized as 'mainstream' were prioritized, since they were easier to access, and had a greater chance of positive outcomes in education or training. Not only did this marginalize socially excluded young people, who were vulnerable to difficult transitions, but it was also perceived as a de-skilling process for guidance practitioners, which restricted their professional autonomy. The availability of European funding allowed some twenty of the seventy-three careers services nation-wide, and a range of other organizations, to engage in work with socially excluded young people that side-stepped these limitations, and to subvert policy intentions.

The Youthstart Initiative was one of four strands of the Employment Community Initiative which ran in two tranches from 1995 to 1999 within the European Social Fund. Youthstart targeted young people classed as disaffected, specifically those who were unemployed and unqualified (Employment Support Unit (ESU), 1999a). The target group were further defined as:

young people who:

- have learning difficulties;
- are from ethnic minority groups;
- are disabled;
- are single parents;
- are drug or alcohol users;

- are disaffected; or
- are from disadvantaged areas.

(ESU, 1999b: 19)

The three overall aims of the Youthstart Initiative were: to promote effective school-to-work transitions for young people, achieving social integration through integration into the labour market; to empower young people to make choices in their transitions through access to advice and guidance; and to develop the professional skills of those assisting the target group through a range of supporting agencies (EC, 1998; ESU, 1999c). Key activities of funded projects were defined accordingly as 'training and guidance, work to develop training resources, job creation and awareness-raising' (ESU, 2000b: 1).

'Comprehensive pathways' to overcome complex social and economic disadvantage were a distinctive aspect of Youthstart, which advocated co-ordinated inter-agency partnership. Although guidance and support for young people were seen as central elements of the programme, they were linked to employment outcomes in a way that did not easily fit the impartial and person-centred ethos of existing services providing career guidance, youth work and counselling. This contradiction was obscured, however, by the rhetoric of Youthstart's official documentation, which focused on empowerment for young people, client-centred approaches to individual goals and a holistic ethos:

> The empowerment stage concerns activities that give young people the tools and confidence to take control of their own pathway. . . . It is about empowering young people to plan their own future and to understand and capitalise on their own potential.
>
> (EC, 1998: 12)

Such pathways were in fact defined in terms of their employment-related direction and destinations. Although an acknowledgement of 'soft' outcomes (such as self-confidence) was a hallmark of the Youthstart Initiative, the programme's assertion of 'holistic' and 'person-centred' approaches is open to question (see Colley (2003) for a fuller discussion of this point).

The official literature produced by the Youthstart Initiative presented a clear view of how it interpreted these processes:

> Each of the stages of the pathway is associated with bringing about a *significant shift in the values and motivation* of the young people, their skills and abilities and in their interaction with the wider environment. The overall objective is to move the young person from a position of alienation and distance from social and economic reality, to a position of social integration and productive activity.
>
> (EC, 1998: 6, emphasis added)

It proposed 'empowerment activities', of which mentoring was identified as a key element. These would use: 'self-evaluation methods and feedback sessions to reinforce the acceptance of values and attitudinal change amongst the young people' (EC, 1998: 12, emphasis added).

These policies contain normative assumptions: *which* values and attitudes are to be instilled in young people, and in *whose* interests? They present young people's negative perceptions of how they will be treated in training and work as one of the main obstacles to their gaining employment (ESU, 2000b; see also Social Exclusion Unit (SEU), 1999). The implication is that 'correct' perceptions would present a positive image of working conditions and harmony of interest between employers and employees. It also implies that young people inhabit a world outside participation in 'mainstream' learning and employment opportunities that is somehow unreal; that they do not engage in productive activities; and that alienation is not a characteristic of the lives of working people who are employed.

At the heart of European policy promoting engagement mentoring, then, we find two key assumptions, expressed in the central goals of the Youthstart programme. The first is that the solution to social exclusion lies in re-engagement with the labour market and/or formal learning routes into it. The second (in marked contrast with the community mentoring model) is that the specific role of mentoring is to facilitate this re-engagement, by altering young people's values, attitudes, beliefs and behaviour in order to engage their personal commitment to becoming employable. This is frequently couched in terms of empowerment, raising aspirations, and making young people more realistic about the world of work.

I shall return to the question of empowerment through mentoring in Chapter 7, and we shall see in Chapter 3 the extent to which the New Beginnings scheme reflected these goals, assumptions and rhetoric. They are certainly fundamental to policies for social inclusion. After the election of the New Labour government in May 1997, the Select Committee on Disaffected Children recommended the use of mentors in all programmes aimed at remedying disaffection, stating also that:

> The key task in tackling disaffection should be to provide challenge, restore motivation and engender key skills. Maximising formal educational achievement for these young people must be at the heart of intervention, whatever the nature of the project concerned. . . . All interventions should have the aim of reintegrating disaffected young people into mainstream education and training opportunities.
>
> (House of Commons Education and Employment Committee, 1998: xxxvii)

The ICG MAP Report emphasizes that:

> the mentors' primary task of *influencing behaviours, and by implication attitudes*, is a fundamental one . . . attitudes [are] the most difficult, as attitude training needs

to engage each individual, and the attitudes then become incorporated into the individual's own frame of reference and values base. MAP is seeking to tackle the most difficult area (i.e. attitudes training) first.

(Barham, personal communication, cited in Ford, 1999a: 18, emphasis added)

The report from the UK Youthstart projects defines and proselytizes mentoring in this way:

Mentoring is a useful way of re-engaging disaffected young people in self-development, training and employment. Mentoring features strongly in the dissemination and mainstreaming of learning from Youthstart projects.

(ESU, 2000a: i)

It goes on to explain that part of the mentors' role in supporting young people as they enter employment is to 'endorse the work ethic, and . . . challenge any negative perceptions the young person may have about entry to the labour market' (ESU, 2000a: 7).

Similarly, the *Guide to Relevant Practice in the Learning Gateway* provides a summary of the tasks of personal advisers, and then emphasizes the following point:

In order to achieve all of these tasks, it is important for the Personal Adviser to recognise that many of the young people entering the Learning Gateway need support to change their attitudes and behaviours. Until they do so, these will continue to be barriers to their reintegration.

(DfEE, 1999e: 9)

There is much emphasis on generating 'realistic' objectives, and challenging those which are 'unrealistic' (see Colley (2000a) for a detailed critique of vocational realism in guidance for young people). The outcomes sought are summarized thus:

The focus of much of the Learning Gateway activity is on developing employability, active citizenship and personal development, with a view to progression to mainstream learning.

(DfEE, 1999e: 32)

While it could be argued that promoting issues such as personal development or active citizenship could hardly be seen as evidence of employment-dominated goals, a DfEE-sponsored evaluation of the *Learning Gateway* pilots illustrates the fact that outcomes such as these may indeed be dominated by employers' rather than young people's needs. 'Development of life skills' is defined as:

improving the *personal effectiveness of young people in the work place* by assisting them to gain skills in areas such as problem solving, confidence building, development of interpersonal skills, team working, punctuality, diagnoses of personal strengths and areas for personal development and life skills, *which employers regard as essential for applicants to have in order for them to seek employment.*

(GHK Economics and Management, 2000: 56, emphases added)

The way the personal is subsumed into the work-related is striking in this extract. The list of such goals could go on, as Piper and Piper's (2000) review of similar schemes demonstrates. They show that mentoring for the 'disaffected' is almost invariably tied to employment as the immediate or eventual outcome, and raise crucial questions about the way in which claims of empowerment frequently underpin these employment-related goals.

There is therefore substantial evidence to support the identification of a distinctive model of engagement mentoring around two central foci: the re-engagement of young people with formal learning and the labour market; and the transformation of their personal attitudes, values and beliefs (in short, their dispositions) in order to engage their commitment to develop 'employability'. With the enthusiastic backing of the New Labour government, engagement mentoring has recently moved from marginal status to prominence in mainstream policy and practice, and core funding has replaced much of the short-term and piecemeal funding on which previous projects had to rely. Still, however, the evidence base for this practice remains limited. This prompts the questions: Why has *engagement mentoring* arisen as the dominant model of mentoring for social inclusion? And why has it arisen *now*?

To answer these questions, we need to consider the economic, social and political context in which engagement mentoring has flourished at the end of the twentieth century. I begin with economic changes in the world of work and their influence on dominant discourses surrounding young people's career transitions. I then go on to examine broader policy approaches to social inclusion in response to this context.

Globalization and youth transitions

The concept of globalization dominates discussions of our historical era. It is impossible to do justice to such a vast subject here, and I refer readers to other authors who have analysed globalization in greater depth (e.g. Beck, 1992; Giddens, 1990; Harvey, 1997; Lyotard, 1973; Sassen, 2000; M.-A. Waters, 1994; M. Waters, 1995). However, in order to understand engagement mentoring as an intervention with socially excluded young people, it is important to recognize the impact of globalization upon perceptions of the world of work and therefore upon young people's school-to-work transitions.

There is widespread consensus that the landscape of employment has been transformed in the last quarter of the twentieth century. The most common themes are the introduction of new technologies, the decline of manufacturing and the dominance of the service sector, which have intensified economic competition at all levels. Institutional structures have adopted 'flatter', less hierarchical forms, and an economy based on services rather than manufacturing, on knowledge rather than physical labour, now requires flexible approaches to work. At the same time, this is held to have brought an end to lifelong job security and a need for lifelong learning to up-skill the population.

Along with the parallel collapse of the traditional youth labour market that used to see most young people enter work directly from school (Rikowski, 2001b), these changes have led to a shift in the way youth transitions are conceptualized. Talk about transitions and careers has moved from metaphors of linear progression, such as ladders and pathways, to metaphors of uncertainty and risk, such as navigation and fragmentation (Furlong and Cartmel, 1997). Another aspect of the economic imperative of globalization that has received critical attention is the increased marketization of PCET options, and the extensive diversification of that market (Maguire et al., 1999). This individualist notion of 'consumer choice' has resulted in an intense policy focus on young people's transitions, represented in initiatives such as the failed experiment with Youth Training Credits (Hodkinson et al., 1996), and the current restructure of guidance and PCET provision (DfEE, 1999d; SEU, 1999).

A number of empirical studies have also raised complex questions about subjective aspects of choice and decision-making. While some young people still have a good chance of enjoying relatively linear and successful transitions, career trajectories have become differentiated in new ways, mediated by subjectivity as well as by structure. A substantial number of young people now move in and out of multiple trajectories, including various permutations of full- and part-time study and work. They have been able to cope with the instability and dislocation of their post-16 transitions by their negotiation of new identities. These are connected closely with patterns of consumption, particularly cultural forms associated with leisure (Ball et al., 2000), and include differentiated aspects of cultural taste and class distinction within the PCET market itself (Maguire et al., 1999). However, there remains a third group of young people who continue to find themselves at the margins of, or excluded from, formal learning opportunities. Lacking the financial, social and/or cultural resources either to engage with that market or to create new subjectivities that might allow them to adapt flexibly to it, they are significantly disadvantaged in respect of the labour market (Ferguson et al., 2000).

Raffo reports action research to assist disadvantaged young people in entering the creative cultural industries in the 'global city' of Manchester. The project focused on the use of mentoring to help young people develop vital social capital and networks (Raffo and Hall, 1999; Raffo, 2000; Raffo and Reeves, 2000). By matching them with adults already working in creative industries, it aimed to engage them in situated learning in authentic contexts. The development of skills such as flexibility, problem-solving and the application of theory to practice was envisaged as an empowering process allowing young people to forge careers as freelance workers. Unfortunately Raffo offers little empirical evidence of the outcomes of this project. Moreover, there is alternative evidence (e.g. Bates, 1994b) that the ability to enter such industries is often dependent on access to economic capital through families' financial sponsorship of the young person's career. Success may require far broader and more established social capital that can provide personal sponsorship for opportunities. While taking a much less directive stance than engagement mentoring typically proposes, Raffo's conception of the process appears to underestimate the role of social structures in shaping young people's trajectories.

Post-Fordism and employability

One of the key changes in the last quarter of the twentieth century is the shift to post-Fordist forms of work organization. Post-Fordism refers to systems characterized by product diversification, niche marketing and flexible team-working, as opposed to earlier twentieth-century 'Fordist' systems of mass production and a rigid division of labour. Debates about the nature of this change often centre on the argument that it requires new types of skill to function in post-Fordist organizations. Prime importance is ascribed to skills that have been variously termed 'core skills', 'key skills', 'transferable skills', or summarized in the concept of 'employability'. These have acquired 'almost totemic status' within education and training (Green, 1997: 88).

What are these skills and qualities of employability held to be? Why does employability matter? One report compiled on behalf of employers, *Towards Employability* (Industry in Education, 1996), opens with the statement that 'Too many of today's young people are poorly prepared for work' (p. 2), and estimates that 'the cost to Britain exceeds £8 billion a year' (p. 2). It goes on to present a lack of employability as a cause of both individual and social crisis:

> Most young people want to succeed but their lack of positive qualities can destroy employability. A lack of employability then destroys ambition, hope and self-esteem. And without exaggerating the point, in extreme cases, such failures are clearly a contributory cause of the high crime and social disorder rates among certain groups of young people.
>
> (Industry in Education, 1996: 2)

In reviewing employers' requirements, the report emphasizes employers' interests in the display of certain personal qualities over and above the importance of qualifications. The qualities highlighted include being articulate, lively, adaptable, innovative, and willing to learn and get involved, as well as demonstrating 'initiative, motivation, pleasantness and communication skills', and the ability to 'fit in with a team and within a company culture' (p. 9). An important caveat is inserted alongside these requirements, however:

> With this in mind, *employers also set considerable store on the qualities of compromise and respect. . . .* We would not disagree with those who would cite increases in

pupils' self-expression and confidence as one of the modern-day successes of a less formal style of teaching. However, we would counsel that *these qualities must always be developed hand-in-hand with educational attention to context and social expectations.*

(Industry in Education, 1996: 9, emphases added)

Furthermore:

> [Staff] also need the personal characteristics and qualities that enable them to deal more effectively with customers, *to sign on to the values and ethos of the business and to fit into its organisational structure, culture and work ethics.*
>
> Not all of these things will be 'natural fits' to an individual's basic personality, so pre-employment development must have taken place to a point where young recruits will have the social adaptability, personal flexibility and awareness of their own strengths and weaknesses to *'go with' the requirements of the job* and give sufficient signals of this during the selection process.

(Industry in Education, 1996: 10, emphases added)

Engagement mentoring is one aspect of 'pre-employment development' that is used to adapt individuals' 'basic personality', and seems to represent one of the educational 'tools' that the report calls for, to encourage young people

> to look at generic attributes that will promote a good working match to employment, or encourage [them] *to look at their own values, attitudes, human interactions* and working styles.

(Industry in Education, 1996: 10, emphasis added)

Education is firmly situated as a service 'providing employers with usable output from the education system, and providing pupils, as individuals, with a strong chance of gaining employment' (p. 28).

Numerous documents present a similar picture of employability (e.g. DfEE, 1996, 2000b, c; Glynn and Nairne, 2000), although rarely in such a combative way as in the *Towards Employability* report. Despite the fact that this view of employability has been condemned as having 'more to do with shaping subjectivity, deference and demeanour than with skill development and citizenship' (Gleeson, 1996: 97), it has thoroughly permeated policy and practice in the field of youth support and guidance, and in mentoring for social inclusion. In doing so, it promotes three key themes.

First, those working with young people in transition are supposed to encourage them to understand, accept and cope with working life at the periphery, without expectations of full-time or permanent employment. This includes the inevitable insecurity and stress of 'portfolio' careers (Wijers and Meijers, 1996), of daily and weekly fluctuations in the availability of work (Vandevelde, 1998), and of part-time, temporary, subcontracted and freelance working (Bridges, 1998).

Second, it promotes the view that young people need to re-invent their own identities as marketable products. The realization of individual potential is equated with the maximization of productivity. Young people's attitudes, values and beliefs consequently need to be transformed. Bridges (1998), for example, has argued that career guidance should focus on transforming clients' attitudes, temperament and *desire*. For him, employability is about '*Who wants to work the most?*' (pp. 13–14). This transformation of personal disposition is also a central theme of the Social Exclusion Unit report *Bridging the Gap* (SEU, 1999), which forcefully promotes the idea that the attitudes, values and beliefs of the socially excluded themselves are a major cause of their (self-)exclusion (Colley and Hodkinson, 2001).

Third, the key challenge for practitioners and mentors working with young people in transition is their clients' resistance to change. Their role thus becomes seen as that of overcoming reluctance to accept employers' demands, and to proselytize vigorously the transformations wrought by globalization (cf. Bayliss, 1998; Wijers and Meijers, 1996). The product of such practice should be young people's willingness to embrace both the rhetoric and the reality of the post-Fordist world of work. This offers another rationale for using the term 'engagement mentoring', since it seeks not only to engage young people with the labour market, but also to engage their commitment to the interests of their employing organizations, and their very hearts and minds to the enterprise. But what of the more general policy context that has embraced engagement mentoring as such a popular intervention?

Policies for social inclusion: individualism and moralization

Much academic critique of PCET and guidance policies inevitably focused until recently on the rise and eventual dominance of the politics of the New Right (e.g. Avis *et al.*, 1996). However, even before the end of Conservative rule and New Labour's first term in office, a debate had arisen about whether Labour policies have represented a sea-change, or simply a discursive reformulation of their predecessors' approach (Levitas, 1996; Lister, 1998). The high profile which the New Labour government accorded to the issues of social exclusion, widening participation and lifelong learning was at first welcomed widely as a reinstatement of concerns for social justice, following years of assertion by the New Right that there is 'no such thing as society', and the Conservative government's unbridled pursuit of free market policies (Keep, 1997). But does having a policy about a particular social problem constitute a promise or a threat?

The reply might well be 'a little bit of both'. The promise of addressing social exclusion has understandably contributed to the development and popularity of engagement mentoring. There appears to have been a grass-roots rejection of the entrepreneurial sink-or-swim ethos of the Conservative government, dominated by the New Right throughout the 1980s and early 1990s. Enthusiasm for mentoring, and the desire to build caring relationships, may also represent a reaction to the bureaucratized support for young people that has been the 'dark side' of professionalizing welfare services throughout the twentieth century (Freedman, 1999). However, engagement mentoring also fits neatly with other aspects of the policy and political context considered here. In this regard, some elements of New Labour policy may indeed contain a threat, insofar as it represents continuity with the New Right agenda.

A central aspect of New Right policies was to devolve responsibility on to individual workers and young people, to ensure that they acquired training to meet the shifting demands of the post-Fordist world of work. One of the key mechanisms for imposing this responsibility has been the marketization of education and training, with its rhetoric of consumerism and choice (Hodkinson, 1996; Maguire *et al.*, 1999). The paradox of this rhetoric was that those supporting young people through their post-16 transitions were 'increasingly forced into modes of intervention located within a tradition of behaviour modification, rather than education for autonomy and choice' (Jeffs and Smith, 1996: 25). Since the election of New Labour, numerous commentators have pointed to the way in which this government has continued to develop policies based on that individualistic approach, in marked contradiction to the communitarian rhetoric of the social exclusion agenda (e.g. Ferguson *et al.*, 2000; Lister, 1998; Stepney *et al.*, 1999). In important respects, New Labour has shifted away from the crudely simplistic view of the New Right, and substituted a more complex discourse of individualism.

One of the most important policies flowing from these moves has been that of welfare-to-work, replicating the earlier 'workfare' programme in the United States under Democrat President Clinton. Freedman (1999) argues that this has been a key influence in policy-makers' interest in the use of mentoring as an intervention with socially excluded youth. It helps to explain the ties between engagement mentoring and the goals of expected labour market destinations. Such outcomes are credible only in a period of economic upturn when employment levels are high, and become increasingly difficult to legitimate in times of recession leading to high unemployment (Brine, 1998). In this regard, it is not surprising that engagement mentoring has become established during just such an upturn.

On the other hand, this also points to the increasing ideological value mentoring will have if, as seems highly likely, the current economic recession in the US leads to a global recession that once again finds unemployment levels soaring. In such a scenario, engagement mentoring appears to offer a partial but high-profile response to the fear of social unrest which may underpin the social exclusion agenda promoted by New Labour and the European Community (Brine, 1998). In doing so increasingly through the use of volunteers, and often with less than adequate funding for mentor training and support, it can also represent an extremely cheap intervention with a disproportionately high 'feel-good' factor for the expenditure (Gulam and Zulfiqar, 1998).

The welfare-to-work ethos is particularly evident in what is arguably the most important policy document to underpin the current expansion of engagement mentoring, *Bridging the Gap* (SEU, 1999). This report has as its central proposal the establishment of *Connexions* as an integrated mentoring and support service targeted at socially excluded young people. (For a more detailed critique of *Bridging the Gap*, see Colley and Hodkinson, 2001.) Its analysis posits a causal relationship between non-participation in structured learning between the ages of 16 and 18 and longer term experiences of social exclusion. It represents social exclusion almost entirely in terms of deficit and deviancy, an approach which Watts (1999) has claimed is typical of New Labour policy. A litany of lacks – poor physical and mental health, lack of qualifications and skills, teenage parenthood, drug dependency, unstable families – are underscored by selective quotes from young people that compound a portrait of feckless idlers staying in bed until late in the afternoon, then loafing on street corners and engaging in petty crime.

Bridging the Gap represents young people's attitudes, values and beliefs as the major reason for their exclusion. The report chastises them, along with their families and communities, for maintaining an unfounded pessimism in their job prospects, and for their 'lack of any purposeful activity' (SEU, 1999: 8). It is not surprising, then, that the report's major proposal focuses on engagement mentoring, which poses the need for young people to re-invent themselves because they are 'the wrong sort of people, living in the wrong places, displaying the wrong attitudes' (Jeffs and Spence, 2000: 40).

There are strong parallels with the three chief indicators by which Charles Murray controversially defined the 'underclass'. They are single-parent families with absent fathers, criminal behaviour often linked to drug abuse, and unemployment in the form of 'large numbers of young healthy, low-income males [who] choose not to take jobs' (Murray, 1990: 17). Similarly, such a focus on attitudes, values and behaviours is the hallmark of discourses which place a moral interpretation upon social exclusion, and pathologize those considered to be socially excluded (Jeffs and Smith, 1996; Lister, 1998; Reid, 1999; Watts, 1999, 2001a). Their very appeal to dominant moral codes restricts the space for policy debate, and legitimates particular policy innovations.

These policies contain a strong element of Calvinistic moralism. We can detect a resonance between the Prime Minister's Foreword to *Bridging the Gap*: 'The best defence against social exclusion is having a job, and the best way to get a job is to have a good education, with the right training and experience' (Blair, 1999: 6), and Thomas Carlyle's proclamation in his Edinburgh speech of 1886: 'Work is the grand cure of all the maladies and miseries that ever beset mankind.' This has been seen as a new authoritarianism towards the poor (Stepney *et al.*, 1999) as well as towards young people (Jeffs and Smith, 1996; Jeffs and Spence, 2000), relying at least as much upon the stick of coercion as upon the carrot of incentive. The WASP work ethic has come to redefine key notions that used to underpin 'Old' Labour policies:

> According to Gordon Brown [*Labour's Chancellor of the Exchequer*]: 'The government's strategy is to provide employment opportunities for all – the modern definition of full employment in the 21st century' (Budget speech,

1998). What this means for the unemployed is that the efficiency of the market demands that they must compete with each other through their perseverance and skill levels, or suffer the consequences of benefit withdrawal.

(Holden, 1999: 537)

However, Ecclestone (1999) has pointed to a paradox in these policies: despite the policy focus on individual *responsibility*, individual *autonomy* is in fact seen as transgressive. It is construed as risky within the current discourse of lifelong learning, resulting in increasingly directive and compulsory approaches to propel the socially excluded into the 'liberating possibilities' of education both for their own good and for the good of society (Ecclestone, 1999: 335). Moreover, this redefinition works in the opposite direction, and 'risk' comes to signify almost any instance of independent activity that transgresses dominant norms. Participation in formal learning and employment thus becomes a 'guilty obligation to others' (Ecclestone, 1999: 340). It is not difficult to see how engagement mentoring could be used as a pulpit for preaching this obligation.

A sign of the times

This historical perspective on mentoring suggests that it is impossible to understand its power dynamics purely in terms of the micro-level interactions between mentor and mentee. Engagement mentoring is located within a far larger and more complex web of power relations that are specific to our historical era. The most fundamental structural forces in our society include capitalist economic and social relations. They also include gender and the patriarchal oppression of women, and other deep-rooted inequalities relating to youth, race and disability. These continue to influence youth transitions and social trajectories, including through institutional practices such as planned mentoring. Such macro-level power relations are bolstered further by the contemporary political climate. Engagement mentoring at the turn of the millennium therefore has to be viewed as a social phenomenon created in part by this context. We must keep these aspects in sight to understand fully the experiences of individual mentors and mentees.

So far, then, I have traced the emergence of engagement mentoring, describing its key features and the context that informs it. This entire discussion, however, begs a more fundamental question, one that has vexed the field incessantly: What does mentoring actually mean? And how can we define it?

Chapter 2

Unravelling myths of Mentor

The difficulty of defining mentoring

Perhaps the most persistently tantalizing question I have come across in the study of mentoring – among researchers, professionals, mentors and mentees alike – is also an apparently basic one: What does mentoring mean? How can we define it? It seems to be a vexing question for those involved in its practice, as some of the mentors at New Beginnings found:

Jane: [Mentoring] means such a lot, because I think it's very difficult to define.

Karen: Mentoring is difficult, because no one ever tells you exactly what it should be.

Rachel: I'm really confused about how the mentoring. . . . The mentoring side of the [training] course was very sort of: 'OK, this is where you are, this is what you're like' . . . but when you got there, you didn't know what you were doing.

The training provided for the students who volunteered as mentors at New Beginnings and the views of the scheme's staff are described in Chapter 3, while the interpretations of mentoring that individual mentors and young people developed are explored in the case stories in Chapters 4 to 6. These accounts reveal a wide variety of meanings adopted by different participants within a single scheme.

These difficulties in defining mentoring are hardly surprising. Although the past twenty-five years have produced a vast amount of academic literature on mentoring, it has failed to achieve any consensus. Most recently, Roberts has reviewed that literature comprehensively, seeking a lexical definition which might resolve 'whether or not we are talking about the same thing' (Roberts, 2000a: 148). He analyses over eighty works, and concludes that definitions of mentoring are both myriad and elusive. Piper and Piper warn that mentoring may mean all things to all people, a 'ubiquitous and chameleon-like approach which is everywhere in name but nowhere in substance' (1999: 129). Reams of academic literature have not only failed to rescue mentoring from the 'definitional quagmire' that Haggerty identified in 1986 (cited in Roberts, 2000a: 149), but have made the problem worse. One early literature review complained that this was hindering the research process itself:

> The phenomenon of mentoring is not clearly conceptualized, leading to confusion as to just what is being measured or offered as an ingredient in success. Mentoring appears to mean one thing to developmental psychologists, another thing to business people, and a third thing to those in academic settings.
>
> (Merriam, 1983: 169)

I do not propose to drag readers into the swamp of a detailed semantic discussion here. A more useful way to clarify what we mean by 'mentoring' is to consider two broad approaches that have been taken to this problem. In doing so, we will need to look beyond youth mentoring to other contexts in which mentoring has been widely used, such as initial and continuing professional development for business managers, teachers and nurses. It will also be particularly helpful to identify the few critical analyses of mentoring that have emerged, and the important points of debate they have raised.

Mentoring: functions or relationship?

One of the main ways in which researchers have tried to define mentoring is in terms of mentor functions. Alleman (1986) elaborated nine functions of a mentor, ranging from coaching to personal sponsorship. Kram (1988) proposed a dualist typology of 'career-related' and 'psychosocial' (personal support) functions which still underpins many research enquiries into mentoring (e.g. Roberts, 1998, 2000b; Scandura, 1998). However, since mentoring is now practised in so many different contexts, the list of functions it might incorporate grows and grows. If we defined mentoring by its functions, it would create an effect similar to the *lipsmackinthirst quenchinacetastinmotivatingoodbuzzincooltalkinhighwalkinfastlivinevergivincoolfizzin* . . . Pepsi-Cola advertisement. We would find ourselves confronted with a litany of mentoring functions that may never be exhaustive: teaching, coaching, advising, guiding, directing, protecting, supporting, sponsoring, challenging, encouraging, motivating, befriending, inspiring, *esteembuildinrolemodellininformationgivinskillsharincareerdevelop innovicenurturinrisktakingradeimprovinaspirationraisinhorizonbroadenintargetsettinkingmakinselfre generatincriticallyreflectinperformanceassessinfeedbackgivin*. . . .The result is a blur, the concept becomes increasingly hard to distinguish, yet (as in the Pepsi ad) the effect is not to deepen our understanding of mentoring. It simply creates a sense of how wonderful it must be, since it produces so many positive effects.

What is it, then, that makes mentoring special? What sets it apart from the many other instances of these functions, where we call them by their own names: teaching, guidance, advice and so on? To switch similes: What produces the sense that mentoring, like Coca-Cola, is 'The Real Thing'? Anderson and Lucasse Shannon argue that the distinctive essence of mentoring is its combination of developmental functions *with an 'ongoing caring relationship'* (1995: 29). In a similar vein, Roberts (2000b) finds that mentors expect to provide both instrumental and personal support to their mentees, but place more emphasis on the latter in practice. He concludes that 'a supportive relationship' is the essential attribute of mentoring that distinguishes it from its contingent functions.

Mentoring, as 'The Real Thing', aspires to create a human bond. Merriam (1983) identified a classical model of mentoring in Levinson's study *The Seasons of a Man's Life* (Levinson *et al.*, 1978). Based on Carl Jung's developmental psychology, this is regarded as a seminal work, and is credited with sparking widespread interest in mentoring. In four detailed case studies of men throughout the middle years of their lives, an unexpected finding was the crucial role a mentor had played in the careers of three of them. It describes many of the functions of a mentor already noted above, but most importantly the authors define it as a long-term and intense emotional relationship akin to parental love:

> The true mentor . . . serves as an analogue in adulthood of the 'good enough' parent for the child . . . creating a space in which the young man can work on a reasonably satisfactory life structure that contains the Dream.
>
> (Levinson et al., 1978: 98–99)

('The Dream' is a term used by Jung, and refers to career and lifestyle aspirations held in early adulthood.) These findings rapidly inspired a series of surveys to investigate mentoring among successful business executives, reflected in Roche's report, 'Much ado about mentors' (1979).

Researching mentor relationships

The most successful mentor relationships described by Levinson *et al.* had arisen on an informal basis. The study showed that they were relatively rare, and its authors recommended that mentoring and its benefits should be made more widely accessible. A great deal of research was subsequently devoted to capturing the essence of mentor relationships. Quantitative methods were used to try and identify objective factors for success, and to develop best practice guidelines for formalized mentoring programmes. Such studies (e.g. Fagenson, 1988; Noe, 1988; Scandura and Viator, 1994) typically use psychological survey questionnaires to measure various attitudes, behaviours and outcomes of mentor relationships, but provide little insight into the processes and development of the relationships themselves. They therefore tend to return us to the Pepsi-style list of functions, rather than bringing us any closer to the Coke-style 'Real Thing'. As Merriam argued:

> Mentoring relationships have to first be uncovered and then investigated in the totality of a person's life – both the mentor's and the protégé's. Research focus could thus be upon the dynamics of the relationship itself, the motivations

behind the formation of such relationships, the positive and negative outcomes, the reciprocity of the relationships, and so on.

(Merriam, 1983: 171)

How has the literature of almost two decades met the challenge of this research agenda? We can identify three main trends.

First, a small number of qualitative social psychology studies (e.g. Kram, 1988; Levinson *et al.*, 1978) do give us some sense of the inner workings of these relationships. They focus primarily on mentoring within the work context of education or business organizations, between senior, more experienced individuals and newcomers to a profession or company. They offer insights into the ways that participants perceived themselves, each other and the progress of their relationship over time. They also attempt to situate these insights at least within the institutional context of the workplace, and within the 'totality of a person's life' through some exploration of life histories in the research interviews. They give little consideration, however, to the impact of wider societal factors upon these individual relationships.

Such studies typically define mentor relationships according to successive phases through which they develop. Kram (1988) identifies the key phases as initiation, cultivation, separation and redefinition, reinforcing the notion of mentoring as a linear, quasi-parental relationship. As with parent–adolescent relationships, the stage of separation, where the mentee is capable of and desires more autonomy, is identified as the point at which conflicts may occur. At this stage, mentor relationships may become less beneficial or even destructive for either partner. However, the successful completion of the cycle is represented as a move from initial inequality between expert and novice towards relative equality as peers. With the notable exceptions of Philip's work in the UK (Philip, 1997, 2000a; Philip and Hendry, 1996) and that of Freedman (1995, 1999) in the US, there are no such in-depth qualitative studies in the literature on youth mentoring.

Second, later examples of such case study research offer fewer insights into particular relationships, partly because they do not investigate the broader life histories of individual respondents. They do, however, acknowledge to a greater degree the broader socio-economic and political context that has driven the increasingly formalized use of mentoring. Some refer to the competitive economic pressures on businesses since the mid-1970s to reduce or remove those layers of middle management, especially personnel departments, which traditionally were responsible for individual training and development (Megginson and Clutterbuck, 1995; Shea, 1992). Mentoring became favoured as a way of enabling both the induction of new staff and continuing professional development in the workplace, using the support of experienced colleagues rather than more expensive and time-consuming off-the-job training.

In education itself, highly political decisions brought mentoring to prominence. In 1992, a circular from the Department for Education and Science (forerunner of the DfEE and DfES) substantially increased the proportion of school-based training for student teachers, reducing the influence of teacher educators and higher education institutions. As a result, mentoring of students during their teaching practice became central to their initial education. Researchers identified new institutional pressures upon the mentor relationship as this happened, particularly as mentors had an important role in the formal assessment of students' performance. The mentor relationship thus became linked with professional 'gatekeeping' functions (Gay and Stephenson, 1998; McIntyre *et al.*, 1993; Millwater and Yarrow, 1997).

A third group of writings consists of anecdotal accounts of mentor relationships. These sometimes appear as tributes by a mentee on the occasion of the mentor's retirement or death. Others are written by both members of a mentoring dyad, reflecting back on their relationship once it has moved beyond the final phase of 'redefinition'. These tend to be celebratory stories, bordering occasionally on the self-congratulatory:

> Like the onset of the relationship, the redefinition solidified rapidly and unnoticed. When [Joan] asked Gordon to serve on her doctoral committee it was with the confidence that she would not feel subservient. For his part, Gordon had already seen the relationship as one of equality for months before the consulting work had begun. The relationship is now an easy one, two people who know each other well and get pleasure from collaboration.
>
> (Harrison and Klopf, 1986: 64)

Here, the shift from inherent inequality to shared peer status in the relationship is central.

Anecdotal celebrations also form a significant proportion of the literature on youth mentoring, particularly more popular representations found in the educational press (e.g. Times Educational Supplement, 2000) and at events such as the National Mentoring Network conferences. These narratives, however, notably lack the shift towards a growing sense of equality contained in professional tales of mentoring. The tendency to promote stories of happy endings is hardly surprising, for who would wish (or dare) to wash any dirty linen about unproductive or failed relationships in public, let alone define such failures as mentoring?

This third category underlines the inherent weaknesses of much research into mentoring, including more serious studies:

> The literature on mentoring is biased in favour of the phenomenon . . . it warrants neither the enthusiasm about its value, nor the exhortations to go out and find one . . . [M]entoring is not clearly conceptualised. . . . The majority of published articles consists of testimonials or opinions . . . [T]here are no studies of the negative effects of mentoring, or [of its] absence.
>
> (Merriam, 1983: 169–170)

The subsequent literature has done little to rectify the situation. Almost two decades later, Piper and Piper protest that accounts of mentoring tend to be 'programmatic and anecdotal' (2000: 84). Scandura (1998) argues that even the most compre-hensive studies have failed to devote adequate attention to evidence of negative and damaging experiences in mentoring. She claims that this 'dark side of mentoring' has become a taboo subject.

Much research starts from the biased starting point of investigating the assumed *benefits* of mentoring, rather than its full range of outcomes. This may be due to the dominance of evaluation studies commissioned by mentoring projects themselves. The pressure to demonstrate success to funding sponsors may produce research that is conformative rather than genuinely analytical or critical (Stronach and Morris, 1994). Elsewhere, many exhortations to practise mentoring are uttered without any clear definition. Examples may be found in policy documentation:

> We believe that a good mentor can make all the difference to outcomes for disaffected young people. We commend the use of mentoring in work with these young people. Programmes designed to re-integrate young people into the mainstream should involve the use of mentors.
>
> (House of Commons Education and Employment Committee, 1998: xxxvii)

They are also evident in manager- and practitioner-oriented literature. Here is one example of an unsubstantiated claim in a consultancy report prepared for a local authority, suggesting strategies for the social inclusion of young people:

> There is a wealth of information extolling the value of mentoring schemes. . . . Mentoring could be seen as an ideal strategy to re-establish contact with . . . young people [who are either self-excluding or 'dropped off the end' of existing provision].
>
> (Toucan Europe, 1999: 2)

A similar trend appears in academic texts, such as this bold but unelaborated statement:

> There needs to be much more mentoring. The theme of mentoring is gradually becoming more familiar, but in a lifelong learning culture it will come into its own. There will be major problems in raising mentoring from an occasional facility into a mass provision.
>
> (Smith and Spurling, 1999: 146)

Functions or relationship? Appearances or essence? Pepsi or Coke? At the end of the day, neither approach tells us much about the product, except that it must be good, and that it will make us feel good. All this leaves us as far as ever from a definition of mentoring. As a set of functions, it proliferates as it shifts into new contexts. As a relationship, it seems to offer some distinction between mentoring and its component functions. However, such relationships are not only difficult to investigate and portray, but clearly there exist barriers to considering them in an unbiased way.

One possible source of clarification may be found in dissenting voices raised among this imprecise consensus. Although Merriam (1983) noted the biased nature of mentoring research long ago, it is only recently that a small but important body of work has begun to emerge, seeking to uncover and challenge some of the taken-for-granted assumptions that shape the meanings given to mentoring. As indicated in Chapter 1, such critiques signal the need for a closer examination of the dynamics of power in mentor relationships, and this has often been linked with issues of gender.

Power and gender in mentor relationships

Gay and Stephenson (1998) analyse mentor relationships in terms of their power dynamics. They situate different styles and aspects of mentoring on a spectrum which ranges from direction to guidance (see Table 2.1).

This framework presents mutuality of learning as key to the effectiveness of mentor relationships. Although a degree of inequality is seen as inevitable, Gay and Stephenson argue that it should be minimized. None the less, their analysis implicitly ascribes the power to determine where a particular relationship will find itself on this spectrum to the mentor. This is expressed more explicitly by Millwater and Yarrow (1997), who argue that the 'mindset' of the mentor determines the quality of the relationship. The few studies which touch upon the 'dark side' of mentoring also suggest that problems in mentoring arise from mentors' abuse of their superior power (Kram, 1988; Long, 1997; Scandura, 1998). Others suggest that traditional models inherently produce 'unequal access to power, and even power of the mentor over the person being mentored' (Armstrong and Zukas, 1997: 7). They conclude that peer mentoring may be a more egalitarian model.

However, Gay and Stephenson (1998) also offer a different perspective. They suggest (although they do not develop the insight fully) that the formalization of mentoring within powerful institutions such as schools or companies changes the nature of the process. The needs and interests of the institution increasingly

Table 2.1 Spectrum of mentoring styles

Direction	◀——————▶	Guidance
Hierarchy	◀——————▶	Reciprocity
Control	◀——————▶	Empowerment
Inequality	◀——————▶	Equality
Dependency	◀——————▶	Autonomy

Source: Adapted from Gay and Stephenson (1998)

determine the agenda and goals of mentor relationships, rather than allowing negotiation within the dyad itself. The imposition of external goals tends to drive the mentor's practice towards the more directive end of the spectrum. Here we can raise further questions: How does this influence the mentor's role? Does it simply increase the power – and potential for abuse of power – on the part of the mentor? To what extent does the mentor become a vehicle for external interests, rather than a facilitator for the mentee? Does this suggest a different conceptualization of power relations in mentoring, as the mentor relationship becomes *triadic* rather than dyadic? And to what extent might this raise ethical dilemmas, where conflicts of interest might arise?

These are important considerations in engagement mentoring for young people. We have seen how this model is tied to employment-related outcomes decided by policy-makers, and influenced by employers' needs. But there is a danger here that socially excluded young people may be treated as the objects of others' agendas:

> if the individual is understood as essentially passive and dependent on society for defining meanings, values and patterns of activity, then mentoring will be regarded as being concerned with individual behaviour and its modification in accordance with a socially prescribed blueprint. Although constraint may be ruled out, differential status and the demonstration of implicit or explicit benefit will provide the basis for focused behaviour modification, achieved by example or exhortation.
>
> (Piper and Piper, 1999: 127)

In this scenario, mentoring may come to represent a form of 'social cleansing or human resource allocation' (Piper and Piper, 2000: 90), especially when governments are under economic pressure to reduce welfare spending, but fear the social unrest this may create (Freedman, 1999).

Roberts (1998, 2000b) broaches the issue of gender stereotypes in mentoring through the notion of 'psychological androgyny'. He argues that this might be a useful way to combine the effective elements of both (male) power and (female) nurture on the part of mentors, in providing instrumental assistance as well as emotional support for their mentees. His findings are that all mentors experienced a more powerful drive to act in nurturing rather than instrumental ways. However, this psychological approach fails to take into account gender as a social construction which is part of women's oppression in our society. It evades rather than reveals the gender stereotype inherent in the notion of nurture, and it fails to address the location of mentoring dyads within wider relations of power. This leads us to consider a further strand of thought, bringing feminist perspectives to bear on mentoring.

Liberal feminist authors have criticized the classical model of mentoring as hierarchical and directive, based on assumptions of paternalism and androcentric theories of development, even in all-female dyads (Cochran-Smith and Paris, 1995;

DeMarco, 1993; Standing, 1999). Within such traditional frameworks, the mentor is construed as the powerful member of the dyad, and the mentee as the powerless or disempowered. The process is seen as transmitting a reified concept of knowledge from the experienced mentor to the novice mentee, reinforcing established practice and invalidating the new. These critiques call for 'alternative vision[s of] . . . women's ways of collaborating' (Cochran-Smith and Paris, 1995: 182) and '[m]entoring relationships that assume both asymmetry *and* equal participation in conjoined work' (Cochran-Smith and Paris, 1995: 189), based on 'the three common characteristics of mentorship – reciprocity, empowerment and solidarity' (DeMarco, 1993: 1243). Although Standing identifies a 'nurturing *versus* controlling duality' (1999: 4) in common models of mentoring, she criticizes their tendency to subordinate the nurturing element to the process of control.

This view also suggests that the problem of power in mentoring is above all a problem for the mentee. It focuses on the vulnerability of the mentee's position, particularly where that location is compounded by class status and/or gender or other forms of oppression. This is not an unimportant issue, and certainly deserves more research attention than it has received. It is an issue that will be explored centrally in the case stories later in this book. However, about 80 per cent of New Beginnings mentors were female, as is the case for youth mentoring volunteers nationally (Skinner and Fleming, 1999). The same is true of careers service staff, who have formed the core of the *Connexions* service. Social constructions of gender stereotypically represent the role of women as carers and nurturers, both within the family and at work, and this is part of their oppression within patriarchal society.

From this perspective, models of mentoring based on nurture may be problematic for the female majority of mentors. If dominant discourses of mentoring seek to transmit dominant ideologies (Standing, 1999), and if 'mentoring needs to be subjected to a critique that is appreciative of the present political economy and all its attendant contradictions' (Gulam and Zulfiqar, 1998: 44), then a socialist (rather than liberal) feminist critique is needed to address the way in which mentoring impacts not only upon the mentee, but upon the mentor as well. The operation of power within mentoring dyads may be far more complex than the simple contrast between a controlling or a nurturing stance on the mentor's part.

Myths of Mentor

This complexity may be illustrated by analysing one of the most powerful images that has been used to promote the mentoring movement: the myth of Mentor. The original Mentor was a character in Homer's *Odyssey* (an epic poem from Ancient Greece), and this myth appears repeatedly in academic articles, practitioner journals, and in publicity and training materials for mentoring programmes. It is used to claim that mentoring is a practice dating back thousands of years, and this is typical of the way in which myths often serve to legitimate certain practices. The myth of Mentor is frequently used to introduce the mentor's role and define it in a highly rhetorical manner. A more detailed analysis of these images can allow us to unravel *what* is being legitimated, *how* that legitimation takes place and what meanings of mentoring are conveyed. Revealing insights may be gained by contrasting the original tale with modern versions.

Homer's epic tells of the king Odysseus' lengthy return from the Trojan War. During his absence he had entrusted his kingdom, Ithaca, and his infant son, Telemachus, to the care of an old friend, Mentor. Little did he know that he would be absent for twenty years. The better known heart of the poem is Odysseus' account of his arduous journey home after the fall of Troy, but this is framed at the start and end of the poem by a sub-plot. The goddess Athene first assures his return home, then prepares his son for their reunion, and finally assists them to regain the throne of Ithaca from usurpers who have created chaos there. Modern accounts draw on this myth in one of two ways.

Some versions focus on the figure of Mentor himself. He is portrayed as a wise and kindly elder, a surrogate parent, a trusted adviser, an educator and guide. His role is described variously as nurturing, supporting, protecting, acting as a role model for Telemachus, and possessing a visionary perception of his ward's true potential. This is seen as demanding integrity, personal investment, and the development of a relationship with the young man based on deep mutual affection and respect. These characteristics reflect the classical model of the mentor.

Other versions identify that it is not Mentor himself, but the goddess Athene (at times disguised as Mentor) who undertakes the active mentor role in the *Odyssey*. As befitting a deity, most of these accounts focus on her extraordinary qualities and her inspirational character. The most significant of these works in the context of engagement mentoring is Ford's (1999a) evaluation of the ICG's Mentoring Action Project (MAP), one of the most important projects to establish mentoring for social inclusion in the UK.

Ford has done much to challenge weaker aspects of new government policies on mentoring, in particular their narrow focus on employment-related goals for socially excluded young people. He has also highlighted the support which professionals need when engaging in intensive work with that client group. However, his report on the MAP is of interest here because Homer's myth is absolutely central to its preface. He uses this preface not only to clarify his terminology, but also to evoke the image of professional mentoring that he wishes to convey:

> It is illuminating to return to the original source of the word 'mentor', and to discern at least some of the characteristics of behaviour which lent force to the term entering the English language in order to describe *a particular quality of caring relationship*.
>
> (Ford, 1999a: 9, emphasis added)

In a powerfully rhetorical and emotive account of mentoring in the *Odyssey*, Ford associates Athene's image with that of the ideal mentor. But he is highly selective in the mentoring activities he chooses to portray, focusing on her role in encouraging Telemachus, building his morale, inspiring him to adult independence, and illuminating his way as, together with his father, she leads him to overthrow the usurpers. Ford also selects, or ascribes, particular qualities she is supposed to possess: her 'high standards of professional practice' (p. 9), her willingness to act as mentor, and her display of the necessary skills.

This characterization of the mythical mentor is deepened throughout the preface. Mentoring is described as 'selfless caring . . . genuinely client-centred care' (p. 8), 'in-depth care' (p. 10), 'caring for each individual client, which was warm, dispassionate, spontaneous and non-judgemental, and with a readiness to go that "additional mile" beyond the call of duty' (p. 13). This culminates in another concept related to Ancient Greek culture, that of *agapé*: '"love" (in terms of selfless giving) [which] denotes the selfless love which we now associate . . . with the genuine professional' (p. 14). This notion of *agapé* is associated, implicitly and explicitly, with Christian religious imagery. Athene lights the way for Telemachus (like Christ), instils him with courage and resolve (like the Holy Spirit), and displays a quasi-parental love for him (like God the Father). This account creates an idealized identity for mentors, one of devotion and self-denial.

Ford's definition of mentoring also draws heavily on that of Shea (1992), who focuses on the 'specialness' of the mentor, once again 'going above and beyond' the already existing work role (p. 21). This reinforces the idea that mentors should accept the additional burden of work that the role often entails. Shea recounts that, in the *Odyssey*, father and son are reunited to overthrow the usurpers and assure Telemachus' birthright, so this also defines the mentor's role:

> History and legend record the deeds of princes and kings, but each of us has a birthright to be all that we can be. Mentors are those special people in our lives, who, through their deeds and work, help us to move towards fulfilling that potential.
>
> (Shea, 1992: 11)

Yet this notion of 'birthright' for the mentee is already contextualized by the prefatory paragraph that opens the book, situating new forms of mentoring within the framework of organizations transformed by new technology, globalization and competitiveness: 'The goal [of mentoring] is not a particular position within the company. Rather it is the empowerment of the mentoree [*sic*] by developing his or her abilities' (Shea, 1992: 7). Once again we see the common theme in recent literature, including the more critical accounts, of mentoring as an empowering relationship in the context of a new world order. However, as we saw in Chapter 1, the idea that post-Fordist changes in the world of work represent a 'birthright' for young people is highly questionable, and the typical 'inheritance' of the young people enrolled at New Beginnings was a meagre one, described in Chapter 3.

This modern version of the Homeric myth thus presents powerful images of mentors as saintly and self-sacrificing on the one hand, and on the other as almost superhuman in their power to transform their mentees. All of these versions are powerful tales of a mentee's rites of passage in the transition to adulthood, a quest in search of a father and a heroic joint reconquest of birthright – tales which elicit a strong emotional response.

The present according to a past we never had

However, the *Odyssey* tells a very different story from any of these versions. As the action of Homer's epic opens, Odysseus' royal household is in utter disarray after his long absence, and Prince Telemachus is in deep personal crisis. Mentor is clearly responsible for this débâcle, and is a public laughing-stock – a far cry from the wise and nurturing adviser portrayed in some modern renditions. Athene has to step into the breach, an omniscient and omnipotent goddess, but she is by no means a typically female or nurturing character. She herself had no mother, being born directly from the head of her father Zeus, king of the gods. This birth thus casts her as the god of wisdom, a representative of male rationality despite her female form. She is also the god of war.

Athene does indeed carry out a number of the functions that have been variously ascribed to mentoring – advice, advocacy, acting as a role model and raising the young man's self-esteem. Yet there is no sense of any emotional bond or nurture between them. The outcome of her mentorship is that Odysseus and Telemachus are reunited, and re-establish their military, economic and political rule in a bloody and ruthless battle. Following this, Telemachus tortures and executes the household maids who had consorted with his enemies, establishing his sexual domination as well. So we see that the myth of the mentor's kindly nurture and self-sacrificing devotion is not age-old at all. It is a modern creation that contrasts starkly with the brutal actions of the ancient myth. It is a simulacrum, 'an identical copy for which no original has ever existed' (Jameson, 1984: 68): the present according to a past we never had. The present is presented as filtering down from the past. Yet this 'past' is the past(iche) of a 'prequel', a social construction of antiquity filtered through the prism of the specific socio-historical context of today.

This gulf between the original myth of Mentor and its modern rewritings raises a number of questions in the current context, as mentoring becomes an ingredient of almost every education and welfare policy recipe. Why should current accounts of mentoring wish to refer to an Ancient Greek myth? Why do they do so in a substantially inaccurate way? If they are not based upon the *Odyssey*, what do these accounts draw upon? Let us analyse more closely the role that myths can play in the practice of mentoring.

Samuel (1999) warns of the 'idolatry of origins' in seeking to explain modern social practices by referring to myths, and Conkey (1991) argues that the search for ancient origins is a kind of 'seduction'. The greater antiquity we ascribe to a feature of human nature or society, the more natural and essential it appears, and the more continuity and tenacity it gains. Reed (1975), through a Marxist feminist approach to anthropology, argues that Ancient Greek myths in particular have to be understood in their original social and historical context. They played an important role in a society which was at a vital cusp, when gender relations and political power had become intertwined. The patriarchy had been established only recently, and there was still a turbulent struggle to defeat earlier matriarchal forms of rule. Greek mythology is therefore 'a reflection of the enormous difficulties involved in consolidating the father family and the line of descent from fathers to sons' (Reed, 1975: 457). Without that consolidation, disaster would result for the ruling order. The moral of the tale of mentoring in the *Odyssey* is that, unless Odysseus has a worthy son and heir, he cannot be a worthy king, and his household will be destroyed. That is why Athene devotes her enormous powers to mentor Telemachus.

Myths, however, obscure their own moral tales. They are depoliticized and depoliticizing, a 'general metalanguage which is trained to *celebrate* things, and no longer to "*act*" them"' (Barthes, 1972: 144, original emphasis). Celebration, as we noted earlier in this chapter, is one of the main themes in mentoring literature and conferences. Myths serve not only to simplify and essentialize our experience, but also to make the contingent (and often the expedient) appear eternal and immutable. In transforming the merely historical into the natural, they serve a specific ideological function: to recruit universal agreement for ideas which covertly serve the interests of a dominant minority. They generate a discourse that brooks no opposition and acts as a 'régime of truth' (Foucault, 1980: 131). To disagree appears immoral.

The nature of human bonds

One seductive aspect of mentoring is its claim to be 'The Real Thing', a close personal relationship. As we saw in Chapter 1, a major rationale for planned mentoring programmes for socially excluded youth is that they will reproduce the benefits of informal mentor relationships, and make those benefits available to young people less able to seek out such relationships for themselves. However, we need to be clear about the types of relationship that arise in different contexts. In particular, informal relationships are entered into voluntarily, while planned relationships are orchestrated by more artificial means.

Human bonds belong to three types: biological and natural, legal and artificial, or social and voluntary. But we often prefer to refer to our less intimate relationships in terms of other, closer bonds (Almond, 1991). Thus the mentoring of young people in planned mentoring schemes (a legal/artificial bond) is represented strongly in the language of caring and parenting (a biological/natural bond) and of religious imagery (a social/voluntary bond) in Ford's MAP report Preface (1999a). Similarly, the title of the major youth mentoring programme in the US, *Big Brothers Big Sisters*, also represents artificial mentor relationships in biological and natural terms.

This returns us to feminist arguments about power and gender in mentoring:

> The social applicability of a concept of mentoring originating from a myth-ical relationship between two privileged men is open to question. This may

reflect patriarchal relations where power is vested in men and perpetuated in future generations through mentoring. . . . [B]y appearing as a man to influence another man, Athena ensures the central roles remain male. Hence mentoring can be regarded as a process through which a dominant ideology is communicated.

(Standing, 1999: 5)

Such liberal feminist critiques centre importantly on issues of social control and hierarchical relationships in mentoring, which are cloaked by a myth evoking nurture. But these feminists themselves remain within the modern discourse of the myth of Mentor. In arguing that mentors should model themselves on a false image of Athene as a nurturing female, they still beg the question of whether it is indeed *possible* to equalize or democratize mentor relationships according to the alternative paradigms they advocate. Can 'women's ways of collaborating' (Cochran-Smith and Paris, 1995: 182) step outside of the régime of truth embodied in the myth – particularly in relation to engagement mentoring of socially excluded young people? Or is this itself a romantic myth? How are mentors positioned within the power relations of our era, particularly in contexts such as youth mentoring, where the majority of mentors are female? What impact do images of mentors as self-sacrificing and devoted 'beyond the call of duty' have on those who do the mentoring? Of the feminist authors we have considered, only Standing (1999: 15) touches briefly upon this aspect of power relations within mentoring dyads. After highlighting the supposed benefits for both members, in two sentences she briefly acknowledges the often unrecognized burden that falls upon the mentor in addition to her normal duties.

Rather than seeking alternative, but still romanticized, versions of mentors as Athene, a combination of feminist and class perspectives might lead to a different critique of this rhetoric. A socialist feminist perspective situates all human relationships within the context of patriarchal capitalist social relations. These are defined by differential relations to the means of production, and by relations of power connected with class, gender, race, disability and other factors. I will return to apply such a perspective to mentoring in Chapter 7, to develop a theoretical framework for understanding the power dynamics of mentor relationships, and to reconsider how the meaning of mentoring may be defined. But having considered the context which has generated engagement mentoring, and having unravelled the meanings contained in its myths, let us turn to the evidence from my empirical research at New Beginnings. Readers can then judge the policies outlined in Chapter 1, and the concepts of mentoring outlined in this chapter, in the light of mentors' and mentees' actual experiences. Before narrating the stories of individual mentor relationships I encountered, I begin by telling the story of the New Beginnings scheme itself in Chapter 3. As an introduction to that story, I end this chapter with a brief description of how the research was conducted.

Conducting the research at New Beginnings

The research was conducted as a case study of a scheme I have called New Beginnings. All personal and institutional names, as well as the location of the scheme, have been anonymized to preserve confidentiality. New Beginnings was a pre-vocational training programme provided for young people by the Wellshire Training and Enterprise Council (WellTEC) in partnership with the University of Wellshire (UoW). It recruited 16- and 17-year-olds classed as 'disaffected', that is to say, who were not engaged in structured education, training or employment. UoW recruited and trained undergraduate students to volunteer as mentors for these young people. (Training and Enterprise Councils were government-appointed regional bodies responsible for training provision and business development. They were disbanded in 2001, and their training remit has been taken over by newly appointed Learning and Skills Councils.)

I approached the research from within a critical interpretive framework (Anderson, 1989). The main method of generating data was through two sweeps of individual semi-structured interviews with each member of matched pairs of student volunteers and young people. These interviews lasted between forty-five and ninety minutes. The sample was restricted to those who had established ongoing mentor relationships, and on the basis of my experience in guidance and counselling, I set a criterion that they should have been meeting together for at least six weeks, although in practice some pairs had been meeting for much longer. This produced a small opportunity sample. Since I was allowed access to the young people only through the auspices of the New Beginnings scheme for a limited time, I interviewed all those who met the criterion and were willing to take part in the research (two mentors declined for personal reasons). This resulted in interviews with nine mentors and eight mentees (one young person had two mentors), and with a further three mentors whose mentees had left by the time I gained access. Second interviews were conducted when these relationships came to an end, or six to twelve months after the first sweep if they were still continuing.

The reader should note that the sample therefore has significant limitations. While it includes both female and male mentors and mentees, as well as disabled members of both groups, all the respondents were white. Although none of the young trainees at New Beginnings was recorded as being from the black or Asian communities, some of the student volunteers were, but they were not active mentors during the period when I had access to the scheme. In addition, the data necessarily reflect the views of young people who had opted to become involved in the mentoring element of the scheme and who had the skills and disposition, in one way or another, to establish a relationship with their mentor. This sample is therefore likely to produce a more favourable view of mentoring than a broader range of young people or mentors might have expressed.

In order to generate data about the meso-level institutional context provided by the scheme, I also interviewed all the New Beginnings staff members and the managers at WellTEC associated with it, including the economic research officer whose work had partially informed the design of the scheme; UoW staff and managers of the mentoring scheme (except one, who was unavailable due to sick leave); and four professionals from other youth support agencies working in liaison with New Beginnings. This resulted in a total of forty-four interviews, all of which were tape-recorded and transcribed.

Further empirical data were generated by my participant observation of one full mentor training course and two mentor support meetings at UoW, observations from my visits to Cotswold House and contacts with staff there, and participation in the New Beginnings Steering Committee from April 1999 onward. I kept fieldnotes of these observations, written up as soon as possible afterwards, and using notes I had made *in situ* where such note-taking was appropriate. I also kept a reflective research diary alongside my fieldnotes.

Documentary sources of data included 1991 Census Data for the local area and the paper records of the young people kept by staff at New Beginnings, which were collated by my colleague Heather Piper, and I am grateful to her for providing this information. They also included statistical information on the local labour market published by WellTEC and the Wellshire Careers Service. Again, for reasons of anonymity, these sources cannot be fully disclosed.

Narratives of each mentor relationship were synthesized through repeated listening to the tapes and reading of transcripts, starting with the accounts of the young people to ensure these were not submerged by the data of more articulate adults. These stories were subjected to challenge and reinterpretation through discussion with my doctoral supervision team, and public presentation of interim findings to practitioners and academics at seminars and conferences. I turn now to describe the background of the New Beginnings scheme, its planning, design and implementation.

Part II

The mentor relationships

Chapter 3

New Beginnings
An engagement mentoring scheme

Table 3.1 New Beginnings: organizations and people

New Beginnings	A pre-vocational training scheme providing intensive individual support to re-engage disaffected 16- to 18-year-olds with the labour market. Based at WellTEC. Optional mentoring support for trainees offered through a partnership with University of Wellshire (UoW)
WellTEC	Wellshire Training and Enterprise Council
UoW	University of Wellshire. Campuses located in Midtown and Littleville
Cotswold House	Headquarters of WellTEC
Bob Johnson	WellTEC's Economic Research Officer
Anna Jeffries	Senior Lecturer in Education at UoW, manager for UoW's input to New Beginnings
Hugh Davies	Senior Executive at WellTEC
Irene Marsden	Senior Lecturer in Humanities at UoW, manager for UoW's input to New Beginnings
Kath Martin	Senior Manager, WellTEC Youth Programmes
Brenda Mavers	Manager of the Futures Centre at Cotswold House, WellTEC line manager for New Beginnings
Futures Centre	Location of New Beginnings scheme and Futures Club
Futures Club	Mainstream Jobsearch club for unemployed young people
Elaine Peters	New Beginnings' Placement Officer
Maureen James	New Beginnings' Trainer
Paula Modotti	Link Careers Adviser for New Beginnings from Wellshire Careers Service
Renée Jones	UoW's part-time Co-ordinator for New Beginnings
Wendy Chessingham	UoW Lecturer, Research and Development Officer for mentor training provided by UoW for New Beginnings

Introduction

All of the mentor relationships described later in this book were developed within the New Beginnings scheme. As we shall see, New Beginnings was a typical example of the engagement mentoring model. It was both a product of the broad economic, social and political context that gave rise to that model, and of the specific social and economic landscape of its local catchment area, especially factors which impacted on young people's transitions from school. Recognizing this local and institutional context is essential for understanding the mentor relationships discussed in the following chapters.

Since New Beginnings provided mentoring within the specific context of PCET, I begin this chapter by outlining distinctive aspects of post-16 transitions in the geographical area where the scheme was located. I go on to discuss the planning and design of New Beginnings from the perspectives of those who managed and staffed it. Most importantly, I describe how the process of mentoring was envisaged by WellTEC and UoW staff, and then conveyed to mentors and mentees through their induction and training, as well as through the physical environment and informal discourses that shaped the scheme. However, the story does not end there. The scheme had a 'life history' of its own, so the chapter also traces a number of unanticipated external events that came to impact on New Beginnings and the mentor relationships within it.

Inheritance: the landscape of youth transitions in Wellshire

The New Beginnings scheme was based at Wellshire Training and Enterprise Council (WellTEC) in Cotswold House, their headquarters in Midtown. Funding was sought through a bid in 1997 to the EC Youthstart Initiative (already described in Chapter 1), to run the scheme for two years, from January 1998 until December 1999. WellTEC also planned to extend the scheme with its own funding until June 2000.

Wellshire is a mainly rural county, with three major towns, Midtown, Mainborough, and Mostley, and a number of smaller towns such as Sweetland, Littleville and Backerton. The county's population is predominantly white British, with less than 1 per cent belonging to minority ethnic communities, compared with a national average of about 6 per cent. It is a relatively prosperous area of England, and although a number of large manufacturing employers have either closed down or substantially down-sized since the 1980s, there is still a significant manufacturing base alongside a strong service sector. The main areas of employment reported by Wellshire Careers Service in 1997 are shown in Table 3.2. The destinations of school-leavers entering employment and training the previous year are shown in Table 3.3.

At the time of bidding for funds for New Beginnings, the countywide unemployment rate of 3.7 per cent was approximately one-third of the national average

Table 3.2 Wellshire employment by occupational areas

Occupational area	%
Wholesale, retail, catering	22
Other private and public services	22
Manufacturing	21
Transport and communications	14
Finance and business services	10
Construction	6
Agriculture, mining and utilities	4

Table 3.3 Wellshire school-leavers' employment destinations

Employment	%
Clerical	22.5
Service (e.g. hairdressing and care work)	18.5
Elementary (e.g. labouring and cleaning)	11.5
Skilled engineering	9.5
Other skilled trades (e.g. welders)	9.0
Plant and machine operators	8.0
Skilled construction (e.g. bricklayers)	7.5
Sales	7.0
Agricultural and related	4.0
Science and associated	2.5

(DfEE, 1997). WellTEC's Annual Household Survey (AHS) showed that the national targets for education and training (widely believed to be unachievable nationally) had been almost exceeded two years early. Despite the generally favourable local labour market situation, 70.5 per cent of young people in Wellshire were staying on in full-time education after compulsory schooling, slightly above the national average of 67.9 per cent (DfEE, 1998b). The bulk of these young people were staying on in their school sixth form, particularly in Mainborough and Mostley, although there were also further education (FE) colleges in the area, including Wellshire College located in Midtown.

Within this positive overall picture, however, there were variations both within the county and for young people. Although still below national levels of unemployment, Midtown had almost twice the number of unemployed as Mainborough or Mostley. Youth unemployment (aged 16 to 24) in Wellshire was 50 per cent higher than the county average. Throughout the county, WellTEC had identified 204 young people aged 16 to 17 as not participating in education, employment or training, representing less than 2.5 per cent of school-leavers. This compared very favourably with a national average of 13.7 per cent non-participants among the same cohorts (DfEE, 1998b).

Alongside areas of considerable wealth and privilege, all the major towns and three of the wards in Midtown in particular had some decaying housing estates. These were concentrated in a section of the population which suffered poverty and deprivation. Over 4 per cent of the population in one such ward were from minority ethnic communities. Within this picture, which differs somewhat from the county averages, the WellTEC AHS showed that almost two-thirds of the unemployed were not claiming benefits. The overwhelming majority (87 per cent) of these non-claimants were long-term unemployed. Women, young people and single parents were disproportionately represented among them. In addition, due partly to the prosperity of the area as well as its rural nature, there was a poor infrastructure of public transport which restricted travel-to-work areas for those without cars.

In these respects, Wellshire and Midtown displayed similar 'acute polarizations in terms of poverty, housing, lifestyle and occupation' to a city such as London (Ball et al., 2000: 6), although not such a high proportion of the population was afflicted with disadvantage as is the case in London. Global competition was a factor in the local economy, affecting both the employed and those seeking entry to the labour market. According to Bob Johnson, WellTEC's economic research officer, employers had increasingly high expectations of applicants when recruiting, and employees felt the pressure of intensified work targets and longer working hours. However, as a provincial town, Midtown did not offer its youth the same 'socioscape' of new forms of work, consumption, leisure and cultural identities as the cosmopolitan 'global city' described by Ball et al. (2000) in their study of young people in London. Culturally, its dominant traditions were those of the labour aristocracy, skilled craft occupations and youth transitions rooted in the apprenticeship system. Those traditions may still be discerned in the school-leaver destinations given in Table 3.3. Nevertheless, they had been weakened, particularly for those at the disadvantaged end of the polarization that has taken place, by large-scale cuts in the manufacturing workforce and the shift to high-tech and service industries.

Cohen suggests that such a weakening of traditional working-class cultures has its own impact upon youth identities. At the height of such a culture, he argues that:

> growing up working class took the form of an apprenticeship to an inheri-
> tance: it involved a strong combination of these two codes, spanning familial,
> occupational, recreational, sexual and political practices, and organising them
> into a single normative grid.
>
> (Cohen, 1986: 63)

This creates a strong sense of identity for young people, although Cohen stresses he is not suggesting the existence of an idealized 'golden age' of working-class culture, outside forms of capitalist and patriarchal oppression. Weakened codes or 'grids', however, can produce a scenario that may be particularly apposite to the situation of young people in Midtown at the wrong end of economic and social polarization:

The bad news is that strong communal grids generate a strong collective conscience centred on generational continuity; any break in this, especially in the transition to work, will be experienced as an exclusion from its 'body politic'. Young people in these areas are under much greater than normal pressure to find decent well paid work, and will feel more than usually depressed and worthless if they are unsuccessful. . . . *To be a member of a weak grid family in a strong grid community is to have the worst of all possible worlds.*

(Cohen, 1986: 68, emphasis added)

Both the historical tradition of Midtown and the relative buoyancy of its labour market indicated that it was just such a 'strong grid community'. Although most of the young people whom I interviewed were from families who seemed to subscribe to a strong work ethic, they did experience various social problems and fragmentation of their post-16 transitions. This may be seen as resulting in 'weak grids' for individual young people, several of whom experienced mental health problems in addition to their disrupted patterns of transition. Such a legacy is much bleaker than the globalized 'birthright' to which Shea (1992) so enthusiastically proclaimed their entitlement, as we saw in Chapter 2. It has to be considered as a factor shaping the dispositions and 'horizons for action' (Hodkinson *et al.*, 1996) of the young people who were recruited to New Beginnings. In many ways, their inheritance was that 'worst of all possible worlds'.

Planning New Beginnings

The initial ideas that led to the formation of the New Beginnings scheme arose out of a tentative discussion between Anna Jeffries, a senior lecturer in Education at UoW, and a former colleague of hers, Hugh Davies. Davies had become a senior executive at WellTEC, and wanted the TEC to be involved in the European Youthstart Initiative. Although WellTEC had an excellent reputation among education and welfare professionals in the surrounding region for its proactive and innovative approach to youth training, some of its managers felt that more needed to be done to offer suitable provision for young people who had become disaffected from the PCET system. Mentoring had proved popular in early projects under the Youthstart banner, and appeared to be an ideal element to bring the partnership together: WellTEC would offer training and work experience for disaffected young people, while the university would recruit and train students to act as mentors.

Together with her colleague Irene Marsden, a senior lecturer in Humanities at UoW, Anna was keen to become involved in projects beyond the university itself. Both had worked with disadvantaged young people in their previous professional careers, and both were committed in their academic careers to maintaining an involvement in the field of practice. Their interests also coincided with other institutional priorities UoW had at that time, as Anna pointed out:

> I think the initial response from us [to WellTEC's approach] was wide enthusiasm, 'Yes, let's do it!' for two reasons, I guess. One was that it sounded like an interesting and useful way of putting something back into the community. Probably about that time, the university was spending quite a bit of time thinking about its links with the community . . . and this idea seemed to fit with that, putting something in. But also, I suppose, we thought that there would be the likelihood of the students getting an interesting opportunity as well – that it's a valuable learning opportunity that students could engage with.

As the idea progressed to the stage of bidding for funds, Kath Martin, senior manager for WellTEC's youth programmes, took charge of its progress. Kath was engaged in what she termed a 'personal crusade' to improve YT provision for disadvantaged young people. She was highly critical of the practices of training providers who, due to outcome-related funding régimes, had failed to achieve progression for certain young people who were difficult to integrate into work-based training:

> We used to call it the 'revolving door syndrome'. These young people would go to the Careers Service, they would register, they'd be referred to one of, say, three or four providers, they would go to one supplier, they would be, you know, attendance spasmodic, and they'd eventually be sacked, and then they'd go back to Careers, and they'd be referred to another supplier, because the first one would say: 'I'm not having him again, or her'. And then they would go round this revolving door, and they could spend two years going round there and earning enough money to survive. But again, they were coming out very cynical, and I think the actual system had damaged them more.

Her answer was to develop provision delivered directly by the TEC itself. Although Kath thought the WellTEC–UoW partnership was 'a gem of an idea', her conception of that partnership was quite different from Anna's initial vision, determined more by the funding criteria than other considerations:

> I mean, we needed partnership, the buzz things in the bid were innovation and they were partnership. So we thought the innovation was the mentor, because when we were writing this back in 1996, there wasn't a lot of mentoring going on. . . . That really, when it was sent in, it was really a high point of the bid, you know, the mentor support and the partnership with the university.

An engagement mentoring scheme

Kath Martin had carried out research during 1996 and 1997, funded by the first tranche of the Youthstart Initiative, 'to improve WellTEC's knowledge of disaffected youth, their location, numbers, motivation and aspirations' and to develop inter-agency networking with other support services for young people, such as the careers, probation, social and youth services (New Beginnings bid application). The findings were used to inform a bid for the second tranche of Youthstart funding to establish New Beginnings as specific provision for disaffected young people. This proposed a detailed package of pre-vocational work preparation, to include:

- access to careers guidance on induction, and thereafter as necessary, from a linked careers adviser
- individual assessment of basic and key skills
- one-to-one or small group training in-house with the scheme trainer
- weekly reviews with the placement officer to discuss progress and personal issues
- the chance to sample different occupational areas
- opportunities to undertake pre-vocational, basic skills and National Vocational Qualifications (NVQs)
- tailored work experience placements with supportive employers, with a facility to begin part-time and gradually progress to full-time
- fortnightly workplace visits from the scheme's placement officer
- planned progression to further training opportunities
- the option of being matched with a volunteer mentor to provide weekly one-hour support meetings, in addition to the mentor-type support offered by staff
- referral to an established network of support agencies where necessary
- a training allowance of £45 per week (just above the level of Income Support welfare payments), plus reimbursement of travel expenses over £10.

This is broadly in line with the European Youthstart Initiative's priorities outlined in Chapter 1, with one exception: the needs of minority ethnic youth were not addressed in the New Beginnings bid.

Kath assembled a team of staff she had 'hand-picked' for their commitment to working with socially excluded youth. The team was led by Brenda Mavers, manager of the Futures Centre at Cotswold House, which also provided a base for the Futures Club (a mainstream jobsearch programme for unemployed youth) and Futures Plus (a programme for disaffected school pupils). Under Brenda's supervision, Elaine Peters worked as the New Beginnings placement officer. She had responsibility for liaising with employers to generate and support work experience placements. She inducted young people referred to the scheme, and held weekly meetings with them to review their progress and produce a personal development plan (PDP) recording their timetable and goals for the coming week. Elaine was responsible for matching young people with mentors if they chose to take up that option. She also dealt with any disciplinary issues arising for the trainees, and worked closely with Maureen James, the scheme trainer. Maureen carried out initial assessments of entrants to New Beginnings, as well as basic and key skills training at Cotswold House. She had very close individual contact with the young people, in a role that was, in some ways, less formal than Elaine's.

One aspect of the scheme's design resulted from concerns of both WellTEC and UoW staff about safety for the students and the young people who would participate in mentoring. Both sides were worried about the possibility of impressionable young students being led astray by local youths involved in criminal or drug-related activities. There was also a perceived potential threat of abuse of mentees, or accusations of abuse by them against their mentors. This perception of risk resulted in strict rules governing the location and conduct of mentoring. It was to take place only at Cotswold House, in a dedicated room for mentoring sessions, and other contacts or exchanges of details between mentor and mentee were expressly forbidden. When the young person left the scheme for whatever reason, their relationship with their mentor had to be terminated too.

While New Beginnings benefited from the personal commitment of its staff to the needs of socially excluded young people, its character was inevitably shaped by the fact that it was primarily a TEC-based provision. As Brenda Mavers explained, the TEC had a dual allegiance:

> We are a company who . . . we have two customers. We have the kid, who's our customer – I would say that's our main customer – but of course, businesses are customers of the TEC, you know, so we have to in some ways always get the best for the business as well.

'The best for business' related particularly to the local labour market situation already identified above, in which employers were experiencing a shortage in the supply-side of the market due to very high staying-on rates in school sixth forms and FE. A commitment to plugging this gap was included in the funding bid for New Beginnings, and Bob Johnson explained how the scheme was developed partly in response to employers' needs:

> That's why, from a business point of view, we are interested in projects like New Beginnings, because it's very difficult for us to make much progress against this tide of people continually staying on academically for longer . . . and the idea is therefore that we look at the people who aren't going into either route and trying to get more of them into a job with training, and for people who aren't able to make the grade, if you like, for going into a Modern Apprenticeship, then schemes like New Beginnings will help us to make them ready to go into a National Traineeship or a Modern Apprenticeship.

The employment-related nature of the scheme was thus produced out of a dual rationale. On the one hand, it aimed to lubricate a 'tight' local labour market by increasing the supply of employment-ready young people. This was linked closely to the *raison d'être* of the TEC itself. As Brenda Mavers often pointed out, 'We're in the business of training and employment'. On the other hand, in line with the underpinning philosophy of New Labour's social exclusion agenda, it promoted structured routes to employment as the best solution to social exclusion.

Matching the needs of employers with those of disaffected young people was not, however, straightforward. We have already considered in Chapter 1 employers' tendency to bemoan the lack of employability in school-leavers. Bob Johnson's research showed that Wellshire employers were able to select from a large pool of women returners to the labour market, as well as from students seeking part-time work and underemployed graduates from UoW. These were often seen as a better investment than unemployed school-leavers 'unable to make the grade', although this preference is by no means specific to Wellshire employers or to the current period (see Casson, 1979; Hasluck, 1999). The young people available in theory to expand the supply-side of the labour market 'will consist primarily of those school leavers who are unable or unwilling to continue in education or training (which may be indicative of their abilities, motivation and attitude)' (Hasluck, 1999: 31). There was, then, a strong likelihood that many of the beneficiaries of New Beginnings would end up being channelled into the lower end of the labour market, already well represented in the Wellshire school-leaver destinations cited above: services such as hairdressing, care of the elderly, clerical or retail work and catering (most of which were stereotypically undertaken by young women); unskilled work such as cleaning, packing and labouring; and the less skilled areas of motor vehicle work and construction (stereotypically undertaken by young men). These represent the limited range of occupational areas offered to the trainees at New Beginnings.

At the same time, WellTEC staff recognized that they themselves were in competition with others to recruit and retain the young people. Employment agencies were seen as a big draw for 16- and 17-year-olds, who could earn as much as £120 a week in packing or other unskilled jobs – far more than the £45 a week offered at New Beginnings. There was also the 'grey' economy, where a number of the young people could obtain money through semi-legal means, such as baby-sitting and casual labouring, or more hazardous occupations such as street robbery and drug-dealing (cf. Watts, 1999; Williamson and Middlemiss, 1999). All of these considerations meant that, although the design of New Beginnings had a neatly rational basis, which apparently provided for symmetrical needs on both sides of the local labour market, the problems it addressed were less compatible in practice.

Despite the assertion by Kath Martin that she had faced no constraints in designing New Beginnings, and despite the caring commitment that all of the staff expressed, the scheme's location within the TEC contributed a strong work-based training and employment focus. The local labour market situation meant that young people were directed into the lower end of the labour market. This was compounded by the prescriptive employment destinations demanded by the Youthstart Initiative which funded the scheme. Moreover, the bid application for New Beginnings identified a need to 'drive forward the disaffected young person' to adopt values, attitudes and behaviour that would render them 'employable' within the framework of employer demands. All these factors indicate that New Beginnings was a typical example of engagement mentoring in practice.

How did this design for the scheme – its institutional context – impact upon the mentor relationships it initiated? Millwater and Yarrow (1997) suggest that the beliefs and ethos which participants bring to mentoring – their 'mindset' – are crucial in determining the character of the mentoring process. In addition to the beliefs that participants may already have had, their mindset was likely to have been influenced by the induction and training they received at New Beginnings, as well as by more general interactions with the scheme's staff and its environment. Let us consider in turn the way in which firstly the young people, and then the student mentors, were recruited to New Beginnings, and the 'mindset' towards mentoring that their induction might have engendered.

Involving young people in mentoring

Many of the young people came to New Beginnings via the same route. At some point after leaving school or dropping out of PCET provision, they would try to claim welfare benefits at the local Jobcentre or Benefits Agency, which would refer them back to Wellshire Careers Service, where all unemployed 16- and 17-year-olds were required to register. Others came on to New Beginnings directly from school, as a progression from the Futures Plus programme, and a number were also referred by their social workers. None of the young people self-referred, and there was no outreach activity by the scheme. The first step for all of them would be to have a careers interview with Paula Modotti, the careers adviser linked with New Beginnings. She used particular criteria to refer young people onto New Beginnings:

> It wouldn't necessarily be directly concerned with academic achievement. It would be much more likely to be what I suppose you might call social factors. So if a young person is perhaps living in a hostel, or not living at home with parents, or has been a regular non-attender . . . or for some reason may be reluctant to take part in mainstream education or employment or whatever. We have a lot of young people who are pregnant, you know, they would be [referred]. We see a lot of young people that could be identified as being a problem in actually being what Futures might call 'job ready'. . . . Just, I suppose, reluctance, reluctance, yes, unreadiness is perhaps a better word than reluctance, for whatever reason . . . or with substantial barriers for no fault of their own.

It seemed that young people would be referred directly to work-based training provision, rather than considering a wider range of options more impartially:

Helen: Are there any circumstances in which you maybe have a young person with some sort of social problems, that you'd think New Beginnings isn't really the right thing for them? Where you'd sort of maybe think about a different kind of provision?

Paula: Yes, I mean, if I was in any doubt, then I would refer them to New Beginnings and allow the young person to go through the early assessment procedures and perhaps in discussion with staff at the Club, you know, maybe refer across [to the Futures Club]. So there is a facility to be able to go from New Beginnings to the Futures Club, and from the Club to New Beginnings.

Although Paula described cases where young people had expressed a desire to consider full-time education, she did not refer them to Wellshire FE College, and she had no idea what provision the college made to support young people with social or other problems. (Wellshire College in fact had a learning support unit with a wide range of flexible support provision including a 'befriending' service, which claimed to be particularly successful in integrating young people who had been persistent non-attenders or schoolphobics.) A similar process of automatic referral to New Beginnings was practised by local social workers for young people leaving care.

Moreover, welfare benefit regulations created pressure on young people to participate. Although under-18s are ineligible for unemployment benefits, in inner-city areas some are able to claim welfare payments on the basis of 'severe hardship' if no suitable training provision is deemed to be available (Maclagan, 1992). In Midtown and the surrounding area, the very existence of New Beginnings, as a scheme claiming to offer intensive support for the most disadvantaged, was considered to negate this eligibility, and education maintenance allowances (EMAs) had not been introduced at that time. For most young people out of work and under 18, this meant that participation in New Beginnings was presented as their only access to any legal income. Thus both the manner of referral from the Careers Service and the local interpretation of benefit regulations meant that there was a strong (albeit covert) element of compulsion for young people to participate in the scheme.

The option of mentoring was promoted to the young people in the induction that Elaine Peters carried out with them. If they did not agree to it, she would continue to raise it in her weekly reviews with them, particularly if her judgement was that the young person would benefit from having a mentor:

> The way that I explain it to the young people is . . . I always say that mentors are somebody specifically for them, that that mentor will not see anybody else, they are coming to see them and it's somebody who's not getting paid to see you, it's somebody who wants to help you get into work, and most of them accept that, and that's why it's worked.

The young people whom I interviewed generally presented a common version of how mentoring had been presented to them, and this explanation is typical of their accounts:

Helen: So how did they explain to you what a mentor was?

Hayley: Well, they just said, 'It's someone that you can talk to, like about your problems and that. . . . ' Or if there was anything you'd like to tell people. You know, you could sort of tell things to the mentor that you couldn't tell people that you know.

No further training was provided for the young people to promote a more positive image of mentoring, to help them understand the process of mentoring, reflect upon what benefits they might have derived from the experience, or come to terms with ending relationships and moving on from them, although it has been suggested that this is at least as essential for mentees as for mentors themselves (Freedman, 1999; Phillips-Jones, 1999; Skinner and Fleming, 1999). Brenda Mavers felt that: 'We don't have time to explain mentoring to young people – and besides, explaining it to these kids is far too complex.' However, Elaine used her brief weekly reviews, and feedback from Maureen, as a careful and conscientious checking process that the young person was happy with their mentor. If they were not, she always intervened to re-match them with another mentor.

Contrary to Elaine's assertion that most young people agreed to have a mentor, relatively few actually took up this option. Over the life of the scheme, eighty-eight young people were recruited to New Beginnings. Their records show that less than half of these were matched with a mentor, and a substantial number turned up for only one or two meetings, never establishing ongoing relationships. Of ninety students trained by UoW for the scheme, only twenty-two became active mentors, indicating more realistically the number of functioning mentor relationships that developed.

In the light of this, it is important to note the types of young people who did engage with mentoring. Brenda Mavers described them as the most 'vulnerable' and 'malleable' trainees at New Beginnings, 'a group that will do what they're told'. Readers can judge from the stories in Chapters 4–6 how accurate these judgements may have been. However, it is likely that those who opted for mentoring were either better disposed than others to forming relationships with adults, or more needy in that regard. It is also possible that some of them took up Elaine's persuasive pressure to accept a mentor through a willingness to comply with her authority, without demanding any clearer understanding of what they were entering into.

If we accept the typology of disaffected young people that characterizes different groups in three ways, as temporarily side-tracked, essentially confused or deeply alienated (Williamson and Middlemiss, 1999: 13), the young people whom I interviewed certainly did not appear to belong to the 'deeply alienated' category. They became involved in mentoring willingly, but with little understanding of what it might entail. It is not surprising, then, as we shall see in the case stories which follow, that many of them imposed their own familiar frameworks for relationships upon the mentoring process: those of parenting, sibling support, and above all friendship.

What were the outcomes for individual young people at New Beginnings? How did these relate to its employment goals? Of the eighty-eight who were recruited to New Beginnings, thirty-nine – almost half the total – were recorded either as 'disappeared' or dismissed. What New Beginnings provided may not have been what they needed or wanted, but under local labour market and social security conditions it was what they were often compelled to accept. To leave or be sacked from the scheme was, for most, to lose their sole entitlement to a legal income. This created frictions between WellTEC and UoW staff. While Kath Martin and Brenda Mavers made it clear that they would not tolerate violent behaviour, and claimed that only two young people had been dismissed from the scheme for this reason, the scheme's records showed that many more had been sacked for breaching rules on time-keeping and attendance. UoW staff felt this was inappropriate for a scheme which purported to offer support for young people who had already found themselves excluded from the education and training system. Anna Jeffries linked this specifically to the employment goals of New Beginnings, revealing the difference in ethos between her approach and that of the TEC staff:

> The more heavy-handed constraint seems to be the work-related focus, which has led to one or two disasters in my view. Young people who haven't turned up for whatever reason have been sacked as if they were on some kind of an employment programme. I had thought that the whole point of working with these young people is that you were working with the ones who *don't* turn up, therefore you should expect [that]. The notion that you can be sacked from a programme that is entirely aimed at disaffected kids seems to me to be the most ironic of all situations to be in . . . , it doesn't seem to make any rational sense. . . . It is within bounds that the work-related boundary is an important one, and I simply feel that I disagree with that, but I think my disagreement is simply based on a different notion of what young people need.

The different ethos which Anna and Irene embraced was associated with a long tradition of critical thinking and of educationalists' resistance to instrumental, employment-related policies towards young people. These differences may well have helped to produce some of the contradictory aspects of the mentor training programme that will be considered in the following section of this chapter. We shall see the consequences that dismissal had for some young people in the stories of Adrian and Hayley in Chapter 4. Adrian's case in particular reveals that the number dismissed may in fact have been even higher than recorded. Although he was sacked from New Beginnings, his notes show him as being transferred to the mainstream Futures Club, and therefore as a positive progression. There is a possibility that this manipulation of destinations may have been used in other cases, given the pressure on schemes such as New Beginnings to demonstrate their effectiveness.

Recruiting and training the volunteer mentors

In the early stages of New Beginnings, WellTEC staff were enthusiastic about the use of undergraduate students as volunteer mentors for young people on the scheme. Brenda and Kath both argued that using university students guaranteed the recruitment of mentors of 'a certain calibre', 'people with enough intellectual prowess to look at what the programme was all about', rather than 'just taking the general public off the streets'. This approach distanced New Beginnings from the community-based model of mentoring discussed in Chapter 1.

They also thought that the students would prove useful in relieving the burden on Elaine and Maureen at times when trainee numbers were large. Although the staffing of the scheme was designed to accommodate twelve or at most fifteen young people at a time, busy periods such as the end of the school year in July sometimes saw twenty-five or more enrolled. Kath explained:

> It takes some of the strain off my staff, and that would be definitely one of the reasons why I'd want to continue it, that it's like an hour and a half that they can put off that the kids attended and somebody else is dealing with them.

There was an expectation from the TEC staff that using students would also result in a form of peer mentoring, since they thought the students would be only two or three years older than their mentees. Kath noted that 'Brenda and I are very conscious that we're old farts . . . ' and hoped that the students would be able to relate to the young people on a common level, apparently independent of the TEC, and therefore with greater credibility. (In fact a substantial number of volunteers were mature students, and New Beginnings staff quickly came to prefer older mentors.) The main contradiction in this view, however, was that the non-authoritative peer relationship was seen primarily as a vehicle for communicating the TEC staff's message to young people who were reluctant to take it on board. Kath outlined the role she hoped mentors would play:

> Mentoring was about befriending, and helping us, perhaps using a different way of talking to the young person, to help that young person to see what we were trying to get . . . trying to help them with. So the focus was very clearly about getting them into employment. That was very clear, that that's what the mentoring process was about. It was about when we were saying [to a young person], 'Well, I think, you know, we think you should do this . . . ' that perhaps somebody else saying it in that different way, or coming at it from a different angle, would help the young person hear it, 'cos you can say what you like to some people, can't you, but unless you're saying it in a way that they're willing to hear it, you're wasting your breath. So it's to help us with that communication.

For Brenda, this sometimes focused on the need to convey 'realistic' aspirations to the young people and accept the low-level work placements that were on offer.

Both she and Elaine Peters complained on several occasions that student mentors were too encouraging to young people with ambitions beyond the limited range of occupational areas New Beginnings offered.

Renée Jones was co-ordinator of UoW's input into New Beginnings. She had a target to recruit and train a total of ninety students as volunteer mentors throughout the life of the scheme. Of those who volunteered to join the scheme, 80 per cent were female. The age range was broader than expected by WellTEC staff, with 40 per cent being mature students. They were recruited through publicity tables at the Freshers' Fairs each year, by presentations given in some course induction lectures, and through individual approaches to some students by lecturers in Anna Jeffries' and Irene Mason's departments. About one-third of the volunteers were following teaching degrees, and another third were from social science degrees. The rest were from a variety of courses offered at UoW, such as business management, sports-related courses, creative arts, history and English.

The leaflets promoting the opportunity to volunteer at New Beginnings emphasized the employment-related purpose of engagement mentoring:

> We need volunteers who will offer support and encouragement on a regular informal basis so that the young person can achieve their goals of entering the world of work and training.

They also marketed the scheme heavily on its potential benefits to the students, focusing on the chance to gain practical experience; to help young people and develop related skills; to improve the students' own CVs; and to gain formal accreditation and personal satisfaction. UoW was a 'new' university founded in 1992. Many of its students had not achieved at the higher levels at school or college, and came mainly from upper-working-class and middle-class families. At that time, some 25 per cent of its intake were mature students, and many of its courses were vocational degrees. This emphasizes a parallel purpose for mentoring at New Beginnings: to enhance the employability not only of the young people, but also that of the student mentors as well.

In liaison with the WellTEC staff, Renée had prepared a training course for the mentors. Both the TEC and the university were concerned that the training should be adequate. Accordingly, it was delivered in a weekend block, plus several evening sessions. The total input was equivalent to four full days, similar to that for a module on a degree course. Mentors would have the opportunity to gain academic accreditation for their work at New Beginnings on submission of a reflective learning journal based on their experience of mentoring (although only two mentors ever took up this option). Another academic rather than vocational advantage for the students, more widely taken up in practice, was that their experience might provide a basis for the projects and final year research dissertations that many had to undertake for their degrees.

Wendy Chessingham, a UoW lecturer in social sciences, developed a training pack and mentor handbook to accompany this course. Although we have already seen that the UoW managers of New Beginnings had a different view of mentoring for disaffected young people than the WellTEC staff, the training pack was dominated by the idea that the mentors' main goal was to help get the young people into employment. It did not draw on any of the existing literature on mentoring, nor did it offer any suggested readings on mentoring itself. Mentoring was defined in summary sentences at the end of each section. The following are typical examples from the handbook, and convey the 'mindset' promoted to the students who volunteered:

> Job prospects in the Midtown area are actually very good. It is our aim to help improve these figures further. Within your role as Mentor, by offering encouragement and support to your assigned young person, you could make a difference to the above unemployment figures.
>
> The aim of your role as a Mentor is to support the Personal Development Plan (PDP) that is developed between the TEC and the young person, to discuss the PDP with the young person, and to contribute to any changes within the PDP that you and your young person agree on . . . you must maintain a positive outlook and remember that your aim is to encourage and promote the worth of training.

A rationale was given based on a highly instrumental view of the purpose of learning:

> What is the purpose of education and training? . . . Primarily education and training can lead to a particular role within the workforce. . . . Young people who you may meet through mentoring may not have [key] skills which can make them attractive to the workforce. You must use your role as Mentor in order to encourage the realization that such skills are attainable.

At times there were glimpses of an alternative view, although it invariably remained undetailed and swept aside by the continuing injunctions to mentors:

> Many young people, some of whom you will meet through your role as a Mentor, do not wish to conform to the values and expectations that society upholds with reference to employment and training. . . . This may of course relate to the 'types' of jobs that are on offer to young people through employment and training. These positions can often be menial and monotonous and for very little money. . . . Your role as a Mentor is to encourage the minimization of disaffection.

Unfortunately, there was no attempt to explore in a deeper or more critical manner, either in the pack or in the training sessions, the more complex issues surrounding disaffection from education, training and employment.

Promoting employment and training was thus presented as the key goal of mentoring in the training pack provided by UoW. But what of the process of mentoring itself? How was mentoring interpreted in the course that the students attended? Mentors generally found themselves confused about its meaning, as we have seen from their comments in the introduction to Chapter 2. In the first session of the training course, led by Renée Jones, small groups were given thirty-four different statements about mentoring and asked to sort them into those with which they agreed and disagreed. Some of the statements described basic aspects of interviewing skills, such as 'Getting mentees to "open up"', 'Using appropriate language', and 'Building relationships'. Some described approaches that were firmly emphasized as incorrect in later sessions: 'Being a stand-in mum or dad', 'Using a stick and a carrot', and 'Being prepared to disclose things about yourself'. The majority, however, reinforced the messages of the training pack: 'Sharing values', 'Helping mentees keep to deadlines and schedules', and 'Smiling, being encouraging and optimistic about personal development plans – or other processes being undertaken by mentees'. None of these statements, however, was linked by the tutor in the feedback discussion to research evidence, nor to any frameworks for understanding different models of mentoring and their consequences for practice. As a consequence, mentors struggled with confusion and dilemmas about their role.

Further sessions of the course focused on four propositions about mentoring. First, there was the firm emphasis on *directing* the mentee towards employment-related goals. Second, the students were taught introductory counselling techniques that were *less directive*, while at the same time mentoring was defined repeatedly as *distinct from counselling*. Third, the need to maintain strict boundaries was firmly stressed, as were the scheme regulations which forbade exchanges of contact details or meetings outside Cotswold House between mentor and mentee. Fourth, apart from the PDP, the rest of the mentoring process was conveyed as being problem-focused, with the oft-repeated exhortation to get mentees to 'open up'. Some of the individual case stories – for example, that of Jane in Chapter 4, or Karen and Rachel in Chapter 5 – show how the contradictions between these statements led to confusion and dilemmas for the mentors.

There was a second major element to the training course, which was to teach students about the nature of disaffected young people, and to shape their expectations of the mentees with whom they would be matched at New Beginnings. I was particularly interested in this, as it seemed highly likely that mentors' 'mind-set', and therefore their mentoring practice, would be as much influenced by their perceptions of disaffected youth as by their beliefs about mentoring itself.

Once again, the written training pack drew on the discourse that later produced *Bridging the Gap* (SEU, 1999), containing a litany of deficits and deviance in explaining disaffection. The pack defined youth as 'being in limbo between childhood and adulthood', and young people as 'liv[ing] for the day not for the future'. Young people likely to be referred to New Beginnings were described repeatedly as having little inclination to begin work or training; as rejecting social norms and expectations; and as fantasizing or deliberately telling lies, engaging in criminal activities, abusing alcohol and drugs, having suffered child abuse, or being schizophrenic or suicidal. Their families' role was generally portrayed as ranging from demotivating to neglectful or abusive. While some acknowledgement was made to structural inequalities, this was done in a one-dimensional and negative way that construed the disaffected as passive victims thereof, and focused on their resultant deficiencies. Mentors were urged to display empathy and a non-judgemental stance in relation to the young people, as many other reports on engagement mentoring schemes have emphasized (ESU, 2000a). Unfortunately, the training course did not include any sessions which helped students to question their own personal value-judgements, or to consider more deeply the difficulties of achieving empathy, and the story of Karen and Sharon in Chapter 5 illustrates these problems sharply.

Some students commented that aspects of the training had generated a sense of fear about the young people whom they might be mentoring, particularly as it included warnings about the 'security risk' which had led to strict rules that mentors and mentees should have no contact outside Cotswold House. One mentor's comment offers an example of these concerns:

> *Rachel*: A general awareness guy came in and sort of tried to scare people that all these kids were going to be taking drugs. . . . When they started saying that we weren't insured to go out [of Cotswold House], things like that were a bit off-putting.

My own observations of the training session also highlighted the very negative ways in which disaffected young people were portrayed. One session presented by a local youth worker focused on worst-case scenarios of neglect and abuse of young people by their families. Even Elaine Peters objected to this after attending the same session. She felt that it conveyed an extreme portrayal that did not fit any of the young people whom she had encountered at New Beginnings. Yet it had clearly impacted upon students' expectations as they prepared to begin mentoring.

The environment at New Beginnings

In addition to the training course, the students who volunteered to mentor at New Beginnings were also going into a particular environment at Cotswold House, and having informal discussions with the front-line staff there. What sense did this convey of mentoring and of disaffected youth?

Both Elaine Peters and Maureen James spoke warmly of their enjoyment while working at New Beginnings, and talked very fondly about some of the young people. On more than one occasion I saw a trainee rush into the office, burst into tears on Elaine's shoulder and disappear with her into the mentoring room, to emerge much calmer a while later. Others who had left the scheme would come back to chat at lunch-times, or to bring a new baby to visit, and these young people clearly felt that the Futures Centre was a safe and welcoming place. Despite Kath Martin's declaration to me that she did not want 'her provision' to become a 'nice warm place for tea and toast', Maureen described to me how she would provide just these facilities for young people who were homeless, or who came in for their training preoccupied with other problems:

> They come and sit and talk to me, and it's good. I love it. I think it's because I love the young people, because they absolutely fascinate me . . . the things they come out with!

She and Elaine liked to tell stories of how vulnerable and naive the young people could be, and how they would have to help them in many ways. Care-leavers, for example, had to be taught very basic life skills: what cleaning materials to use in the kitchen, the fact that you had to wash trainers, how to fill in simple forms, that you couldn't heat a tin of baked beans in the microwave oven. Some trainees would have to be taken to their placements, and would cry if Elaine or Maureen prepared to leave, 'just like taking a child to nursery'. The induction sessions they ran for students at Cotswold House were interspersed with exclamations about the young people: 'They're so sweet!', 'They're real characters', 'Love 'em!', 'Bless!'

However, not all the young people were regarded so fondly. Adrian's story in Chapter 4 will show how some young people were labelled as 'taking the mick' or 'swinging the lead', and were disliked by New Beginnings staff as a consequence. This view was also routinely incorporated into some young people's written records, where ten of them are recorded as 'lazy' or 'did not want to work'. Where idle or rude behaviour, or poor attendance and time-keeping were evident in a work placement, this created problems for Elaine, who had to work terribly hard to generate and sustain placements from local employers:

> It's also working your placements as well, because if you know that you've sent a bad [trainee] to somewhere, then it's always quite nice to send a good one next time [*laughs*] just to keep them sweet . . . it's working like that as well so you're not losing all your placements in one go, so it's working them as well as the young people really.

Maureen sometimes linked her perceptions of young people's laziness to her belief in benefit dependency, the comfortable life that she thought could be had on benefits, and the way it undermined the work ethic:

> We've got some [young people] now that have no intention of working. The family hasn't worked, they've not grown up in an environment where you get up for work, so I think the income is always going to be from the Benefit Office, and it's a difficult thing to get past that, you know, why should you get up for work when you can get all this off the state, you know, it's a bit of a tricky one. . . . One boy at the moment, he's living with a girl five years older than him

who's got a child, they're in a council house, so money is not a problem, they've got plenty of benefits coming in.

Maureen held particularly strong views about teenage pregnancy. Although only fourteen of the forty-six girls on New Beginnings were recorded as being or becoming pregnant, she asserted:

Maureen: A lot more of the girls are pregnant than not. We've got two that aren't, but. . . . And some of them, some of the girls think this is, you know, the goal in life . . . is to get pregnant, but sometimes, you know, each month they come in and [*wailing*] 'I'm not pregnant', and you think, 'Well, thank God for that!' [*laughs*]. And some of them say, [*worried tone*] 'I think I'm pregnant' . . . [*resigned tone*]. 'Right . . . '. We looked at options, and none of them would ever look at an abortion or anything like that.

Helen: Really? You talked that through with them?

Maureen: 'Well, have you thought of your options?' 'What do you mean?' 'Well, you don't have to have it, it's early yet, you don't have to have it . . . the quality of life for you, for the baby, who's going to look after it, who's going to finance it?' . . . But it's never any of them said, 'OK, yeah'. . . . They just go, 'Oooh, I couldn't do that, I couldn't . . . '. You know, they don't seem to understand it's difficult . . . when they bring the babies up afterwards and they're struggling. . . . It's difficult having a baby, it's not something you shove away in a drawer.

One of the mentors, Rachel, gave a different perspective on some of these encounters, however:

I overheard someone in the next room [at Cotswold House] one day, and it turned out that two of them, two of the girls had become pregnant and that straightaway they [*New Beginnings staff*] would say, [*angry tone*] 'Well we can't do work experience with you, you have to completely change this!' and it was . . . the way she was talking to them, it was . . . it must have scared them. . . . It was scaring me, the way she was going, 'Hmm!' . . . like this. . . . It was . . . it was a bit crazy. . . . It was completely . . . got them both in the same room and said, [*hectoring tone*] 'Well, so-and-so's in the same boat as you now, you're both pregnant. . . .Well, these are your options . . . ' like, fired them at them. 'You won't be able to do your work experience now! . . . ' It's just a bit, like, overwhelming to overhear something like that . . . I think there would have been other ways of doing that.

The very different ways the environment at New Beginnings impacted on mentor relationships and the individuals within them is explored further in the case stories in Chapters 4 to 6. Finally, let us consider how that environment was itself transformed by the unexpected impact of events beyond New Beginnings, as they compounded problems within the scheme.

Unexpected problems

As I have suggested, like any new project, New Beginnings was experiencing some internal problems as it got underway. By the end of its first year, in January 1999, Renée Jones was becoming increasingly concerned about the fact that only a small proportion of the mentors whom she had trained were actually being used. Although this was discussed at the Steering Committee in May 1999, by its July meeting the situation had worsened. Renée felt there were communication problems with WellTEC staff, who were not liaising with her about the matching. She complained that she was getting 'flak' from angry, unmatched students who felt cheated of an important volunteering opportunity after devoting so much time to the training. Moreover, she feared that this might have negative consequences for her recruitment in September 1999, threatening her chances of meeting her overall target. 'I'd be the one with egg on my face!' she protested.

WellTEC staff, meanwhile, brought complaints to the New Beginnings Steering Committee about the unreliability of some students allocated as mentors, and about mentors' lack of availability when pressure was greatest at the scheme – the start of the summer, which produced a large influx of young people just at the time when most students were going on holiday or taking up full-time vacation jobs. At the same time, students were complaining about the lack of support for them from both institutions, and there was a dispute about whose responsibility this was. Brenda Mavers eventually concluded that, far from her initial view of students as ideal mentors, in practice they were too demanding on her staff, and therefore they were 'too much trouble'. Kath Martin concurred:

> I definitely want to continue with the mentoring, but I think I'd perhaps look at recruiting other people, perhaps some of the ancillary staff that are working in school, the dinner ladies.

Although these problems tended to be discussed at the Steering Committee as weaknesses in the design of New Beginnings itself, external factors played their part in creating or exacerbating them. The original Youthstart Initiative funding for New Beginnings was from January 1998 until December 1999, and it was planned to continue the scheme until the end of that academic year in June 2000, supported by discretionary funding from WellTEC. The hope was that Labour's social inclusion agenda would give programmes such as New Beginnings more stable central funding rather than short-term bids from special initiatives.

However, in mid-1998, the Labour government published its Green Paper *The Learning Age* (DfEE, 1998a), as a prelude to major changes in national post-16 provision the following year. This created wide uncertainty about the future, and

WellTEC organized a major restructure in early 1999. Staff were scrupulously reticent about discussing the impact of this restructure, and I guessed they had been told that it was highly confidential. All my attempts to gauge opinion were firmly discouraged. However, the impression I gathered from my visits to the Futures Centre office was that, while staff were trying to appear upbeat, they were shaken badly by the changes. Brenda Mavers took a lot of time off work sick, and Kath Martin confided to Anna Jeffries that Brenda was suffering stress due to the restructure. Moreover, the imminent appearance of the White Paper *Learning to Succeed* (DfEE, 1999d), due in July 1999, hung over them like a sword of Damocles. Just a week before its appearance, Bob Johnson told me:

> I was speaking to somebody from Government Office the other day who does know what's in the review, you know, but wasn't allowed to say. The only thing he could say is, 'It's going to be fundamental', which I think implies the complete reconstruction of the system that we have for post-16 provision.

When the sword fell, it was worse than they could have expected. The White Paper proposed the total abolition of TECs, to be replaced by Learning and Skills Councils in respect of their remit for post-16 provision, bringing together a new common funding régime for training and college-based full-time education. In addition, the development of the new Learning Gateway (DfEE, 1999e), as an initial step to increase participation and towards the formation of the *Connexions* service, presented a dual threat to the territory on which New Beginnings had staked its claim. On the one hand, the proposed introduction of education maintenance allowances (EMAs) for young people at college introduced competition from FE colleges for the New Beginnings target group. On the other hand, the leading role allocated to careers services in the Learning Gateway, and the introduction of personal advisers in a mentoring role for young people, shifted the balance of power in respect of WellTEC's autonomy and control over New Beginnings and its trainees. In particular, it undermined the rationale for providing volunteer mentors.

Over the summer of 1999, no mentors were matched. Staff sickness, including that of Brenda Mavers, had almost forced the closure of New Beginnings – small wonder that the active mentors found less and less support available. In October 1999 the WellTEC managers informed UoW staff that the New Beginnings brand name was being dropped, that they had terminated their European Youthstart funding before its due date of December that year, and had cancelled the proposal to allocate discretionary funding beyond that date. The training and work experience aspects of the provision would remain in a similar form, but these would be integrated with the former Futures Club under the aegis of the Learning Gateway. Engagement mentoring moved from the margins into the mainstream, but disrupted the New Beginnings scheme as it did so. As Anna Jeffries mused after these developments:

How do I feel about the end of it? It would be nice to think that we were all talking about 'What next?', you know, what bit of money we could chase next, and what I'm puzzled about is that we're *not* talking about 'What next?' What I'm puzzled about is *why* we're not. Are we not talking about 'What next?' because we don't like what we've done and we're glad it's all over, and we've got through it all, thank God, let's slam the door on that! Or are we simply not getting involved in talking about 'What next?' because there are so many big areas of uncertainty for the TEC staff? And I think it's probably the latter, really, I think, I hope, I don't know. . . .

Epilogue

The institutional setting that New Beginnings provided for mentor relationships may be seen within a set of power dynamics connected to other contextual levels. The scheme itself bore the imprint of the European Youthstart Initiative which funded it. This imposed both particular specifications on the scheme, notably its employment goals, and a general ethos, namely the disciplining of young people within the bounds of employability under a banner of empowerment. It connected with the political imperatives identified in Chapter 1: welfare to work, New Labour's social exclusion agenda, and the way that agenda constructs disaffected youth and poor communities. It served employers' interests in the context of local labour market supply problems and far wider concerns about global competition. In these respects, New Beginnings clearly fits the definition of engagement mentoring. Moreover, it promoted a second aspect through which mentoring might transform dispositions. It sought to influence the dispositions of the student mentors themselves, within the discourse of graduate employability to which the university and individual students had to respond.

Each of these contextual levels brings to bear the power of the ruling class and their representatives, however removed some of these may appear from the operation of the scheme itself. They shaped the way that the scheme controlled and prescribed the roles both of the young trainees and the volunteer mentors, the way that professionals liaising with New Beginnings operated referrals to the scheme, and even the implementation by the Benefits Agency of entitlements to benefit within the most stringent interpretation of their regulations.

The partnership managing New Beginnings represents another level of institutional context – the way in which the interests of WellTEC and UoW acted upon the scheme, interacted with each other, and had to respond to the wider political and economic context that we have already considered. Policy-makers set a high value on partnership itself, and it provided access to funding, which in turn impacted on individuals' jobs and prospects of continued employment. The kudos of partnership with HE was an attraction for WellTEC, and at that particular time UoW was prioritizing work that demonstrated its commitment to the local community. All of those involved had a personal commitment to help socially excluded young people, but individuals and their institutions reflected very different values in relation to that commitment. In the end, more powerful forces removed control of the provision from both institutions, resulting in New Beginnings' untimely demise. This, then, was the backdrop for the engagement mentor relationships that were formed between student volunteers and young trainees at New Beginnings.

I continue by narrating the stories of some of those relationships in the following three chapters. A brief description of each of the mentors and mentees in these stories is given in Table 3.4. The case stories in Chapter 4 focus on the positive agency that young people brought to the mentoring process – an agency which is so often ignored by practitioners, managers and policy-makers in this field. These stories reveal much about the positive potential of mentoring, particularly from young people's own perspectives. However, they also reveal the complexity of the power dynamics involved. The positive outcomes identified by the young people were often in conflict with the expectations of the scheme and of the policies that promoted it, resulting in negative consequences for the young person in some cases. I hope readers will be able to compare these accounts with the official and rhetorical stories about mentoring discussed in the first two chapters, and to draw some of their own conclusions as they do so.

Table 3.4 Mentees and mentors in the case stories

	Mentee	Period of mentor relationship	Mentor	
Name	Annette	April 1999 to March 2000	Jane	Name
Age at first interview	17		32	Age at first interview
Background	Former school non-attender. Expecting a child November 1999		Former secretary and personal assistant	Background
First interview	July 1999		May 1999	First interview
Work placement	Business Administration at New Beginnings		BA Applied Social Sciences (Year 2)	Degree course/year
Status at scheme	Left scheme October 1999, completed NVQ Level 1			
Second interview	March 2000		March 2000	Second interview
Status	Full-time mother		Looking for work as professional mentor	Status
Name	Adrian	January to May 1999	Patricia	Name
Age at first interview	17		37	Age at first interview
Background	Former schoolphobic. Mental health problems		Former personnel manager	Background
First interview	May 1999		February 1999	First interview
Work placement	Filing clerk		B.Ed. Secondary Business Studies (Year 2)	Degree course/year
Status at scheme	Sacked May 1999			
Second interview	May 2000			Second interview
Status	Unemployed			Status

continued . . .

Table 3.4 continued

	Mentee	Period of mentor relationship	Mentor	
Name	Hayley	October 1998 to February 1999	Ged	Name
Age at first interview	18		46	Age at first interview
Background	School career disrupted by family breakup and moves to different areas		Former marketing manager. Redundant for several years	Background
First interview	July 1999		January 1999	First interview
Work placement	Assistant at local youth centre		BA Applied Social Sciences (Year 3)	Degree course/year
Status at scheme	Sacked February 1999			
Second interview	April 2000			Second interview
Status	Full-time at FE college, nursery nursing work placement			Status
Name	Sharon	December 1998 to May 1999 (with a nine-week break from January)	Karen	Name
Age at first interview	17		20	Age at first interview
Background	Attended special school for learning difficulties		Came directly from sixth form to university	Background
First interview	May 1999		February 1999	First interview
Work placement	Elderly care		B.Ed. Primary Physical Education (Year 2)	Degree course/year
Status at scheme	Had to leave after 18th birthday			
Second interview	April 2000		May 1999	Second interview
Status	Unemployed, part-time baby-sitting			Status

Sharon

Name	Sharon
Age at first interview	(as above)
First interview	January to February 1999
Background	
Work placement	
Second interview	

Neil

Name	Neil
Age at first interview	17
Background	Attended special school for learning difficulties
First interview	May 1999
Work placement	Catering
Status at scheme	Progressed to mainstream youth training with placement employer
Second interview	March 2000
Status	About to become employed part-time with same employer
	January 1999: ongoing at March 2000

Rachel

Name	Rachel
Age at first interview	21
Background	Came directly from sixth form to university
First interview	February 1999
Degree course/year	BA Creative Arts (Year 3)
Second interview	May 1999

Keith

Name	Keith
Age at first interview	30
Background	Former sales manager, long-time Labour Party member and trade union representative
First interview	May 1999
Degree course/year	BA History and Social Sciences (Year 3)
Second interview	February 2000
Status	Employed at WellTEC as Learning Gateway personal adviser

continued . . .

Table 3.4 continued

	Mentee	Period of mentor relationship	Mentor	
Name	Lisa	July 1998: ongoing at February 2000	Yvonne	Name
Age at first interview	17		21	Age at first interview
Background	School refuser from Year 10 following mother's death		After sixth form, spent one year as carer in respite home for disabled children	Background
First interview	June 1999		June 1999	First interview
Work placement	Various		BA Applied Social Sciences (Year 2)	Degree course/year
Status at scheme	Sacked late 1999, enrolled at Futures Club			
Second interview	February 2000		January 2000	Second interview
Status	Unemployed			Status

Chapter 4

'I know I'm only young, but I know what I want'

Resistance and agency on the part of mentees

Introduction

The case stories in this chapter focus primarily (although not exclusively) on the young people being mentored at New Beginnings. I do not wish to suggest by this that the young people exerted sole or primary control in the cases discussed here. There is ample evidence that they were also subject to the power of others: mentors, New Beginnings staff, other professionals working with them and policy-makers. However, evidence of their agency challenges some of the key assumptions about the power dynamics of mentoring discussed in Chapter 2. To recap, two general assumptions tend to be made: first, power is usually considered only in relation to individual interactions between mentor and mentee, rather than analysis of wider power relations that impact upon the dyad. Second, the power dynamics of mentoring are seen as one-directional. Mentors are assumed to determine where the relationship is situated on the spectrum of direction–guidance, and therefore to control the degree of empowerment for the mentee. The independent exercise of power by the mentee is not generally considered at all.

More specific assumptions about engagement mentoring are that young people can be 'empowered' for their own and society's good by the directive but benevolent imposition of external goals for mentoring, tied to employment-related outcomes, and determined by employers and policy-makers. The moralistic nature of current policy thinking entails an assumption that, while many young people will comply, others may refuse to do so. Compulsion to participate and sanctions for non-participation are therefore seen as justifiable.

In Chapter 3 we have seen how the New Beginnings scheme perpetuated this approach, despite the positive commitment of its managers and staff to support socially excluded young people. Within that context, these assumptions might lead us to expect that some young people would happily engage with mentoring at New Beginnings, while others would vote with their feet and withdraw. In practice, there was a great deal more complexity in the play of power within the mentoring dyads I studied. Far from a polarization between buying into or opting out of the process on the part of the trainees, I found contestation and struggle, resolved in different ways by the young people, their mentors and the New Beginnings staff. I begin with the story of Annette and her mentor Jane, where this struggle produced a crucial turning point in their relationship at an early stage, and continued to influence its progress much later on as well.

Annette and Jane

Annette

The first time I met Annette in the summer of 1999 she was 17 years old, and doing well on the training programme. Her placement was at the New Beginnings office itself, as a clerical receptionist. She was working hard towards completing her NVQ Level 1 in business administration, as she was pregnant, and was due to leave the scheme soon to have her baby in October. Brenda Mavers was very pleased with her performance, and told me that she would have created a permanent post for Annette if she had been staying on. There had been some problems with her pregnancy, though, and she had had to take a lot of time off sick. Annette appeared to be an assertive young woman – Elaine Peters had assured me that she would speak very frankly. At the same time she was guarded in discussing her private life, and I guessed that her mentor would have had to deal with these characteristics.

Annette's mother had died when she was 6 years old. Conflicts with her father arose as she grew up, and eventually he placed her into local authority care. She described this as the starting point of a period of rebellion: 'Well, me and my dad weren't getting on. He got remarried after my mum died, and then I got put into care, but 'cos I wanted to be with my [older] sister I wasn't going to school, and then I moved in with my sister, and I didn't go at all. I know it just sounds stupid now, but it seems like everyone, the school and everything was just nagging at you.' She now took a different, more mature perspective: 'That's what it seemed, but now when you think about it and you look back, you think, they were only doing it for your own good, but when you're at school, you don't see it like that. 'Cos I wanted to wear what I wanted to, and what make-up I wanted to wear, and my jewellery I couldn't wear. I just thought I was different from everyone else and I thought, well, just 'cos they can't do it, doesn't mean that I couldn't. But you regret it all in the end.'

Although the staff at New Beginnings and the TEC often promoted the notion that unemployment among parents was a major cause of disaffection among the young people, Annette's father had continued to work, and this itself caused problems. He was a long-distance lorry driver, which frequently kept him away from home. Annette established a close relationship with her older sister: 'It feels like, when my mum died, we all stuck together, and that's why we're all dead close. 'Cos with my dad always wanting to work when my mum died, like, my sister, she was the one that took care of us.'

A sense of family seemed very important to Annette, and organized the priorities in her life. It had influenced her on-and-off participation in New Beginnings, where she had first started at the age of 16. After three months she had left to work in a chip shop, partly because a few hours there each week paid her more money than the New Beginnings training allowance, and partly because it gave her more time to spend with her sister. Her growing sense of aspiration was also important to her identity. She had become 'fed up' with working at the chip shop, and initially had been compelled to come back to New Beginnings when she tried to claim welfare benefits: 'It was when I moved in with one of my friends and I wasn't getting any money, but I was claiming Income Support, but they said that I had to be on a scheme, so I came here about six or seven months ago. Even if I didn't want to do it, I had to do it for the money.'

Despite that financial compulsion, and two placements in retail and elderly care that she did not enjoy, Annette described how she had eventually settled in her placement at Cotswold House. She seemed to have engaged with the immediate goals set for her at New Beginnings, particularly that of passing her NVQ Level 1 in business administration. 'I'm sticking to this now,' she declared, 'even though sometimes I'm fed up with it, I always think: well, I went wrong at school and I've regretted that, then one day I'll have my NVQ in business admin, I've got it then, haven't I? And that's something I wouldn't mess up. I messed up at school and, like, my dad always used to say that all my brothers and sisters would just be the same, we won't get nothing out of life, so I've got to achieve something.' Annette had a clear plan of how she would pursue this goal, despite having had quite a bit of time off sick due to problems with her pregnancy: 'If I don't get my NVQ done within this three and a half weeks, I'll come in for odd days and finish it off, like, when I leave. It's nearly all finished, I've just got three units to do now.'

Annette's determination to achieve something, and her sense of new-found maturity, had strengthened her engagement with the goals of New Beginnings. But they also created longer term plans that conflicted with the aims of the scheme. Now living independently in her own council house in Midtown's South Side with her steady boyfriend, Annette's main ambition was not to progress into employment at Cotswold House, but to become a full-time mother and establish her own family. She talked about this future assertively and with a sense of excitement: 'Like, I know I'm only young, but I know what I want, and that's what I *did* want, a baby. It'll be brilliant because me and my boyfriend, we're really close anyway, we're dead close, so that's what we both really wanted, to settle down now. Like, I wouldn't think there's nothing wrong when two people who are settled, settling down, there's nothing wrong with having a baby. It's lovely when you see the scan, it's the best thing you can ever see! And feeling it kick and everything, that's when it hits you then, 'cos you know it's really there.'

Perhaps because of her own experiences of losing her mother and then being put into care, Annette would not consider looking for a job at least until her child was old enough to start school, and, even then, childcare arrangements would take first priority, so she was not sure whether she would go back into clerical work at that stage. Her view of future employment prospects, though, was pessimistic, and revealed some enduring resentment about the way young people were compelled by the benefits régime to join schemes such as New Beginnings. I asked her how easy she thought it would be to get a job when the baby was old enough. She replied, 'I don't really know, though, 'cos I think the jobs and that are going to get worse before they get better.'

'What gives you that idea?' I asked.

'Well,' she continued, 'with all these schemes coming out now, and there's going to be more schemes coming out, they'll get all the other people on them. 'Cos you can't beat them, you can't keep, like, putting them off, 'cos they always win.'

'Who always win?' I queried.

'The dole,' she replied, 'they always get you on schemes at the end of the day.'

Annette seemed angry about this, and about other injustices she felt she faced, such as negative attitudes towards young single mothers, and prejudice because of where she lived. Her other dream of 'settling down' was to save enough money to get out of the South Side: 'It's the area that puts you down, so I'd like to leave in the future. It's all right my side, at my end, but it's on the other side, but when you say to people that you live such-and-such, they always look down at you to think: "Why do you live there?" and things like that, because of the estate, what it is.' She longed to move back to Sweetland, where she had been in care and which she remembered fondly.

Jane

Annette's mentor was Jane, a mature student in her early thirties studying for a degree in applied social sciences. Jane was married with a small child, and she described her situation as comfortable and stable. Since leaving school at 16, Jane had worked as a secretary and personal assistant until she left work to have her child. This had precipitated a dramatic personal epiphany, which Jane described with some passion. Having experienced postnatal problems, she had set up a local self-help group for new mothers, and through this she discovered a powerful sense of emotional connection with other women. She found that being needed by others created a much greater sense of reward than she had ever experienced in her secretarial job. 'Once I started doing that, and I got feedback, and I got people saying "Thank you for helping me", it was like, "*Wow!*" you know! It was better than a pay-packet!' she laughed. 'You know, for somebody to say, "Well, you've really helped me", that meant a lot to me, and I think that must have been what inspired me.'

Jane felt that she could no longer countenance going back to work in an office, and began to think about a career change so that she could 'work with people'. Pursuing this discovery raised another issue that seemed fundamental to her values and beliefs: 'I was concerned in the way I was giving information or listening to people, feedback, the way I reacted, body language, everything . . . I was concerned that there must be a right way and wrong way, and I didn't want to offend or upset anybody. That's when I found out about counselling courses. So then I went on to do a counselling course at night school.' After completing her counselling certificate, she sought vocational guidance and chose a degree rather a counselling diploma as a way of broadening her education and expanding her career options.

Having a clear theoretical framework, and reflecting on her practice in relation to theoretical versions of 'the right way' to do things, was a constant theme of Jane's explanations of her activities as a mentor. As a student of applied social sciences, she would have been expected to carry out such reflections in her academic work, no doubt reinforcing her personal concern to 'do the right thing'. Person-centred counselling theory had come to dominate her thinking, and had been her own chosen focus throughout the different elements of her degree course so far. She related mentoring closely to counselling as similar forms of dyadic helping, and planned to explore their similarities in her final year dissertation. To this end she had volunteered for three different schemes: 'I'm using what I'm doing at New Beginnings, and I'm also using work with the Wellshire Probation Service on mentoring, and then counselling that I'm doing for a group in Mainborough, they work with just young people, counselling young people. What I'm doing the dissertation on is the similarity of skills that you need in counselling and mentoring, to work with somebody in a helping relationship, to give them confidence, and so it's working on a self-concept and how somebody feels about themselves in order to move on in life. That's my dissertation.'

A note of explanation may be helpful here. Person-centred counselling is a therapeutic intervention, based upon the premise that the human psyche is characterized by a purposive drive to positive personal growth (Rogers, 1951). The 'perceived' self, in healthy growth or through a helping relationship, becomes ever more closely reconciled with the genuine or 'real' self, and the real self, in turn, approaches an 'ideal' self through a process of 'self-actualization'. A helping relationship is defined as: 'a relationship in which at least one of the parties has the intent of promoting the growth, development, maturity, improved functioning, improved coping with life of the other' (Rogers, 1951: 39–40).

The counsellor not only assists the client in this process, but has the responsibility of pursuing these goals in her own person. It is only in this way that she can achieve what have come to be known in this body of theory as the 'core conditions' of the helping relationship: empathic understanding (the ability to enter the client's frame of reference and see the world as they see it); unconditional positive regard (the capacity to demonstrate caring for and abstain from judgement upon the client); and genuineness or congruence (the extent to which the helper's words accurately reflect her thoughts and feelings, and therefore convey trustworthiness to the client). There is a recognition that these conditions cannot be achieved without constant effort on the part of the counsellor or helper, and that conflicts and tensions will often arise.

It did not surprise me that this approach connected with Jane's experience of discovering what she really wanted to do and be, once she realized her own disaffection from office work, and experienced the pleasure of helping others. The chance to volunteer as a mentor at New Beginnings was therefore a golden opportunity for Jane. It would assist her academic studies, providing a field in which to generate data for her dissertation. It offered engagement in relationships with young people identified as needing help and support. In addition, it would give her voluntary work experience that would be a major advantage in pursuing the future careers to which she aspired.

Establishing a mentor relationship

Bringing Annette and Jane together was not an automatic or easy process. Elaine Peters had thought that Annette would benefit from mentoring ever since she started at New Beginnings, mainly because she was 'very quiet' and 'quite shy in some ways'. Annette, however, had refused the offer repeatedly, and Elaine put this down to her previous experiences of being in care. 'We always get some that don't want mentors,' Elaine explained, 'especially if they've been in contact with Social Services, or they've been in care, because they've talked to so many social workers, they've talked to the Probation Services, they've talked to that many people they don't want to talk to anybody else. . . . They've explained their life so many times that they're not bothered.' Given that so many young people were refusing the mentoring option, Elaine tried a different tack: 'I put it across in different ways as well . . . like Annette didn't want a mentor. . . . But when she decided that business admin was the area that she wanted to go into, and Jane had been in from an admin background, I introduced it, you know, "Jane's been in an admin background, she may be able to help you . . . give you some guidance into your career or whatever" . . . and she's done it and it's worked out fine.'

Jane had felt very uncomfortable to be introduced as 'someone working in an office'. It identified her with the former self she had rejected. In addition, the deceit undermined the basis of trust her person-centred approach demanded, and so she made clear her real situation to Annette from the start, and felt that this had not caused any problems. Although Annette seemed bemused by the thought of someone becoming a student at age 30, she was far more interested in Jane's identity as a mother than as a student or former secretarial worker.

Annette told her version of how she had come to be involved in mentoring: 'Well, every time we had an induction with Elaine Peters, she kept saying if I wanted a mentor, and I kept saying no. I didn't want one at first, I'm not that good really at talking to people that I don't really know.'

'So you didn't fancy that, having to talk to someone you didn't know?' I asked.

'Then when I seen one of my mates, she had one. . . . So I decided to have one,' she replied.

I was not sure whether Annette's friend had convinced her, or whether she had simply complied with Elaine's constant pressure to accept a mentor. Such compliance would be understandable, as Annette came to engage more with the goals of New Beginnings, to trust the staff and to establish herself in her placement there, where Elaine and Brenda were now her managers as well as her training providers. This explanation might be supported by her response when asked how she had been matched with Jane: 'I don't know. . . . Well, I just came in one day, and Elaine said she'd got me a mentor.' I had noticed that Annette and Jane's names were never inscribed on the whiteboard at New Beginnings for all-comers to see, and wondered if Annette had any hand in the invisibility of her mentor relationship, since she worked there. Perhaps she had been reluctant because she felt some stigma was attached to having a mentor.

Annette certainly had a very limited idea of what mentoring was or what its purposes might be. She told me that Elaine had explained a mentor's role as: 'Someone to come in and talk to you, or you can talk to them if you didn't feel comfy speaking to any other person here, you could always speak to them, or tell them about your placement.'

Annette had her own view: 'I'd say mentors were more like social workers or something like that, more than anything.' Social workers, however, were a mixed blessing in her eyes, given her experiences in local authority care: 'Sometimes they were a bit of a pain, because they were always nosy, and they wanted to know everything, and they always used to say, like when I said that I wanted to live down there on the South Side, they didn't really want me to, 'cos of the area. They were always trying to butt in, 'cos I'd had them for quite a few years, and they thought they had some sort of control over me.' This feeling of being controlled, as at school, was something Annette clearly resisted in asserting her own independent choices, and I guessed that this must have taken considerable strength and determination on her part.

As might be expected, Jane had a much more constructed view of mentoring that drew mainly on her affinity with counselling-type interventions: 'I see it as a relationship with somebody . . . very difficult to define, but there's a relationship to offer understanding and to offer the things that counselling offers, empathy and just quite a neutral position as a mentor.' The difference was that counselling demanded a 'professional distance', whereas, for Jane, mentoring was more akin to friendship, 'more relaxed'. As an inexperienced practitioner also, she seemed to prioritize unconsciously some of the 'core conditions' of client-centred practice over others: 'I also see mentoring as in counselling, where you've got to take on board whatever they say, because they can go quite deep and maybe try to shock you, or . . . I don't know, some things that come out are quite shocking, but to act in a non-judgemental way, you can't be judgemental . . . or you can't show any sort of "Oh my goodness!" you know, you've just got to take it all on board, and I think the more you can do that, the more they'll open up and confide in you, so I think that just that neutral position for them to be able to talk openly about anything at all, for somebody to be there, and they know it's not going to go back to the TEC or anybody else . . . you know, confidential.'

There is a tension here between the conscious effort to demonstrate empathy on the one hand, and the unawareness of her lack of congruence as Jane talked about *being* shocked but not *showing* it. There is also a tension between Jane's desire to help and some of her underlying values, which were revealed further as she discussed her views about disaffected youth a few moments later. 'I mean, some of the things they talk about, you know!' she exclaimed. '"My sister had a baby and my granddad brought it up." But that's normal! "Sister didn't want it, so my granddad had it, my dad married so-and-so, had a baby, they didn't want it, so my sister had that one", and it's all so intermingled and. . . . But it's normal, you know, it's what they accept, and you can sit there and think "*Oh! What?!*", but the more they talk, the more it's how life is for them.'

Towards the end of our interview, when I asked how Jane viewed Annette's long-term prospects, I got a rather indignant outburst I was not expecting at all: 'It seems to be, the more I talk to them I didn't realize how much, but it's: "Oh, I'll decorate the baby's bedroom when this cheque comes," or: "My boyfriend's gone on the sick, so when he gets his big cheque, we'll do this." The boyfriend is off work – a 22- and a 17-year-old, fully healthy people, but they've no intention of doing anything, and not an education to get them where they want to go. It's this cheque, that cheque, social, income support, but it's the only thing they know, and to me, like you said, what's the future? Who can make such a difference to make them change? Who can make such a big impact to say "That is not the way you're going to go for the rest of your life"? Who can do that? I don't know.'

A critical incident

Nevertheless, as Jane and Annette began to establish their relationship, the tensions emerged not from their mutual perceptions of each other but from an externally located contradiction: the goals of mentoring as defined by New Beginnings. Annette seemed clearly aware of the official view, which had been put across to the mentors in their training programme, that their role was primarily to encourage the young person to implement their personal development plan (PDP). However, she had her own thoughts about the purpose of mentoring, as she described the things she and Jane discussed together: 'We talked about everything really, but like, mentors are mainly for work, but it wasn't really work that I did talk about.'

Annette used her time with Jane to help her figure out how to deal with arguments she had with her boyfriend, to talk about her family, and in particular, to discuss her concerns about her pregnancy, given that Jane already had a small child. 'She put my mind at rest when I was having problems with the baby,' Annette explained. 'Like, 'cos she had a little girl as well. She just said, like, "Don't worry, it's like all people have different pregnancies, and you're stuck with one of the bad ones, everything will come out fine".' At the same time, she seemed at pains to avoid portraying mentoring as problem-focused in a way that might be stigmatizing: 'I just think mentors are really good, and like some people have different opinions, but I think that they're worth having. 'Cos there's always people out there with worse problems and things like that, that can find even that there is no one that they can talk to, but by having a mentor, they find it easier. It's like with me though, I go in for just someone to talk to, not 'cos I have problems, because I'd already got the job here and everything.'

At first Jane struggled with the way Annette chose to introduce her own agenda and to resist the official view of what the mentoring sessions should cover. She drew on the 'right things' she had been taught to focus on in her mentor training course, explaining that: 'I tried to do the things, the training that she needed, and the educational thing, and work placements, and talk about all of those, you know, the sort of textbook of, you know, how it's supposed to be . . . go along that line of the PDP plan they have.' Annette, as we have already seen, felt that these were not especially useful topics for her to explore with her mentor, and Jane described how Annette began to steer their meetings in a different direction. At their second meeting, Annette brought along a photograph of herself as a little girl on holiday with her mother.

The photograph and the stories it generated dominated that mentoring session and had a profound effect upon Jane, who recounted it in faltering and emotional tones. 'The second time I saw Annette,' Jane recalled, 'she brought me photographs of her and her mum . . . and they were sitting on a holiday wall with the sun behind them . . . and she was the age my daughter is now. So she was 5, Annette was, and her mum's got her arm round her.' Jane acted out the gesture and swallowed hard before she could continue.

'And they've got ice-creams . . . very happy and pigtails and sunny, and she was showing me all these photographs of her and her mum . . . and then . . . she said: "And my mum would be your age now", meaning my age.' Again Jane paused and sighed. 'And that day I got home and cried my eyes out . . . I completely cried my eyes out, but I'm . . . *sure* it was because . . . Annette was 5 on this photograph with *her* mum of *my* age, and I just put it all. . . . And my husband said, "Why are you crying?" you know. I *really* was upset, and it was just . . . it just affected me, you know, seeing them on holiday so happy and then to think that she had died . . . I don't know why, but the way that she told me about it, how it had . . . how her life had gone completely . . . different since then . . . going into care and, you know, breaking up with her brothers and sisters, and I thought, that is *so cruel*, you know, what happens to a family when somebody dies . . . and it just affected me, and I got home and I cried my eyes out, and I thought: "Can I do this?" you know, but then . . . I did, I just went back the next week. But again, I used the learning diary to put that in. Something triggered off inside me, but I'm sure I put myself, you know, I'm thinking *myself* and *my* daughter. . . . The photograph was so sunny and so happy, and then you see this girl who's gone through so much, and she's only 17. . . . Her family breaking up and . . . I think when somebody tells you, you can read case studies in books and all kinds, but when somebody sits in front of you and tells you, you know, you just want to hug them a lot of the time.'

Jane lowered her voice to a whisper, and acted out a hug as she continued, 'You just want to say "Come here", you know, "there's somebody to share that with you". My husband has actually said to me time and time again: "Do you think that this is what you want to do, you know, you get so involved", and I've said "Oh, it doesn't affect me", and what-have-you.'

This account is a dramatic one in more than one respect, and it raised a number of questions for me about how Jane saw her relationship with Annette. I was somewhat shocked to hear her talk about such depth of emotion following what had been only their second meeting, and I found this difficult to regard as genuine. I found myself questioning her apparent wish to be needed as a problematic motivation for her involvement in mentoring. As a former careers adviser whose training had also been steeped in the counselling tradition, alarms bells sounded in my head about the way in which Jane seemed to be transgressing the boundaries of the relationship, and her denial of this even though her husband pointed it out. I was also interested in the way Jane often referred to her learning diary as she did here. Rather than using it for critical self-reflection to learn from such episodes, what seemed important to her was to have a record of them that she could revisit and thereby re-experience their emotional intensity.

A defining moment

None the less, their mentoring sessions continued to centre on Annette's priorities, until Jane took stock: 'Well, I'd worked with her for a few weeks, and then I'd read the training manual to see whether I was doing it the right way. . . . Because what happened is, we got into such . . . a relationship talking about her pregnancy, her mum, dad, all of these things, social workers, and I had to stop and think: am I going along the right lines?' The New Beginnings training pack for mentors, however, emphasized the need to go through the young person's PDP every week. Jane thought, 'Oh gosh! I'd better do that', and asked Annette for her PDP the following week.

Jane continued the story: 'Annette goes: "Oh! . . . No!" and she was *shocked*. . . . And I said, "Oh, I thought we might have a look at it and see what you've been doing", and she says, "Well, I *always* tell you what I've been doing, you know, I do this, that and the other . . . ". I said, "Well, if you like, you could bring it in next week, and we could go through it." And I think she's a bit shocked that I mentioned it, you know, but I'd looked in the mentoring stuff to try and see whether I was doing the right things, really, and it said you should be going over the plan. She brings a booklet she goes to the hospital with for her scans and things, she brings me that every week, but she doesn't bring me this plan, so I talk to her, I ask her what work she's doing 'cos she's on placement with the TEC, so she tells me what she's been doing there, and what training she's doing. We do talk about those things, but I don't think that she wants to. I don't think she wants to.'

Jane never asked for the New Beginnings planner again, and in a later conversation with me she identified this as a crucial turning point in the relationship: 'I think that was the moment when Annette really began to trust me.'

Differing perceptions of the relationship

We have seen how deeply Jane felt about her relationship with Annette through her emotional account of its earliest stages. By the time I was able to interview Annette some weeks after my interview with Jane, the contrast in their perceptions of the relationship was marked. There was no doubt that Annette liked Jane as a person, and she compared the genuineness she perceived in Jane with her previous experiences of social workers who 'just pretended to be nice' because they were paid to do so. She valued Jane's interest in her, and the way she had taken on board her personal concerns rather than continuing to push the training plans from New Beginnings.

However, Annette also talked about her sister, friends and other staff at New Beginnings as people with whom she could talk over her worries and from whom she could get support. It struck me that Annette often talked about her mentor in the past tense, and also that she gave a very different description of the stage their relationship had reached. Not only had they not met for some weeks, but Annette explained several times that 'I only had Jane for about three weeks, four weeks, so I don't know that much really about her.' This also contradicted the account Jane had given me several weeks earlier, that they had already met eight or nine times. One of Annette's comments also seemed to convey a definite sense of ending: 'I wouldn't mind seeing her again, but like I was having a lot of time off as well, when she was leaving.' There seemed to be a large gulf between the degree of involvement the mentor felt, and the helpful but tenuous relationship perceived by the mentee. Their very different accounts clearly showed that mentoring occupied a far more significant and emotive place in Jane's experience than it did for Annette.

I was interested to know how Jane perceived the current hiatus in the relationship. I knew that she had had exams at UoW, and also that she had planned to find temporary work during the summer holidays, which, with Annette's sick-leave, would have made meeting up difficult. In a telephone conversation with Jane she seemed quite upset about the break: 'I want to visit Annette when she finishes to have the baby. I really miss her. I miss the contact. I think about her all the time.' She repeated the story about the mentoring session when Annette had brought in her childhood photographs, and how she had gone home and cried afterwards. Once more, I felt uncomfortable about the strength of Jane's feelings. Whose needs were uppermost in Jane's desire to see her mentee again – Annette's or her own? Jane had recently begun the training course at Wellshire Probation Service where she would be mentoring young ex-offenders, so I guessed that she would be moving on to this new work to fulfil her need to be needed.

A new stage

In late October, however, I called Jane again. Irene Marsden had heard that the New Beginnings staff had made an exception to their strict rules about mentor relationships not going outside the confines of Cotswold House. Brenda Mavers, at Jane's request, had agreed that the pair could continue meeting at Annette's home now that she had left to have the baby. Jane talked excitedly about the difference she perceived in the relationship. A key factor was that the mentoring now took place in informal settings. For Jane this meant that 'We're *never* stuck for things to say', and was much preferable to the closed environment of the mentoring room provided at Cotswold House, which she had found inhibiting.

Perhaps more important, though, was the deeper level of connection she felt she had achieved with Annette: 'I'm amazed! Annette is a different person than she ever appeared at the TEC. She's not reserved, not acting a part. I feel I've finally got to know who she really is.' Just as Jane had discovered the person she 'really' was after quitting secretarial work to give birth, she seemed to ascribe a similar change to Annette now that her mentee had followed the same path.

I carried out second interviews with both women in March 2000. Annette had had her baby, of whom she was very proud. She was pleased she had completed her NVQ before leaving New Beginnings, and was often busy decorating each room of her immaculately clean and tidy house in the latest fashionable styles. Annette thought that her relationship with Jane had shifted away from mentoring to a different basis. 'Well, it's something different now,' she explained, 'because it's like how a friendship should be now. Not just like someone you talk to on advice and things like that. I don't know what it's like. It was like a cross between a teacher or a counsellor the way it was at Cotswold House, but, like, it's different when she's sitting in your home and you're talking to her there, it's just, the atmosphere's different and everything.'

The enthusiasm that Jane had shown in our telephone conversation seemed much dampened by the time I interviewed her six months later. She made the same point about the shift in the relationship as Annette had done: 'It was more, I don't know, perhaps more of a friendship,' Jane said, 'towards a friendship rather than me befriending her and always being there for her. She was asking me, "How's your work going?", you know, "How do you manage with your little girl and your work?" I think she feels that that's the polite way, when somebody's in your house, you don't just let them talk to you and help you all the time.'

Jane explained that this made the relationship more reciprocal, and part of this was that she felt the reward of some gratitude from Annette: 'She's, you know, "Do you want a drink?" and she's asking me, so she's balancing the relationship out a bit, in her way, she's balancing it up. She thinks, "Well, Jane's really good coming round here". I've been taking some clothes of my daughter's that I've kept from when she was young, you know, and washed them through and given them to her, so I think she's perhaps quite grateful, and you know, she's balancing it up.'

However, there were contradictions again between their accounts. Jane told me how Annette always had a long list of questions to ask about caring for the baby, while Annette told me she did not really need to ask Jane about such things any more, since the health visitor dealt with the very few problems that arose. One incident had pleased her greatly: 'Annette asked me if I thought she could ever become a social worker. I said, "Oh, I do! I think you'd make a good social worker, yeah." And Annette said, "Because I've been thinking since I've had the baby and I've been at home, I've been thinking about going back to college and doing something. . . . " Now, that was the first time she has ever herself. . . . At the TEC it was, "You're doing administration, you're doing computers", but she did it purely because she was going through the system. She didn't want to do it, she didn't want to be an office worker, but this is the first time she's said to me, "Do you think I could?" And I said, "You could".'

Annette, on the other hand, despite considerable probing on my part, asserted that she had not thought at all about her career plans since leaving New Beginnings, and had not discussed them with Jane. Perhaps that was a vulnerable issue she did not want to share with me in our interview, but I was struck by the similarities between Jane's account of Annette's rejection of office work, and her original account of her own experiences of career transformation *en route* to university.

More problems for Jane related to the fact that Annette was busy with her new baby, and with her network of friends and relatives, as well as health professionals who gave her advice and support. Annette told me how she spent her time now she was no longer working at New Beginnings: 'I just go to my sister's a lot. I just go up there and keep her company, while my nephew's at school. Then the baby's just got her injections, she's had two lots of injections, but she's got to have some more. If you want, you just take her every Tuesday to have her weighed, but we've got to do that as well tomorrow.' Discussing the best times for mentoring meetings reinforced a sense of how hectic Annette's schedule was. 'I wouldn't say on a Monday,' she calculated, ''cos my boyfriend has his mates come round, 'cos he goes to football, and it gets a bit too busy. And not on a Wednesday or a Monday morning, 'cos my auntie comes here and I go there. On a Thursday, I think, would be best. Mornings, though, I'd rather have the mornings, then it's not so chaotic.'

Despite the shift to informality and friendship, their relationship in fact seemed to be drifting apart. Annette thought that she and Jane had met only four times in the five months since she had left New Beginnings, and their last meeting had been over three months ago, before Christmas. Jane was clearly finding this a problem too, given the pressures of completing her dissertation and undertaking her other voluntary work. 'Annette's a different one than perhaps my other [mentor] relationships at the moment,' she said laughing, 'because of getting hold of her and getting together, so we do have these phases when she first had the baby, you see . . . I went every week, because I knew she was there and she wasn't going anywhere . . . mmm. . . . Now with Annette it's different, because it's not a dead-set arrangement. I was going there every week, but then, you know, I go one day and she's not in 'cos baby's ill or what-have-you, so I try again the next week and she's not there, or with other people.'

Jane was becoming frustrated with this situation, particularly as it was a fairly long drive for her to Midtown. She had tried sending letters and leaving notes encouraging Annette to contact her, and pointed out with some annoyance that 'I always put a twenty-pence piece in, and I say, "Give me a ring and we can arrange to meet up", but she never does. She's a naughty girl!'

I asked Jane whether she had thought or talked about ending the relationship, and received a somewhat vague reply: 'Mmm . . . no, we wouldn't. . . . That's the plan I have written about as well, is: how do we end these relationships? Because I think there's a feeling of loss . . . for me and for them. . . . '

Jane felt disappointed and annoyed that her efforts often went unrewarded, yet she avoided her responsibility for drawing the relationship to a point of closure. Annette still welcomed Jane's interest and concern for her, but the contact was not one that Annette prioritized now her need for support was being fulfilled elsewhere. As at New Beginnings, their relationship was once again petering out.

Coming together and growing apart

Both Jane's and Annette's personal dispositions and shifting identities seemed to influence the formation and subsequent course of their mentor relationship. Annette's history of losing her mother and being placed into care by her father meant that establishing a stable family life, rather than education or work, was the overriding value in her life. Jane was a deeply caring person with a strong moral desire to 'do things right' and connect with others in helping relationships. Both women had experienced recent turning points in their lives (cf. Hodkinson *et al.*, 1996) that connected motherhood with career transition and identity transformation. This brought them initially into the framework of New Beginnings, but later led to conflict with the scheme.

On the one hand, although Annette's new-found maturity had enabled her to engage successfully with the employment-related goals of New Beginnings, this was only a temporary priority for her until her child was born. On the other hand, although Jane intended to apply the New Beginnings guidelines for mentoring, their directive nature conflicted with her commitment to more person-centred principles. When Jane tried to connect their mentor relationship more firmly with employment-related outcomes, and demanded to see Annette's PDP, Annette resisted and refused to comply. She asserted her own agenda of seeking reassurance and support for her pregnancy from Jane, in the absence of her own natural mother. Annette's substitution of the maternity clinic planner for the PDP planner is a graphic symbol of her agency, and changed the course of the mentor relationship. Jane had to make a choice, and supported the younger woman's agenda – not only because of her ethical beliefs, but perhaps also because of her own identification with Annette's mother, indicated by the session when Annette brought her childhood photograph. That decision may also be related to the emotional investment Jane had already made in the relationship, and her fear of its rupture or loss. During Annette's pregnancy, then, we can see that both women were able to fulfil needs through the mentor relationship. For Annette it served a vital purpose, and, despite her initial doubts, she valued the support it had provided through an anxious time.

Yet we can also see that there were differences in the class backgrounds and social values of these two women that would also loosen their bond. Annette still resented the fact that she and her boyfriend had been forced onto training schemes under threat of losing their benefits, but received only a few pounds a week more than their benefits would have paid. She saw their future prospects as something of a battle with the state, in which 'the dole' held the ultimate balance of power.

She fully intended to work in the future, and hoped her boyfriend would get into steady work, but opportunities to gain decent employment that would pay well and securely enough to enable the longed-for move to Sweetland were being restricted on two fronts. First, Annette felt up against other people's prejudices about where she lived and about teenage single parenthood. Second, she perceived that 'the dole' was in fact restricting the supply of real jobs by converting them into training schemes which the unemployed would then be forced to join.

Jane, on the other hand, despite her frequent references to the empathy and non-judgemental approach which she saw as central to Rogerian counselling, at times seemed to represent typical middle-class values. Rather than reflecting empathy by entering Annette's frame of reference, Jane seemed to absorb and reproduce dominant discourses about disaffection. The empathy, unconditional positive regard and congruence demanded by person-centred approaches were countered by Jane's deep shock at hearing about Annette's life and family. Jane's avowal of 'what is normal' for the disaffected, of 'how life is for *them*', attempted to be non-judgemental, but revealed a moral judgement in the very way that it was contrasted with her own perception of dominant social norms. She adopted a discourse of deviance as she talked about Annette's situation in terms of benefit dependency, unwillingness to work, teenage pregnancy, lack of respect for educational values, and eventually Annette's rejection of Jane's own helping intervention. Jane's comments about illegitimacy and 'healthy people with no intention of doing anything' paralleled closely Charles Murray's controversial definition of *The Emerging British Underclass* (1990) that we encountered earlier in Chapter 1. Jane saw her task in mentoring as that of altering these deviant values and behaviours, but she had a pessimistic view that disaffected young people might not be susceptible to such helping interventions. The distance she believed they had to travel to social inclusion appeared too far. The 'core conditions' seemed to have disappeared altogether.

Once outside the institutional context of New Beginnings, and during the period immediately surrounding the birth of Annette's child, Jane's interest in the relationship had revived. Away from an environment that had reinforced her concerns about the deviance of socially excluded young people, she was able once again to focus on compensating for deficits, sharing her knowledge and experience, making gifts of her own child's outgrown clothes, and reflecting back Annette's success as a parent. As this basis for their bond diminished, however, and Jane's frustration and possible sense of rejection grew, she reverted to the values that had been promoted at New Beginnings, focused on education as a route to employment, and she chose as the highlight of this stage of mentoring Annette's remark about going to college and aiming for a career similar to Jane's. Once again, the way she recounted this incident shows how she reinscribed Annette's experiences in terms of her own epiphany.

Both Annette and Jane thought their relationship had evolved from mentoring towards informal friendship. For Annette, it seemed a natural continuation that Jane would visit her from time to time, and she enjoyed the contact, but she did not pursue it actively herself. She did not make the effort to be at home for planned meetings, nor did she use the money Jane left to phone her. For Jane, however, friendship implied more commitment in the relationship, something she hoped was indicated by Annette's more reciprocal attitude when they did meet at her home, and which she sought to deepen by gift-giving, with the assumption that Annette would be grateful for Jane's social and material help. Her inability to take responsibility as the mentor for recognizing the relationship had outrun its course and creating a sense of closure linked to her own emotional needs – a sense of loss she could not face, and which she ascribed to her mentee as well.

In these ways, we can return to consider their dispositions in a different light. Not only did Jane and Annette draw upon individual aspects of their own personal histories in positioning themselves in relation to each other, to the scheme, and within wider social structures and ideological discourses. Gender and class also contributed to their perspectives. Gender brought them together in their common concerns about motherhood and the primacy of family, filtered through social constructions of women's role. However, while caring was located firmly within family and community for Annette, Jane aspired to centre her developing professional identity on caring also, and we see how this created a mismatch of aspirations as both women progressed in these directions. Annette no longer felt the need for an outsider's help, but Jane was disappointed in this and found it hard to let go.

Class also played its part. While Jane strove consciously to present her non-judgemental professional persona, her middle-classes prejudices, her resentment and fear of the underclass surfaced with less awareness. Her interpretations of Annette's transition and aspirations beyond New Beginnings revealed an imposition of her own values that could only contribute to her own frustration and disappointment if Annette did not in fact pursue them. At the same time, Annette felt the weight of discrimination loaded against her in what she saw as a battle against the state which she and her class were doomed to lose. She resented the combination of coercion and sanctions that welfare to work represented, seeing it as a dead-end condemnation to cheap labour. Her tacit knowledge of the labour market, and of its filters that directed her and her peers into its lower end with ever-diminishing pay and conditions, may only have been reinforced by her experience of being compelled into the New Beginnings scheme.

A successful mentor relationship or a failed one?

The story of mentoring between Annette and Jane undermines the simplistic assumptions identified in the introductory paragraphs to this chapter. Tensions arose in the relationship due to contradictions related both to the institutional setting and wider political constructions of disaffection and of the purpose of mentoring. Annette's power of agency was instrumental in determining the direction of the relationship (including its ending). She rejected employment-related goals as a focus of her mentoring sessions with Jane, and saw a battle ahead with government agencies in order to survive as she pursued her own family values. These values did not fit with the dominant moral code, nor with the policy imperative of employment as the solution to social exclusion. However, Annette asserted her own agenda within the relationship, and there is no doubt that she greatly valued the support she was able to obtain from Jane, and the relationship they had formed together.

Jane still lived in hope of altering Annette's attitudes and values in line with her own, and grasped at any sign that this transformation might be occurring. At the same time, Annette was drawing on the social inclusion and survival strategies of her own community, so that Jane's cultural resources gradually counted for less. Despite Annette's success as a parent, and her moral conviction that 'a child needs its mother when it's young', as a teenage parent and drop-out from formal education and training systems she would probably register as a failure within the framework outlined in *Bridging the Gap* (SEU, 1999). All these complex interactions between the two individuals, their personal histories and social backgrounds, the context of New Beginnings and the wider social setting indicate the futility of prescribing either the content or the outcomes of mentor relationships.

Like every individual relationship, that of Annette and Jane was in many ways unique. However, other young people also demonstrated their own power of agency within their mentor relationship, and in relation to the New Beginnings scheme. Before moving on from a focus on the young people's role in mentoring, let us look briefly at two other case stories that illustrate similar dynamics.

Adrian and Patricia

Adrian had been schoolphobic, and had suffered depression and anxiety, agoraphobia, and an eating disorder in his early teenage years. He lived with his mother, and had not seen his father for several years until the latter had recently returned to Midtown. There were constant conflicts at home with his mother, which had worsened since his father's reappearance. Aged 17, he described himself as feeling very 'dislodged' and 'confused': 'I can't seem to figure out, am I an adult or am I still a teenager?' Adrian described his post-16 choice as a stark one, between coming to New Beginnings and committing suicide. He had summoned up the courage to go to the local careers office because he desperately wanted to show his father that he could achieve something. The careers adviser had referred him to New Beginnings. When I first talked to him in May 1999, Adrian had just been sacked after five months on the scheme.

Somewhat to my surprise, he was still very happy that he had chosen New Beginnings, mainly because of his relationship with his mentor, Patricia. Adrian had specifically asked Elaine to match him with an older, female mentor. Patricia was in her late thirties. She was a student teacher who had been involved in workplace mentoring in her previous career as a personnel manager. Adrian recounted with pleasure their meetings in the mentoring room at Cotswold House, where Patricia listened to him talk over his problems and offered him advice about how to resolve conflicts with his mother, or how to ask for more training to overcome his boredom at work.

As he explained, 'To be honest, I think anyone who's in my position, who has problems with meeting people, being around people even, I think a mentor is one of the greatest things you can have. I'd tell any young person to have a mentor. What Pat has done for me is, you know, it's just to turn me around and give me positive thoughts. If I wouldn't have had Pat, I think I'd still have the problems at home. You know, she's put my life in a whole different perspective.' Although mentoring was not the spark for a major turning point in Adrian's life, it reinforced that turning point, and was crucial in helping him establish his sense of a new, more powerful identity.

Adrian's work placement was as a filing clerk. He was sacked from New Beginnings because he breached the rules on lateness and absence at this placement. This caused major problems for Elaine Peters, who had to work extremely hard to get employers to offer placements, and did not want to lose them because of the young people's behaviour. Elaine had waited in her car outside the local crematorium one day when Adrian had given a grandparent's funeral as his excuse for not going to work. She checked out his story in a similar fashion when he pleaded absence for a dental appointment. His non-appearance on both occasions led to disciplinary action. Elaine interpreted this behaviour as showing that he had gained in confidence, and no longer needed the individual support New Beginnings provided. Her feeling was that Adrian had been 'swinging the lead' and that 'he didn't really want to work'. Adrian was dismissed from the scheme, although this was not stated in his records. He was offered a place at the Futures Club, paying less than half the New Beginnings weekly allowance, and his departure was thus represented as an outcome of positive progression.

Adrian and Pat both gave a different view of these events, however. Pat was concerned that Adrian had unidentified learning difficulties that were causing him to miss work through fear of getting things wrong. She thought that perhaps a lack of basic literacy and numeracy skills made something as apparently simple as filing a difficult task for Adrian, and that he was frightened to admit to the problem. She tried to advocate on his behalf with New Beginnings staff, but to no avail.

Adrian told me that he had become demoralized in his placement, which did not at all match his modest career aspirations and interests of becoming a computer operator. He felt he had not been given any proper training, but was unfairly condemned to all the 'crap jobs' nobody else wanted to do. He felt depression creeping on again, and some days he simply could not face going into work – hence his false excuses to Elaine. It seemed likely that both his and his mentor's accounts each reflected part of a wider process. However, the greatest blow for Adrian was that his dismissal abruptly ended his relationship with his mentor in a kind of double punishment. The strict rules of the scheme meant that they were not allowed to keep in touch, and his feelings about this were predictably strong.

'That was an unhappy time for me, you know,' he asserted, 'to just be cut off, just to be severed away from someone who you explain to and talk to and poured out your heart to, and I was very angry, to be honest.'

Twelve months later, I interviewed Adrian again. He was still unemployed after a number of brief false starts at the Futures Club and on other schemes. Now over 18, he was anxious about his future, and saw 'time running out' as he passed the age limit of all the transitional support available – a cut-off point that is reinforced by the end of *Connexions* support for over-19s. Even so long after leaving New Beginnings, Adrian still identified his mentoring experience there as providing a major benefit: he now had the capacity to seek out new mentors for himself. He explained, 'I think now I will attach to somebody, one person, you know, and I'll attach to them. You see that person, and you think, "Yes, I'll hang around with her or him".' He was able to describe how he had done this in his subsequent work placements, and how this was the role in which he saw his current personal adviser at the careers service – another mentor he was regretfully about to lose.

Although he had not successfully entered the labour market yet, Adrian talked a lot about the fact that he now felt like an adult, in contrast with his feelings of confusion in our earlier interview. His father had helped him to get a council house on the South Side of Midtown, which Adrian was enthusiastically decorating in what sounded like an extremely idiosyncratic style. He now had a group of friends, and enjoyed going out to the pub with them at weekends. Although there were still problems in his relationship with his mother, the fact that he had moved out made these easier to cope with, and he seemed to have overcome his mental health problems at that time.

The wrong sort of transformation

Adrian had developed resistance to the New Beginnings scheme in reaction to the limitations it imposed. On the one hand, he seemed to be making progress towards social inclusion in terms of the dominant discourse. He had absorbed well the lessons about the new world of work, and aspired to work in IT 'where the future lies'. He was enthusiastic, almost evangelical, about the new-found confidence Patricia had encouraged in him. On the other hand, because of both of these developments in his identity he clashed with the constraints of the scheme. Working in IT did not fit the narrow pattern of labour market entry for young people at New Beginnings.

Consequently, without negotiation, Adrian was filtered into a clerical job which was below his aspirations but still above his level of ability. Paradoxically, his enthusiasm and verbal articulacy, combined with his embarrassment about his basic skills gaps, meant that although he was not yet capable of completing even simple filing tasks, and in spite of Patricia's intercession, the New Beginnings staff did not bother to assess his needs in this regard. Unlike Annette, therefore, Adrian was unable to comply with the requirements of the scheme while using mentoring for his own purposes. With Patricia's support as his mentor, Adrian had rapidly achieved a dramatic personal transformation – but it was the wrong sort of transformation, and within the terms of the scheme the mentor relationship had failed. The very agency he exercised within that relationship eventually placed him beyond the pale, and he was once again excluded. The advocacy of his mentor was swept aside by the structured, employment-related rules of the scheme. Nevertheless, acquiring mentors elsewhere was a skill that he had learned. In addition, the personal confidence that Patricia had helped him to develop had eased his difficult transition to adulthood. Like Annette, Adrian's story is one that highlights the enormous potential of mentor relationships with socially excluded young people, but also reveals the limitations of the engagement mentoring model.

Hayley and Ged

The first time I heard mention of Hayley was at a mentors' support meeting convened by Renée Jones at UoW in December 1998. In a round table discussion about problems that mentors had experienced, her mentor Ged talked about his feelings of extreme frustration with 'the *Doctor Who* girl'. Hayley's obsessional hobby revolved around this science fiction TV series, and the New Beginnings staff were keen to find a mentor who could relate to her after one mentor relationship had failed. They appealed to Ged, who had declared his own interest in sci-fi on his New Beginnings application form, and so their relationship began. As Hayley put it, 'He's a *Star Trek* fan, but they thought that was close enough.'

I had interviewed Ged in January 1999, but by the time I was granted access to interview the young people at New Beginnings Hayley had just turned 18, and had also been sacked from the scheme. Brenda Mavers refused to put me in contact with Hayley. She said that relations had broken down irrevocably with the family, as Hayley's mother had complained to the careers service about her dismissal. 'We're about employment here,' Brenda stated, 'employment is what we are here for, and Hayley wasn't looking for that. She needed counselling or psychiatric help, and that's not what we are here for.'

When I asked Elaine Peters, she rolled her eyes, shook her head, and said to me: 'Oooh, that's a funny one, you don't want to talk to that one. We had to sack her, and she left under a cloud.' However, Ged agreed to help me if he could, and I interviewed her in July 1999.

Hayley was quite a boisterous young woman, often talking loud and fast, and laughing noisily at her own jokes. She had moved around the country repeatedly, especially after her parents had split up in her early teens. Hayley adored her father (Ged had described her as 'a Daddy's girl'), and she had gone to live with him after the separation, but, as Annette had found, problems arose when he started a new relationship and remarried. Hayley stayed with her grandparents for a while, then came back to Midtown to live with her mother and her learning-disabled brother. Hayley's mother was claiming benefits while studying A levels full-time at Wellshire College in order to go on to a degree at UoW. However, Hayley resented her mother's preoccupation with her studies, and there were constant conflicts between them.

All the moving around had disrupted her schooling, and, although she managed to gain eight GCSE passes, her school-to-work transition had been severely fragmented. Hayley had a lot of experience helping to look after her brother, and her great ambition was to become a nursery nurse. However, she ended up with a number of false starts at a college and a training provider, and was eventually referred to New Beginnings. All this had happened in what Hayley perceived as a haphazard and generally unlucky manner. 'It was sort of a bit of a muddle,' she told me, 'my life's a muddle.'

Nursery nursing, like computing, was regarded as an unrealistic option for the young people who came to New Beginnings, and this was made clear to Hayley straight away: 'They said, "No, you can't do that," and it sort of put me on a downer.' Careers guidance from Paula Modotti steered her in the direction of animal care, although she had no interest in this, resulting in two brief and unsuccessful placements. At the same time Hayley had agreed to accept a mentor when this option was introduced, but her first relationship did not establish itself well. 'She was a bit bossy. She'd say, "Why don't you do this, why don't you do that?" I couldn't really talk to her about things.' So the New Beginnings staff set about trying to find a mentor who would have something in common with Hayley's love of *Doctor Who*.

Ged was a mature student in his late forties, who had come to university to study applied social sciences after being made redundant from his career as a marketing manager some years earlier. He had been attracted to the volunteer mentor programme at New Beginnings for two reasons. First, his particular interest in his degree was youth offending, and he believed that young people 'went off the rails' because of the general social problem that adults did not offer them enough time or one-to-one support. He was vehemently opposed to what he saw as 'labelling' of young people by terms such as 'disaffection'. 'I know who they're attaching it to,' he said, 'but I don't know what it is or why it is, whether it's just jargon for the sake of jargon. To me, it's mainly yuppie terminology, if you like.' He also explained, hesitatingly, that his interest in mentoring at New Beginnings was 'a mix between that and my personal circumstances . . . because my wife died six months ago . . . because I needed something outside of what I'd got to focus on.'

Ged doubted that New Beginnings was right for Hayley. He thought that she was highly intelligent, and at the same time far too immature to cope with employment. For both reasons, he felt that college would have been a more appropriate environment for her to take time to develop herself and her abilities. However, he explained how his wife's death had caused him to question the way he had previously tried to impose on others his own deeply held values about education and the need for ongoing personal development. While he sometimes felt frustrated with Hayley's retreat into sci-fi fantasy, he did not see his role as pushing her to engage with any formal structures of progression until she was ready to do so.

Hayley really enjoyed her meetings with Ged. However frustrating he found them himself, he clearly made an effort to work with her interests, and he showed a great deal of warmth and patience. She roared with laughter as she told me how they would both turn up at Cotswold House with bagsful of sci-fi materials: 'Ged used to end up bringing things in to show me, and I'd bring my bag packed with books and autographs and things like that.' She liked the fact that Ged was 'slightly zany', and that he colluded with her in avoiding discussion of her training or PDP: 'Sometimes, instead of talking about what we were supposed to be talking about, me and Ged, they'd come in and we'd be talking about *Star Trek* or *Doctor Who*, instead of what I'd done over the last week! Sometimes, me and Ged, we were known to go over the hour. I mean, they said they could hear us laughing half-way down the corridor!'

She also greatly valued the time he took, in contrast to her first mentor, to listen to her and help her talk through the problems she was having at home with her mother. Ged would use story-lines from *Doctor Who* to try to put these problems into perspective, and help Hayley find ways of dealing with them. She acknowledged her temper tantrums that had sometimes got her into trouble at New Beginnings, which Ged perceived as related to ongoing mental health problems. 'I'll keep things bottled up,' she explained, 'and then I sort of suddenly flare.' Talking things over with Ged had changed her: 'I don't think I keep things bottled up as much. I wanted things to be different and a bit better with my mum. I wouldn't say that we have a perfect relationship, but it's improved.'

Eventually Hayley was found a placement at the local youth service 'drop-in shop' in Midtown. She quite enjoyed it, and she got on well with Jeanie Andrews, the youth worker who ran the centre. However, after a few weeks, Hayley went in feeling low. She locked herself in the toilet to cry, and Jeanie called Elaine Peters to let her know there was a problem. Elaine thought that there had been another temper display, and two days later she sacked Hayley from New Beginnings, in spite of the fact that Jeanie had assured Elaine that she was happy to continue the placement. As in Adrian's case, Hayley also suffered the double punishment of losing Ged as her mentor automatically.

Both of them found this distressing, especially in the abrupt way it was enforced. Hayley had felt very upset, and explained: 'I would have probably liked to have seen Ged at least one more time after I was, you know, dismissed, maybe not necessarily carried it on, but at least to have said a proper goodbye.'

Ged was also taken aback: 'It came completely out of the blue for me. Elaine just phoned up and said she'd finished Hayley off the scheme. That was it. It just ended.' The dismissal also hit Hayley's family hard financially. It came two weeks before her 18th birthday, when she would have been able to claim unemployment benefits. She lost £90 in training allowances from the scheme. Then, as one of the very few young people officially dismissed from New Beginnings, she was deemed by Employment Service regulations to have lost her place through her own fault and was ineligible for benefits for several weeks thereafter. Hayley thus suffered a triple punishment.

I interviewed her again nine months later, in April 2000. She had had high hopes of getting on to a childcare course the previous September when, after signing on unemployed for six months, she had been put on New Deal. Despite the efforts of her personal adviser, there had been a mix-up at Midtown College, and once again Hayley missed the start of the course. Nevertheless, the personal adviser organized a tailor-made package for Hayley at the college, and at the time of our interview she was doing three days a week at college and spending the other two days on a work placement in a primary school and its nursery. She was really enjoying the work, and said that her supervisors were pleased with her performance. There would be a place for her on the nursery nursing course in September, if her tutors judged she was capable of succeeding on it by the end of the summer term. She had also become a volunteer helper at her brother's disabled gymnasts' club, and had qualified as a sports coach.

Hayley no longer felt that she wanted or needed a mentor. Her head of department at college sorted out any practical problems with her courses, and she knew about the student counselling facility that was available. She finally felt on track to achieve her ambition of going into childcare. 'I got there eventually', she said. When I asked if there was anything final she wanted to add about her experience at New Beginnings, she said: 'I just got over it, basically.'

'So it was something to get over?' I asked.

'Yeah,' she replied, 'it took me a while to get over it, I mean for a while afterwards, I was still slightly bitter about it, but, you know, now it's just something that's happened and I'm getting on with, now I'm getting on with college.'

Resisting transformation and 'employability'

For three years after leaving school, Hayley had refused to give up her ambition of working in childcare, despite missing out on the annual cycle of college courses, and despite the lack of opportunity to pursue this career at New Beginnings. She seemed to have accepted a stalemate situation on the scheme, perhaps in order to escape the isolation of being unemployed in Midtown, where she had not been at school, and therefore had no friends of her own age. Hayley complied with all the technical rules of the scheme. Her timekeeping and attendance were excellent, and she was completing all her vocational access qualifications.

However, she resolutely avoided being driven into occupational training she did not want to do, and therefore spent most of her time at Cotswold House. There, her boisterous nature and need for attention, which sometimes spilled over into temper, may well have been a problem for the hard-pressed staff. Finding Hayley a mentor who could occupy her for at least some of the time must have been a priority. Although aware of her mental health problems, and of the unlikelihood of finding her work through the scheme, the staff maintained her participation there without any attempts to refer her for more appropriate treatment. The careers adviser diagnosed her guidance and support needs solely in terms of fitting her into the framework of options available through the New Beginnings scheme, rather than considering Hayley's needs in a holistic way, or exploring the possibilities offered by Midtown College.

Hayley took control of her mentor relationship, using it to distract her from her troubles through seeking fun, entertainment and attention from Ged, and at other times to gain his support in working through her personal problems. She was well aware that this was not what they were 'supposed' to be doing with their time, as was Ged. However, his own personal epiphany, provoked by his bereavement, led him to accept her agenda rather than that of the scheme.

Although more compliant than Adrian, Hayley's resistance also finally placed her outside of the scheme. In spite of the warm intentions and affection expressed by New Beginnings staff towards the young people they recruited, and in spite of their awareness of Hayley's mental health problems, her departure from the scheme was constructed very much as her own fault. Employment outcomes were expected, and Hayley's disposition was clearly not being reformed as employable. In the framework of current government policy, Hayley was a young person who had been given two years of intensive individual support, but still had not engaged with learning and employment. She and her family felt the sharp end of the financial sanctions that were then applied. How this was supposed to help a young woman with unaddressed mental health problems is unclear. Certainly, a much more amicable and protective solution for Hayley could have been negotiated had staff given the situation more objective consideration.

Although she had felt bitter about her dismissal, including the abrupt break from Ged, it had in fact enabled Hayley to pick up the threads of her career ambition of working with children. There had still been setbacks and 'muddle', but the intervention of her personal adviser had opened other avenues, and she was optimistic about her chances of starting the nursery nursing course later that year. She appreciated the way in which Ged had helped her to develop calmer relationships at home. Like Adrian, her own account of mentoring is a very positive one.

Mentoring for social inclusion or re-creating social exclusion?

Annette's, Adrian's and Hayley's stories illustrate the complex but undeniable nature of young people's agency within their mentor relationships. I do not argue that their agency dominated other sources of power in these cases, but that young people can exercise power rather than being passive recipients of mentoring. Their stories reveal how their agency runs up against other sources of power – individual, institutional, and social – in problematic and complex ways, with unpredictable outcomes.

Each of these young people engaged with New Beginnings to very different degrees. Annette eventually settled into the scheme and progressed to achieve her qualifications, though with no intention of going on into YT or employment. Adrian felt his life transformed by his mentoring experience, but this only compounded his difficulties in engaging with the limited employment goals of the scheme. Hayley complied sufficiently to remain within the scheme for almost two years, while resisting progression to employment that she did not want. Eventually, her failure to adapt her disposition resulted in her dismissal, but this enabled her return to the career path of her choice. Although an explicit aim of New Beginnings was to end the 'revolving door' syndrome, some young people were simply rotated out again by the scheme itself. Having had the official opportunity of an avowedly supportive scheme such as New Beginnings, and still not becoming 'employable', there was the risk that their exclusion from officially defined patterns of an acceptable career could be increased.

All three of them valued their relationships with their mentors, and found their experiences of mentoring helpful. However, they contested the imposition of employment-related goals within their mentor relationships. They used their agency to gain some breathing space from the pressures of their lives, and from training or work, within the mentoring sessions. This suggests that the mentoring process, in these cases, was far from wholly driven by the mentor, nor could it be controlled by the scheme. The outcomes, nevertheless, demonstrate how young people's agency conflicted with other, more powerful individuals and factors in the setting. As a result, potentially positive successes were sometimes converted into further instances of failure. Let us turn now to consider some other case stories which focus more specifically on the experiences of the mentors.

Chapter 5

'To suffer and be still'

Surveillance, self-surveillance, and the transformation of mentors' dispositions

Introduction

Many studies of mentoring suggest that mentors benefit by increasing their own social and cultural capital. One expectation of the New Beginnings scheme may be that mentors were likely to gain greater benefits from their participation than the young people, since university students could capitalize on the more substantial cultural resources they already possessed. Employers, for example, have been willing to allow their staff time to volunteer for industrial mentoring in schools, in part because of the transferable skills it is thought to develop in mentors themselves. Gardiner (1995) produces a far longer list of benefits for mentors than for mentees in her study of the *BEAT* project, an engagement mentoring scheme for young offenders in Birmingham, many of whom were from black and Asian communities. Nevertheless, her study also contains hints that all might not be positive in terms of outcomes for mentors.

She claims there is a weakness in the scheme related to the role of its community-based mentors. As with New Beginnings, the *BEAT* project included mentoring as a supporting element of a wider programme which included personal and vocational effectiveness, career awareness and realism, and structured vocational placements. However, as in the cases of Adrian and Hayley in Chapter 4, and as we saw more generally in Chapter 3, mentors may not be expected to raise young people's expectations so much as to cool them off and filter them into lower status pathways. The first lesson of good practice that Gardiner advances is that:

> Whilst mentors must view the expectations of the young people with enthusiasm, a balanced outlook of what is a realistically achievable goal for the young people is critical to the success of all the parties.
>
> (Gardiner, 1995: 55)

Gardiner's recommendation seems to suggest that encouraging young people to pursue their own goals was a rhetorical rather than a genuine aspiration for mentoring in that project. Ahier (1996) and Stronach (1989) have argued that vocational and work-related curricula pre- and post-16 are used to influence the adults delivering them as much as to initiate the young people who appear to be its prime objective. Since *BEAT* mentors were sought from poor inner-city communities, engagement mentoring might be seen (to borrow a very different Ancient Greek myth) as a Trojan horse for such adults. It may represent a negative force within the whole community if it promotes a limited concept of career paths available to its members, and deems other aspirations to be unrealistically above their station. Moreover, despite the claims of benefits for mentors, there is considerable evidence that mentoring schemes for socially excluded young people experience difficulty both in recruiting *and retaining* volunteers, suggesting that the experience is not always a rewarding one for mentors (Freedman, 1999; Skinner and Fleming, 1999).

In this light, we can revisit the key assumptions about mentoring discussed in earlier chapters and summarized in the introduction to Chapter 4, this time from the perspective of mentors. Two of these assumptions – that power dynamics of mentoring are located within dyadic interactions, and that mentors control the character of the process – sit uneasily alongside assumptions that mentors are vehicles for empowering young people to acquire employability, and that mentors can and should work to alter young people's dispositions. They rely on a construction of mentoring which disembeds the dyad and both its members, *including the mentor*, from the operation of other echelons of power through social structures. They are also silent about the degree to which mentors are expected to alter their own dispositions in order to present ideal role models of employability – and how different role models are deemed appropriate for different social groupings, according to class, gender and race.

The mentors' accounts presented here challenge simplistic assumptions that they benefit from the mentoring process. All the mentors whom I interviewed seemed to become more anxious and demoralized about mentoring the longer their relationships continued. Few could identify any tangible benefits for themselves or for their mentees, and as we shall see, some felt it had become a thoroughly negative experience. In some cases, the attempt to reform the mentee's disposition through the presentation of the mentor's self as an embodiment of an idealized norm created unsustainable tensions. We have already seen some hints of these tensions in Jane's story in Chapter 4. This chapter begins with the stories of two young students, Karen and Rachel, both of whom mentored Sharon, although they adopted very different approaches.

Karen and Sharon

Sharon

Sharon was 17 years old when I first met her at New Beginnings in May 1999. She had attended a special school because of learning difficulties, and had been referred to New Beginnings when she tried to claim welfare benefits. She lived with her family, who were very poor, and needed an income. Staff at New Beginnings were also concerned about other social problems. They thought she had heavy drinking bouts, and suspected that Sharon's relationship with her uncle might be of an abusive nature. At Cotswold House, she seemed extremely timid, speaking in a whisper, often giving monosyllabic responses with long pauses, and avoiding eye contact. When I interviewed her, even allowing for the fact that I was a stranger to her, I gained a sense of how difficult it must have been for her mentor to spend an hour a week with her in the mentoring room set aside exclusively for talking.

Sharon's attendance and punctuality at New Beginnings could not be faulted. She complied with every formal aspect of the PDP drawn up for her each week. Although she did regular baby-sitting for family and neighbours in the evenings and at weekends, and wanted to go into a career in childcare, staff regarded this ambition as completely inappropriate. Not only was this career off-limits for New Beginnings trainees in general (as we heard from Hayley in Chapter 4), but Sharon's unkempt appearance, apparently poor communication skills and low academic ability were all seen to rule her out as a suitable candidate. She had dutifully attended the placements found for her in hairdressing and in care of the elderly, but the employers had asked Elaine Peters to end the placements because of Sharon's poor presentation, uncommunicative behaviour and lack of initiative.

Elaine explained, 'I don't know where I'm going with Sharon. . . . She's the only one out of the lot that I can't see where I'm going.' At the same time, she suspected that there was more to the contrast between Sharon's formal compliance, which kept her well within the regulations of the scheme, and her non-compliance with more general expectations of developing employability. 'I think Sharon's a little bit of a madam as well,' she said, 'because one week she can do something and the week after she can't, so I think she plays on it a bit as well, she's not quite as innocent as she looks a lot of the time.'

Karen

Sharon was matched with Karen, a 20-year-old student training as a primary teacher. Elaine was looking for a particular kind of mentor for her. 'Sharon, who will hardly make conversation with you, needs somebody perhaps younger,' she explained, 'because they're younger, they're lively, they can talk about what they've been doing at night or whatever to bring her out of herself, so it works.' Karen was thought to be the ideal person, and staff always referred to her as an excellent mentor.

Karen did indeed come across as a very bright and bubbly young woman at our first interview in February 1999. She was extremely talkative, and her words came rushing out. Karen had a very strong belief in her suitability as a mentor for disaffected young people, based on her own past experiences. She was dyslexic, which she had struggled to overcome while it remained undiagnosed at school. Her A level studies had been obstructed by a lengthy illness. Her older brother had been addicted to heroin, disrupting family life for some years. Karen herself had also experimented with illegal drugs until a very frightening incident involving adulterated Ecstasy at a dance club. This history was a major part of her motivation to become involved in mentoring at New Beginnings. 'I've had a lot of strange things happen to me in my life, which wouldn't happen to everybody else,' she laughed. 'I'm very unlucky! But then I think, "No", because I'm a better person because of it. And if I can say to people, "Yeah, but, you know, I've been there, I know what you've been feeling . . . ".'

There was a cathartic aspect to mentoring for Karen. 'I'm very happy now,' she continued, 'but there was a time when I wasn't, and you know . . . I think if I can give an hour of my time to have somebody feel maybe happy for an hour, that that's worth something, and that's good for me as well . . . the thought that I'm helping somebody, because that makes me feel a lot better, knowing that all the bad things that have happened to me can make someone else feel a lot better.'

Karen had had six mentoring sessions with Sharon at that time, and was very enthusiastic and optimistic about the experience. She had a highly personal view of mentoring in contrast to the official version promoted at New Beginnings. 'My idea of mentoring is that I'm there to be a friend,' she asserted, 'and friendship is a two-way thing. You've got to be there for them all the time. I'd be quite happy if there was a real problem to get a phone call from Sharon any time, to meet her somewhere and talk to her.' She offered this definition: 'Mentoring is to be there, to talk, have a laugh, take their mind off things.' At that stage the experience was very rewarding. 'I love going to see Sharon every week,' she declared, 'I feel dead professional doing it. I come out feeling, "Oh great, yeah. . . . We had a good laugh, a good chat."' Karen also felt that her mentoring was having a positive impact on Sharon's communication skills, and emphasized the similarities in their experiences of overcoming adversity: 'She's made amazing progress in six meetings! She's a normal average young girl. She has problems with learning, reading, writing, but why should that stop her? It didn't stop me. She's a lot worse than me, but I know what she's up against.'

Karen's approach meant that she treated the recommended focus on the PDP as irrelevant, although she knew she was supposed to record certain topics on 'the form' (the weekly log for monitoring what had been discussed in the mentoring session). I asked her what went on when she met Sharon. 'We talk about nothing in particular,' she replied. 'We people-watch . . . do strange things, very silly, relaxing things. That's what she needs. We have a lot in common, we're both teenagers, we both have a boyfriend. We talk about holidays, what we'd do if we won the lottery, food, chips! Then we sit and fill the form in together. I say, "Sharon, what are we going to say we've talked about this week?" As far as I'm concerned, housing benefits, the money that she gets, job prospects, go way over her head . . . and, mmm . . . we just tend to sort of make things up!' she laughed.

Karen also made tactful efforts to discuss improvements Sharon could make to her hair, clothes and make-up, as well as introducing informal conversations about a healthy diet and losing weight. She instigated a competition to see who could manage their money best by still having a £1 coin left at the end of week, which Sharon invariably won. Prompted by Elaine, she probed Sharon's relationship with her boyfriend to check that they were not sleeping together without contraceptive measures. In the early weeks, Karen had felt the need for some support in her mentoring, and was disappointed that neither UoW nor the TEC seemed to provide opportunities for this. She relied instead on some chance meetings with Ged (Hayley's mentor, whom we met in Chapter 4) as a chance to talk over difficulties and ideas. Karen's biggest concern was that she had to go away for nine weeks on teaching practice, and she had discussed this with Sharon to prepare her for the break, promising that she would return as her mentor. (Sharon's temporary match with Rachel during Karen's absence is the next case story in this chapter.) Sharon seemed to be enjoying the relationship too. She liked the fact that Karen was lively and talkative, and said that she missed her while she was away.

A dramatic change

Three months later, once I had been granted access to interview the young people, I contacted Karen to ask for her help in approaching Sharon to take part in the research. She told me that she planned to quit as Sharon's mentor, and sounded quite distressed. I asked if she wanted to come and take part in another interview to talk over what had happened, which she agreed to do. Karen's demeanour was quite different on this occasion from the bright enthusiasm she had displayed a few months before. Her tone was flat, she seemed on the verge of tears, the laughter that had frequently punctuated our first interview had disappeared, and her talk was interspersed with growls of frustration. 'I've told the TEC I can't carry on,' she declared. 'It's really hard and like, I find it incredibly frustrating and I really am going spare. You know, I don't think I can do this much longer, because I keep going home and I'm just so wound up, because I . . . just *nothing* . . . she just will not respond to anything.' The 'amazing progress' Karen had perceived in the first few weeks of mentoring had evaporated: 'When we first started, I thought we were getting somewhere . . . I don't think we're going to get any further now.'

Despite Karen's tactful hints and gifts of shampoo and soap, she felt Sharon's personal hygiene was getting worse. This was not only disappointing, but unpleasant for Karen when they met. Sharon's latest work placement was failing yet again, and her communication was deteriorating. As Karen explained, 'She won't talk. Unless you ask, she won't talk, and you'll find that . . . you'll find that you're asking questions and you'll get a one-word reply, or you'll get a gaze, which means that she hasn't got an answer for you.'

The monitoring forms, which Karen referred to this time as 'crap' and 'horrendous', had fallen by the wayside: 'They ask us to fill out those sheets. . . . Well, we've stopped doing it, I stopped doing it, because I can't. . . . What do I write down? "What have you discussed?" Not a lot! What's been on TV and what she's eaten for her dinner, which is chips every night.' Now that the mentoring room had been moved and had no outside window, they could not even amuse themselves by people-watching any more. The environment, designed for verbal interaction, felt sterile: 'We're stuck in a room together. There's nothing to stimulate conversation.' Karen also found the mentoring room inhibiting. 'I always feel tense when I go and sit in that room for some reason,' she said. 'It's like a little police cell.'

When I reminded Karen of her initial definition of mentoring as a two-way friendship, she responded: 'Sharon can't be my friend, because she can't talk to me . . . but she can't talk to anybody. If anything, she talks to me more, because I ask the right sort of questions and I act like an idiot sometimes . . . and I make her laugh and feel comfortable . . . and I can do it because I'm talking to a 5-year-old, because that at the end of the day is what I'm doing.' It seemed that Sharon was fairly skilfully obtaining the entertainment she enjoyed through Karen's company, but at a cost that Karen felt unable to sustain: 'It's very sad, because you don't know what to do for the best. I get very angry . . . I get frustrated, then I feel guilty for getting frustrated, 'cos she can't help the way she is, and I can't help her either. I just don't feel I'm helping her at all. I'm pulling at teeth and it's becoming uncomfortable.'

Karen was also angry about what she perceived as a complete absence of support for the mentors, complaining that 'I just feel that they gave us this training, took up our time, stuck us in there, you know, just said, "Right, there you are, there's your person, get on with it!"' The fact that no one had chased her up to complete the monitoring forms confirmed this perception.

I asked Karen what she thought Sharon might be learning in her work placement, and got a bitter-sounding response: 'I think she's learning to make lots of cups of tea. I think she's learning to be a complete recluse again. She's learning to go into this little shell and not come out.' Karen had broached her intention of leaving New Beginnings with Sharon, giving as excuses her impending exams, her return home for the summer holidays and the teaching practice she would be doing again in the autumn term. The shell metaphor resurfaced as she spoke of her disappointment and personal hurt at Sharon's reaction. 'She's just empty really, I think. . . . She's just like this empty shell,' she said. 'She doesn't seem to bother. You know, I said to her, "Do you mind someone else coming to talk to you?" . . . "No." "Do you mind that I'm going away?" . . . "No, I'll just talk to someone else." Really unemotional.' The rewards of mentoring had also evaporated, and Karen found herself wondering, 'Why the hell am I wasting my time when nothing's happening, and I should give something to me, something better, and that's . . . I always said if I started to feel like that, I'd go, and I do sort of feel like this.'

I asked Karen also about her previous view that mentoring worked because she and Sharon had a lot in common. 'Mmm . . . we're worlds apart', she replied. She went on to talk about 'us' and 'them', referring respectively to university students and socially excluded young people: 'From our point of view, we know what they're growing up with, but from the other point of view, *we're* all at university. Yeah, fair enough, we're not all rich, we're not all from advantaged families, but we *are* at university, we've *made* something of our lives, no matter how hard it's been with what we've got, so we're obviously the people that have got determination, you know, we *want* to succeed. But these people, ugh! . . . They just don't care. You go, like, "Can you not see that there's a better thing?" because a lot of them can't . . . and I think our role is to "make them see" somehow.'

Karen felt that Sharon needed far more specialist help, and would have benefited from a scheme that promoted group activities, rather than the employment focus and one-to-one mentoring of New Beginnings, which she had come to feel was utterly inappropriate for Sharon. She knew that Elaine was also feeling the futility of keeping Sharon at the scheme, and recognized some of the wider constraints that perpetuated the situation: 'If the government are just going to say, "Hey, you can have some money, but you must get them into employment," I mean, not everyone fits that category, do they? And I just think the government doesn't have categories of people like Sharon.'

Sharon in a different light

I interviewed Sharon again a year later, in April 2000. She had had to leave New Beginnings after her 18th birthday, and was signing on as unemployed. She was still with her family, and I visited her in the very dilapidated council house in Midtown where they lived. The house seemed full of people, introduced to me as Sharon's mother and father, her aunts, neighbours and boyfriend. Sharon still gave very quiet and mostly brief responses to my questions, but she seemed much more relaxed than at our previous meeting, and she became quite animated as she told me about her recent engagement. She proudly showed me her ring, and a pair of noisy love-birds her fiancé had bought her. She hoped that they would be able to get a council house locally by the time they married, and settle down to have children of their own.

Sharon said she was checking Jobcentre vacancies each time she went to sign on. She had not applied for any jobs, nor had the Employment Service staff offered any help or obliged her to join New Deal. She was doing more baby-sitting for relatives and neighbours, and described how she took care of the children, playing educational games with them and teaching them to share with each other. Whatever Sharon's prospects of working in a formal nursery (and this did seem highly unlikely), I thought how much she – and the children whom she looked after – would have benefited, had she received some training and education in child-care. This would have meant, however, an acknowledgement by New Beginnings' staff that informal baby-sitting counted as work, even though it functioned as part of the 'grey' economy. Perhaps, as in Hayley's case, some tailor-made college provision would have been more suitable.

Sharon missed Karen, but said that she was able to talk to her fiancé, female relatives and baby-sitting clients in the same way. As I left, she accompanied me to the door. In the few minutes we chatted she greeted every passer-by, and at one point, when another aunt called to her from a house across the road, I was astonished to hear Sharon bellow a reply at full volume. At Cotswold House, Sharon had seemed timid and isolated, but I gained quite a different image of her outside that environment, in a community that offered her its own form of social inclusion and a responsible role for her to play.

From enthusiasm to frustration

Once again, individual dispositions and personal biographies played an important role in this mentoring experience. Karen had overcome considerable social and learning difficulties to succeed at university, and this was a central factor in her perception of mentoring and of the mentor as role model. Sharon deployed different identities in different environments. Elaine Peters may well have guessed correctly that Sharon's unemployable persona at New Beginnings represented her resistance to employment outcomes she did not want. However, in the hope that readers can draw their own conclusions about the impact of these dispositions from the story, I wish to concentrate here on Karen's experience as a mentor, in order to explore other dynamics of power.

Despite Karen's criticisms of New Beginnings, her neglect of discussions on Sharon's PDP and her flippant use of the weekly mentoring record, her initial enthusiasm and optimism fitted the fundamental policy concerns that have informed engagement mentoring. First of all, she described Sharon as 'a normal average young girl', but with particularly major deficits that needed fixing. If Sharon's communication and presentation skills could be raised to employable levels, she might be able to emulate Karen's progress by reforming herself and moving into employment (albeit at a lower level). Second, Karen's self-image as a mentor who 'knows what it is like' to overcome adversity seemed to predict success for her role modelling as an ideally reformed character herself. It may also have provided a basis for empathy towards her mentee's situation. Third, Karen believed in personal devotion to the mentee that was also 'dead professional' – such as Ford's concept of *agapé* (1999a) that we considered in Chapter 2 – as key to the process of mentoring.

We have already seen in Chapter 1 the negative ways in which policy literature constructs youngsters such as Sharon, along with their families and communities. Karen's experience demonstrates the tensions that can arise for a mentor trying to 'bridge the gap'. At an institutional level, we can question whether the careers service system of automatic referral to New Beginnings was appropriate, as well as the adequacy of the various assessments Sharon underwent. It may have been helpful to explore the possibilities of a college referral in close liaison with the learning support tutor, including the use of funds available for students with special needs to buy in speech therapy. Sharon's family could have been advised that her full-time attendance at college would have allowed them to continue claiming welfare and child benefits for Sharon – an amount that would have differed little from her training allowance at New Beginnings. However, once Sharon had started at New Beginnings, it came to appear as a 'choice of the necessary' (Bourdieu, 1986). Sharon's broader needs were not addressed, but it did provide what appeared to be the only means to an income much needed by her and her family. Whether consciously or not, Sharon complied with all the formal regulations in order to stay on the scheme, while making no visible effort to integrate herself in the work placements that would have led to undesired employment outcomes.

Given Sharon's superficial engagement with New Beginnings, and her failure to progress in the expected manner, Karen responded in two ways. Initially, she colluded with Sharon's desire to use her mentoring session each week as an opportunity for entertainment. Establishing a friendly rapport with a young person who had genuine difficulties communicating with others outside her own community seemed to be Karen's first priority, and initially this collusion appeared to be paying dividends. However, when the spatial setting of those sessions was restricted further to impose purely verbal interactions, both mentor and mentee experienced difficulties in maintaining the relationship. Karen began to feel overwhelmed by Sharon's failures, even regression, in relation to the officially prescribed outcomes of the New Beginnings scheme. She focused on concerns that Sharon's 'employability' (hygiene, motivation, communication skills) had worsened rather than improved, and on the apparent impossibility of securing an employment destination for her.

Her frustration reveals a tension. On the one hand, she understood that this was not Sharon's fault, but was due to structural inequalities facing people with learning difficulties that government policies fail to take into account. On the other hand, she reproduced dominant discourses of 'disaffected' youth in her exasperation that 'these people don't care'. The way that these tensions then reflect back upon herself may be seen in her heavily ironic remark that 'our role is to "make them see" somehow', which indicates the normative role modelling she felt under pressure to enact. This comment reminded me of Jane's protest in Chapter 4: 'Who can make such a big impact on them?'

I was also interested in another parallel with Jane's story. Karen appeared to have encountered a major epiphany, a turning point in her identity, where she shifted from being an educational failure and 'wild child' taking risks with drugs, to an educational success story as her dyslexia was diagnosed, and she progressed to university, developing a 'dead professional' persona as a student teacher. This new identity was slighted by the fact that staff did not read the forms she completed or even notice when she gave up on this task. She felt entitled to overt monitoring of her work as an acknowledgement of her role, a validation of her presence within the scheme. Such entitlement would have been central to her experience at university. Yet the offhand stance she encountered reinforced the impersonal power of the WellTEC staff, and denied the 'dead professional' status to which she now aspired. Her comparison of the mentoring room with a 'little police cell' seems to sum up her sense of covert surveillance, combined with an almost physical sense of abandonment and isolation. Feeling watched, but without a direct gaze, her sense of identity was unsettled. Let us move on to see what happened during

Karen's absence on teaching practice, when Rachel was chosen to step in as Sharon's mentor.

Rachel and Sharon

Rachel

Rachel was a 21-year-old student. Unlike most volunteers for New Beginnings, who were studying to be teachers or to enter other caring careers, she was in her final year of a creative arts degree at UoW. She came to my office for her interview wearing baggy combat fatigues and a baseball cap, something of a contrast with the other female mentors, who tended to be neatly and fashionably dressed. Rachel had grown up in a rural village, and described her family background as middle class, stable and supportive. However, like Karen, she had had her own troubled past. She too was dyslexic, and at the age of 15 she had abused alcohol to such an extent that she had had to be hospitalized. However, unlike Karen, she did not see these experiences as relevant to her role as a mentor. She felt they were behind her now, and that it would be counterproductive to share those experiences with a younger mentee.

Rachel began by talking about some fundamental contradictions she had already encountered in the New Beginnings scheme. On the one hand, she explained, the mentors were expected to promote the employment and training goals of the scheme. She understood that WellTEC staff believed students would be effective vehicles for this message because they were close in age to the young people, and because of their informal appearance and non-authoritative role. On the other hand, as someone who projected a very informal and unconventional image of herself, Rachel had developed a strong perception during the mentor training course that she did not 'fit in' with the scheme's ideal of a mentor. 'Me and my friend got there,' she recalled, 'and it was negative just from my appearance and, like, my friend's appearance. It was sort of a bit scruffy, you know, a bit arty, and from then on it was sort of like, "They're not going to pass," or whatever.' One of the things she noticed was that: 'We were the only couple that are not [student] teachers. I thought that was quite interesting. I think they were like . . . slightly wary of us.' Rachel was sceptical about the motivations of student teachers to volunteer as mentors at New Beginnings. She felt that they were only doing it because it would 'look good on their CVs', whereas she herself was 'probably doing it for more genuine reasons'.

Nevertheless, Rachel took the training course very seriously and seemed to have understood well the framework it promoted for mentoring. However, as soon as she met Sharon and began working with her, contradictions surfaced. She found Sharon 'incredibly shy – I've never met anybody so shy in my life', and was concerned that this was being interpreted as 'laziness' by employers. Rachel had already discovered that Sharon's abiding ambition was to work in childcare. She could not understand why New Beginnings staff would not allow Sharon to pursue this, but she was aware that Sharon was not interested in alternative occupations, or even in formal employment at all.

Rachel, like Karen, found the mentoring sessions were subverted by Sharon to provide amusement. This was compounded by the fact that Karen had previously established a pattern of entertaining fun and chatter about herself in the sessions. 'Sharon asks me a lot about what I do, which I didn't expect,' Rachel explained. 'They say, "Don't talk about yourself," but she asks. I can't avoid it. It gets her talking, it starts conversations. She asks about college mainly, and what I've been doing every week, or the next week. Holidays are a big thing. We talk about going out. Her uncle and her family take her to the pub, to karaoke. Baby-sitting, holidays, a friend of hers who's at college. Nothing about jobs comes up. But New Beginnings say getting a job is the main thing.'

Rachel was confused by the gap between the mentors' training and the practical situation she encountered. Like Karen, she found difficulty completing the monitoring form: 'I thought there was a definite programme for each young person, and we'd ask them about it, if they had any problems. But the form is embarrassing! You can't put "holidays", "karaoke"! It's not directing them towards a job, which is what I thought the programme was really for.' All the same, she felt that she was beginning to build up a rapport with Sharon. She was planning to bring in magazine articles to spark discussions, and felt frustrated by the fact that mentoring was confined to the room at Cotswold House. She also seemed to feel a caring championship for Sharon, as she spoke of her personal ambitions for mentoring: 'I'd like to turn round to people and say that she's more than just shy. She's got a personality and stuff, then . . . 'cos I'm saying it to you that the only thing is she's really shy, but I think there is something more there.'

The relationship breaks down

Several weeks later, I heard from Elaine Peters that Karen had returned as Sharon's mentor, and Rachel had been removed as a mentor before Karen's return. I rang Rachel, who seemed quite upset about her experience. Her perception was that she had been 'sacked' by WellTEC staff after a few meetings with Sharon, but she had been given no explanation. In our second interview, she described her feelings about what had happened as 'a bit bitter'. She referred back to her initial experiences of feeling unwelcomed on the mentor training course, expanding on her previous comments. Not only had Rachel felt marginalized at the training course, but she also felt that there were important differences of identity between art students and student teachers. She thought that the latter were preferred as mentors by New Beginnings staff, because they were perceived as 'responsible', 'institutionalized', 'nice and safe'. By contrast, art students such as herself were perceived as 'radical', 'always going up against the boundaries', and willing to challenge rules in a way that student teachers would not.

Rachel declared that she was very confused about what had happened with her mentoring. Her view was that she and Sharon were 'getting on fine', but she had been concerned about a number of other issues: the lack of the mentor support that had been promised, ongoing difficulties with filling in the form to log each week's discussions, and increasing doubts as to whether the provision at New Beginnings was appropriate for Sharon. Sharon evaded any discussion about her employment-related PDP in the sessions. She seemed mainly interested in finding out about Rachel's life at UoW, and discussing what each of them had done at the weekend. 'I was trying to talk about jobs,' Rachel explained, 'but Sharon wasn't interested, only in what I was doing. One week all she talked about was drinking. It's all going on about her social life rather than getting a job.'

Rachel identified the difficulty of pursuing a mentor relationship rather than simply friendship: 'It was easy for me to establish a friendship with her. But there was no back-up for what the course told us mentoring should be. It was hard to keep going back to Sharon and trying to get things out of her. We could have a forty-five-minute conversation, but nothing that had come up in the mentors' training course. I couldn't make it work.' As this had gone on, like Karen, she had begun to find the atmosphere of the mentoring room 'clinical' and 'intimidating'. For Rachel it was 'like being in an exam room'. She observed that 'There were all these posters on the walls about not taking drugs and not doing this and not doing that'. She described these as a kind of injunction to the mentors: 'Perform now! Go on! . . . And if you can't think of anything, look on the wall and say: "Don't take drugs!"'

In my interview with Sharon, however, she told me that Rachel had been sacked by the New Beginnings staff through her instigation. She had told Elaine Peters that she did not like Rachel, and the following exchange took place between us:

Helen: You told me you didn't get on with Rachel so well. Tell me how Rachel
          was different from Karen?
Sharon: She was too quiet.
Helen: What things did she talk to you about?
Sharon: [*Silence*]
Helen: Your placement?
Sharon: Mmm [*nods*]. [*Pause*] I said I didn't like her because she was quiet.
Helen: What makes it work with Karen that didn't work with Rachel?
Sharon: Karen talks more than Rachel.

There is no doubt that the New Beginnings staff intervened appropriately to end a relationship that was not working out for the young person (although it may also be argued that it was appropriate to give constructive feedback to mentors when this happened). What is interesting is that Rachel was deemed unsuitable at least in part *because* she was making more effort than Karen had done to 'do the right thing'. She tried to implement the scheme's recommendations about what a good mentor should do by focusing on the PDP. However, Sharon resisted this, and had the power to remove her mentor for pushing it. One of the sharpest ironies is that Karen, who blatantly disregarded the guidelines for mentoring, falsified her forms and eventually stopped completing them, was regarded as an ideal mentor whom Elaine was sorry to lose, while Rachel was summarily removed. Yet both were left feeling bitterness and failure. At our second interview, Rachel had just decided not to apply for an attractive post for a youth and community arts worker, because she felt she could not put her experience at New Beginnings on her application form, and feared she would be given a bad reference. Her experience of mentoring had not empowered her, nor had it enhanced her employability.

Let us return finally to what Rachel meant by 'being radical' and 'pushing the boundaries' as an art student. 'Looking back over your three years at UoW,' I asked her, 'has it given *you* the chance to push any boundaries, or do anything radical, Rachel? Is that what this experience has been for you?'

Rachel went on to explain, hesitantly at first, that she had been heavily involved in organizing protests against the NATO bombings of Kosovo going on at the time. 'There's a group of us,' she explained, 'we're demonstrating, but we're not doing it 'cos it's like the "student thing" to do. We've got the facilities available, there's big governing bodies that can help us, that agree with us, so we're sort of like, if you're a student and you want to say something, we'll help you, sort of thing. So that in that sense it is easier for a student to demonstrate rather than someone who's got a full-time job and everything.' She added, however, that 'the university aren't liking it a bit'. Their posters were pulled down by the authorities, and she and her fellow protesters were having to be cautious, since their e-mails could be monitored.

I asked if Rachel had been involved in any other campaigns, and she told me that as a lesbian she was also involved in gay liberation marches. I wanted to know how these commitments connected with her experience of mentoring, particularly since Sharon asked a lot about what Rachel did at college, and what she did at weekends.

'What would have happened', I queried, 'if Sharon asked you what you'd been doing this week, and you'd told her you'd been to a demonstration in London about how awful the war was, and then you wrote that on the form . . . what would happen?'

Rachel did not believe that the staff at Cotswold House read the forms at all, since she had had no feedback about them, ' . . . but if they had done,' she suggested, 'I think they probably would have gone: "Why, why were you talking to her about that sort of thing, that's not about getting her a job!" . . . I don't think they would permit it.'

'Do you think they would have a problem if you were talking about gay liberation?' I asked.

'We would have been chucked out of the building probably, I think!' Rachel replied, laughing. All the same, Rachel did not feel it would have been appropriate to discuss these things with Sharon, since they were not within the mentoring remit of developing Sharon's employability.

My final question was to ask Rachel if she had anything else to say about New Beginnings that we had not covered in the interview.

'It's not new beginnings,' she replied, 'it's dead endings.'

Policing one's own identity

I was struck by the idiosyncratic disposition that Rachel projected through her physical appearance and dress, as well as through her talk about being 'radical' and her political activities. I was also concerned that she felt much of this had to be suppressed in order to function within New Beginnings. Politics and sexuality were clearly central aspects of Rachel's identity, but they were also taboo subjects that she believed would not be tolerated. In spite of her certainty that mentor relationships were not being monitored by the WellTEC staff, she policed herself for fear that they might be – just as Karen feared surveillance in the mentoring room she compared to 'a police cell'. As we saw in Chapter 3, Rachel was well aware that conversations could be overheard easily through the thin walls of adjoining offices and corridors. Like Karen's 'police cell' simile for the mentoring room, Rachel's image of it as an 'exam room', in the spotlight of 'performance' with a prescribed script, also emphasized its character of surveillance and isolation. Examinations, of course, represent one of the ultimate experiences for students of being 'on trial', of being individually judged, yet they are often criticized as an exercise in 'regurgitation' of accepted/acceptable accounts. It is a situation of high pressure, of fear and intense anxiety for some, conducted usually in silence, and under the gaze of an invigilator. One receives a distinct and inescapable classification at the end of it on which one's entire learning career will be judged, but there is no feedback.

Where did Rachel's sense of being judged in this way come from? She may have felt inhibited because of the planned nature of this engagement mentoring scheme, and the directive nature of its guidelines. In volunteering for the scheme, perhaps she felt she had also inevitably bought into its principles, and, in doing so, abandoned her right to 'push the boundaries' and challenge the status quo. Her inhibitions may also have been reinforced by her sense of marginalization during the mentor training course.

Yet there is more to her story than that. Rachel had a strict sense of what she could and could not discuss with Sharon in mentoring meetings. This was not determined by what she had learned through her training, although it did provide her with a sense of what her role ought to be. She felt uncomfortable talking about social activities with Sharon, but still engaged in such discussions. So where did she get her sense of taboo in discussing matters that were central to her identity? How did she recognize the code of what was permissible and not permissible? It seems unfeasible to argue that this code could be derived solely or even primarily from New Beginnings as an institution. There was no explicit rubric about unsuitable topics for discussion. Although mentors were advised during the training to avoid discussion about their private lives, this does not explain Rachel's belief that she would get 'thrown out of the building' if she mentioned her involvement in a gay rights protest. She worried about the fact that she discussed holidays and karaoke with Sharon, but was aware that Karen had done so too, and that New Beginnings staff had tolerated this. At the same time, this does not in itself substantiate her belief that, if staff had monitored her discussions, they would have challenged her if she had discussed her anti-war activities while mentoring.

A more plausible explanation may be that Rachel's self-surveillance demonstrates the power of deeply inculcated but invisible normative conventions in society. Such norms are promoted by schooling that reinforces heterosexual and gendered identities, by dominant discourses absorbed from mass media, by political ideology, and by the widespread oppression of homosexuality, which is constructed in particular as a threat to children and young people. Rachel displayed determination and courage to engage in active citizenship opposing dominant social *mores*, university authorities and government policy. However, despite this 'radical' identity, Rachel paradoxically conformed compliantly with the paradigm of engagement mentoring. More paradoxically still, she was sacked as a mentor because Sharon resisted the goals of engagement mentoring within the relationship, and resented Rachel's attempts to pursue them.

Keith and Neil

Other relationships presented similar evidence of a separation of students' identities within and beyond their role as mentors. There is not space here to recount them all, but let us look briefly at one more case story that made a deep impression on me. Keith, a mature student of history and sociology, mentored Neil, a 17-year-old with moderate learning difficulties. Keith was highly articulate, and his responses were constructed thoughtfully and articulately in the light of strongly held beliefs. Neil was a 'lovable rogue' according to Elaine Peters, and all the staff at New Beginnings were fond of him.

Over fifteen months, Neil and Keith had developed what appeared to be a warm, trusting and rewarding relationship. Keith was concerned to avoid prejudice towards Neil's learning difficulties, and this connected with his strong sense of social justice. He had been an active Labour Party member for fifteen years, and a trade union activist throughout his employment, and he spoke of this as a central feature of his life history. He was highly critical of New Labour's social exclusion agenda, describing it as 'virtually encouraging people to suffer and be still'. Yet when Neil was accused of theft in his workplace without any evidence, suspended from his placement and almost sacked from New Beginnings, Keith's role became that of confessor, trying to get Neil to own up to the theft. Thanks to Neil's favourable disposition in the eyes of the staff, and to the employer's failure to provide evidence, his denials were eventually accepted, and he was transferred to another placement. However, Keith had not discussed anything with Neil about his rights in the situation. Although he often offered Neil what he called 'pearls of wisdom' as they discussed issues in the workplace, Keith never raised the question of trade union representation, or recounted any anecdotes about his political experiences.

I challenged Keith about this at our second interview, and asked him why he had never raised his deeply held beliefs with Neil, especially when he had faced an injustice in his workplace. Keith explained it first on a general level by referring to the 'apathy' of young people today: 'Neil's a very different teenager to what I was. . . . Youth aren't politicized in the same way any more.' He continued by being more specific about Neil and his fellow trainees: 'Politically, no, I've never really been able to talk to him on that level. I feel anybody who I'd be able to communicate with on that level might not necessarily be on the programme. I can't imagine that anyone who you're able to have an articulate political conversation with would be here.' This statement seemed to contradict his previous assertions that he did not consider learning difficulties to be a form of inferiority.

Although Keith had gone through various relatively sophisticated arguments with Neil about the need to work in general, and the need to stick at New Beginnings rather than quit because of the problems, he had felt unable to discuss Neil's rights as a worker when confronted with unsubstantiated accusations and dismissal. Despite his frequent criticisms of the Labour Party under its current leadership, Keith had adopted in practice their discourse of 'no rights without responsibilities'. Like Rachel, despite his own self-perception as a radical, Keith had absorbed the imperative of engagement mentoring, and in doing so he was censoring his own knowledge, experience and beliefs. This indicates the deeply powerful nature of disciplinary self-surveillance, causing even the most politicized mentors, such as Keith and Rachel, to suppress some of their core beliefs and values, and to promote an ideology that, on a conscious level, they actively opposed.

Notwithstanding, Keith and Neil's mentor relationship was the most successful one I encountered in this study. It provided a rewarding personal experience, and participation in New Beginnings also had direct employment outcomes for both men. When Keith finished his degree in summer 1999, Brenda Mavers offered him a job at the new Learning Gateway, which he accepted. Neil was successful in his new placement in a factory canteen, where he moved on to structured youth training provision, and worked towards his NVQ Level 1. He was offered part-time employment there once he was 18. These successes, however, spelled the end of their relationship. Keith was told by Brenda that he had to close the relationship by the time Neil reached his 18th birthday and had to leave New Beginnings. At our final interviews, Neil refused to acknowledge this would have to happen. When I asked Keith about how he would manage the closure, it was the only time I found him lost for words. The rules for ending mentor relationships when the young people had to leave the scheme seemed particularly misguided here. Even in this best of all possible scenarios, the dogmatic structure of New Beginnings conflicted with the benefits of a highly successful mentoring experience.

Transforming mentors' identities

The stories of Karen, Rachel and Keith reveal another layer of complexity in the power dynamics operating in engagement mentor relationships. Although their mentoring experiences were very different, we can discern some common contradictions. They all narrated their identities as somehow challenging the status quo – Karen through her highly personal interpretation of mentoring as friend-ship, and Rachel and Keith in more political ways. Nevertheless, on a different level, they all worked to promote the employment-related goals of engagement mentoring, and, in moments of difficulty or crisis, reverted to this as the benchmark for their mentor relationships, as Keith did when Neil stood accused. Their fears and frustrations were related directly to the threat of their mentees' failure to develop employability, which Rachel and Karen read in terms of their own failure to affect Sharon's disposition.

Moreover, the project of altering their mentees' disposition connected increasingly with a sense of the need to *transform their own disposition* in the context of engagement mentoring. Karen needed to present herself as the reformed delinquent now made good. She also experienced the torment of frustration and guilt expressed so visibly and audibly in our second interview, but concealed it by acting 'the idiot' in her mentoring sessions. Rachel abstained from pushing the boundaries of convention, and operated as one of the most conformative of mentors in relation to the goals of engagement mentoring. She censored discussion about parts of her life – her politics and her sexuality – that were vital to her identity, but which also rendered her vulnerable, placing her beyond the pale of dominant ideology and morality. Keith, taking his lead from the New Beginnings staff, focused on the effort to get Neil to face up to his 'responsibilities' to confess to a crime. At the same time, he saw Neil as someone incapable of understanding issues about working-class rights. He therefore censored discussion of his own long-term labour movement commitment and experience, never sharing them with his mentee.

These cases put flesh on the bones of the discourse we considered in Chapter 1, namely that employability now requires the Procrustean re-invention of identity. The pressures which mentors experienced to transform their own as well as their mentees' dispositions may stem from a variety of sources. They reflect in part the power of the scheme and its staff to promote a particular agenda and goals for mentoring. They also reflect the *potential* power of the staff to monitor the mentoring process, whether through the weekly report forms, by overhearing discussions in the mentoring room, or by questioning the young mentee. As discussed in previous chapters, these aspects of the scheme and its personnel are inevitably bound up with the much wider context that has produced the phenomenon of engagement mentoring. Moreover, different elements of this wider context produce power relations that are not imposed directly through individual interactions, but are covert and internalized by the mentors as members of a broader, collective social layer with distinctive class outlooks. Some examples that illustrate this include Jane, Karen and Keith's positioning of disaffected young people as the 'Other'. This poses communication as impossible or severely restricted. For the female mentors in particular, it imposes a painful burden of containment of their own reactions and denial of powerful emotional responses in order to maintain the appearance of the normative role model. This in turn leads to a process of somehow Othering parts of their own identity, as the mentors separate off and marginalize important formative experiences in their own life histories. We can also include in these wider power relations the suppression/oppression of Rachel's sexuality, and the dangerousness of her radical opposition to war pursued by the UK government and its allies.

Keith's story poses its own question about the impact of engagement mentoring on relationships and individual dispositions: what are the consequences when planned mentoring forces an apparently healthy and beneficial relationship to end at a formally defined point? We can only guess how it affected the pair, since I was unable to follow them up after this point. But it seems that this is a neglected aspect of mentoring experiences, worthy of further research investigation, if the longer term effects of mentoring are to be more fully understood. Chapter 6 focuses on just one case story. It illustrates parallel experiences of a mentor and her mentee in relation to the power dynamics of engagement mentoring.

Love's labour lost?

Mentoring as an impossible fiction

Introduction

Chapter 4 focused on the experiences of young people at New Beginnings who resisted the intrusion of employment-related goals into their relationships with their mentors, and who did not adapt their dispositions adequately in line with 'employability'. By contrast, Chapter 5 revealed how mentors' dispositions adapted to covert pressures on them to role-model idealized identities. They conformed to moralized notions of 'employability', as well as to dominant social norms. Even in the case of Keith and Neil, who had established one of the most positive relationships I witnessed, this interrupted Keith's empathy for Neil. For Karen and Rachel, both female and younger mentors, it resulted in a breakdown of their respective relationships with Sharon that bore damaging consequences for them.

This chapter focuses on one mentor relationship that brought the experiences of both mentor and mentee into a parallel trajectory as their relationship developed. Yvonne, a 21-year-old student of applied social sciences, had already been mentoring 17-year-old Lisa for almost a year when I first interviewed them in June 1999, and they were still meeting in February 2000, months after the New Beginnings programme had come to an end. Sadly, however, the length of the relationship was not an indication of success, as in the case of Keith and Neil. These two young women appeared to be going round in circles, failing to make progress, and unable either to draw conclusions, or to draw their relationship to a conclusion. Their stories seemed to represent parallel experiences in every sense of the word – each continued to follow the mentoring track alongside one another, but they never seemed to come together in a rewarding way.

Lisa and Yvonne: the burden of care at the core of disposition

Lisa

New Beginnings staff regarded Lisa as extremely shy, and were concerned about her difficulty communicating with adults. Although evidently bright – she had been an above-average pupil at school and regarded herself as 'clever' – she spoke in a whisper that was often difficult to hear, and gave very brief answers to my questions, often trailing off into silence. She described herself as 'immature' for her age, making much of the fact that her best friend was a much younger girl with learning disabilities. She also talked in a childish voice, and as we drove from Cotswold House for our interview at UoW, she chatted excitedly and sentimentally about some new kittens her cat had just produced. Throughout the interview she behaved in a very coy, almost eccentric manner. She often averted her face and giggled nervously, and it was hard for me to engage her in conversation. As with Sharon, I experienced at first hand some of the difficulties Lisa's mentor must herself have had to confront.

Lisa's mother had died of cancer when she was in Year 10, not long after the start of her GCSE courses. She had taken time off school to help care for her mother in the latter stage of her illness, and when she returned to school she felt she was given little help by teachers to make up the work she had missed. She was also bullied by other pupils about her bereavement, and soon refused to attend school any more. Lisa had then been recruited to the Futures Plus programme for non-attenders in Year 11, managed by the same staff as New Beginnings, and had progressed to the New Beginnings scheme the following summer.

As well as being clever, the other key attribute Lisa identified in herself was that she was a very caring person. She felt a lot of responsibility for supporting her father and siblings emotionally since her mother's death, which understandably had disrupted the family. Lisa had an older brother who lived elsewhere and whom she rarely saw. Her younger brother, who was 12, had become 'really, really bad and naughty' and Lisa found it hard to get on with him. He had begun to develop emotional and behavioural difficulties since the bereavement, which manifested themselves in a number of ways. He was excluded repeatedly from school, swore at adults and vandalized neighbours' windows. He had hit Lisa's friend, and refused to help out with any of the housework.

Despite being referred for bereavement counselling, he refused to attend, and the problems were getting worse. Their older sister had given up her job and remained in the family home to care for her siblings as 'mother-auntie-cleaner', in Lisa's words. Lisa would offer her shoulder to cry on when her sister felt unable to cope, or when she had frequent arguments with her boyfriend. Their father had transferred to the night shift in his job in order to earn enough money to support the whole family, and this in turn meant that the family rarely sat down to eat a meal together. Communication seemed to have broken down between himself and Lisa, something that Yvonne suspected may have been related to the fact that Lisa was 'the spitting image' of her mother, and therefore a constant reminder of her loss. Moreover, Lisa tried to care for her best friend, who had learning difficulties, was overweight and was being bullied at school. This friend also had emotional problems due to 'something that happened when she was young', which Lisa did not wish to specify.

Lisa felt her role was to try and relieve the burden of other people's problems in some way, but it was proving very stressful for her to take them on herself. Yvonne was concerned that Lisa's painful shyness was a sign of low self-esteem. She also suspected that her mentee's constant tiredness and extremely thin physique indicated depression and/or an eating disorder. She tried, unsuccessfully, to persuade Lisa to take up a referral for counselling herself. However, Lisa's hope was that mentoring would ease the burden. She defined mentoring as having 'someone to talk to . . . because I take on my family's problems and my friends' problems as well as my own'. However, after a year of being mentored by Yvonne, she found it difficult to explain how it helped:

Helen: And how does it help, having somebody to talk to?
Lisa: [*Silence*]
Helen: How would you explain that?
Lisa: [*Silence*]

Yvonne

Lisa felt that being clever and being caring were two very important characteristics that she shared with her mentor, Yvonne. Yvonne appeared to be a very confident and matter-of-fact person, and somehow more mature than the other undergraduates of her age whom I met. Her answers to each of my questions were extremely lengthy, and sometimes she barely paused for breath as she talked. Yvonne had a lot to say, and she often expressed it very assertively. She lived in Arlington, at her parents' home, and talked happily about family life with them. She had a particularly close relationship with her mother, whom she identified as her own 'mentor' and confidante. Arlington was a good twenty-five miles from Midtown, so she commuted in an old and sometimes unreliable car to the university campus at Littleville and to her meetings at Cotswold House with Lisa. Yvonne already had considerable experience of practical caring and of taking responsibility for others' needs. She had an older brother with severe learning disabilities, and had helped her mother to care for him from an early age. From the age of 15, Yvonne had worked part-time, caring for children with severe physical and learning disabilities. She had worked full-time at a respite home for such children for a year after completing her A levels, and had enjoyed this job. She continued to work there on a part-time basis throughout her degree at UoW, partly for the experience, but mainly to lessen the financial burden of her education on her family, who were not well-off.

Although Yvonne had felt 'burnt out' at the end of her GCSE courses, her mother had insisted that she went on to sixth-form college. Yvonne hated A levels, especially sociology, which she had picked as an 'easy option'. Having enjoyed her new job, she gave it up reluctantly to go to university, once again at her mother's instigation. Despite her dislike of sociology, it had produced her best A level result, so she started a degree in social sciences. It also seemed to be relevant to her ambitions of returning to work with disabled people. Things had not improved on the study front, however, as she commented on the difficulty of disciplining herself to get through her course: 'I hate it, it's a load of waffle, just strange theories ranting on about life! Why bother?'

It is not difficult to see how Yvonne's life history might have shaped her disposition. She was an intensely pragmatic person, scornful of 'strange theories'. She disliked any form of self-pity, and believed deeply that one had to endure the difficulties life inflicted, such as the obligation to care for her brother, or the frustrations of studying social sciences. She often spoke about the need to 'stick with it' (a virtue) in order to avoid 'getting stuck' (anathema), and I guessed that her success in working with disabled children indicated large reserves of patience, as well as a genuine commitment to care for others. Her mother's influence seemed especially important in this regard. 'That's the way I've always been brought up,' Yvonne explained, 'you don't, you can't just quit. Once I start something I have to finish it. In some form, I have to know that either I've done everything I can and that's it, or there's, you know, there's nothing else to be done anyway. . . . '

For both young women, then, the burden of care was at the core of their dispositions. For Lisa, this was a problem. She had not yet figured out how to cope with it in a way that preserved her own well-being very adequately. She hoped that having Yvonne as her mentor would help, but she was unable to describe how (or if) it had made a difference. For Yvonne, caring generally posed less of a problem. Her mother had brought her up to believe stoically that what could not be cured must be endured. Her pragmatism had proved healthy in caring for others. Nevertheless, it was not entirely adequate for dealing with her academic work. The very mindset that helped her cope in practical situations made it difficult for her to engage in the more abstract, theoretical work demanded by the university. The patience she brought to bear in her caring role rapidly wore thin in this context. Let us move on to look in more detail at Lisa's and Yvonne's beliefs about mentoring.

The dream of mentoring

Lisa had not been sure what Elaine Peters meant when she first talked to her about mentoring, but willingly complied with the suggestion. 'Elaine asked me if I wanted a mentor,' Lisa recalled, 'and she told me that her name was Yvonne, and she's really nice. And I said, "Yeah, I'll try. I'll meet her next week". And then I liked her, so I've been seeing her.'

I asked how Elaine had explained what a mentor was, and Lisa replied: 'She said that she's someone to talk to, and she'll help you if you need it.' Lisa liked and admired Yvonne a lot, and described her as being like a best friend or an older sister. As we have already seen, one of Lisa's hopes was that mentoring would help her cope with her own emotional problems in a quasi-therapeutic way, allowing her to offload the burden of caring for others. In our first interview she said she thought that mentoring had given her more confidence in talking to adults. At the very end of that interview she ventured an explanation of other ways a mentor could help. 'If you don't want to talk about something with family or friends,' she said, 'and you don't want to hurt either of you, a mentor is some-one else to talk to. . . . Your family or friends have done something, and you don't really like it, and you want to speak to them about it, but you're scared it'll hurt them. . . . You talk to your mentor and you can, like, find a more discreet way of putting it.'

Lisa had educational ambitions, too. She very much regretted the fact that she had not been able to take her GCSEs at school, and wanted to go to college to resit them. Her favourite subjects at school had been history, art and English, and she would have liked to study these again, together with maths. She believed, probably correctly, that she was capable of going to university as Yvonne had done. After that, she wanted to go abroad to work, probably in America, though she had no specific career ideas as yet. I asked Lisa if she felt there were obstacles that might get in the way of these ambitions. The forcefulness of her reply surprised me. 'Life is very fair,' she asserted, ''cos people have to be determined, if they want their dreams to come true.' She thought that her mentor could help her by 'telling her what to do', and chiding her if she did not follow this advice.

Yvonne had her own dream of how mentoring should work. As she explained it to me when we first met, her understanding was that the young people would go to New Beginnings for a while. They could talk to their mentor about any problems they had, and this would give them a chance to 'air off' and 'get it off their chests', so that things would start to 'clear in their heads'. They could then concentrate on what the TEC wanted them to do, and settle into their work experience, hopefully progressing to a job. This matched closely the twin aspects of mentoring conveyed in the mentors' training course: a focus on the PDP, but also getting the young person to 'open up' about their problems.

Yvonne's story about mentoring was a neat one of linear progression, with a happy ending that fitted the goals of engagement mentoring. She gave an example of how she had seen it happen for another mentor. 'There was a batch of us that all started mentoring together,' she recalled, 'and one of the mentors finished a couple of months after he started. Luckily, the young person that he started with, he'd gone through the whole talking to him or whatever, and he'd gone out and got himself an apprenticeship, he's gone and got himself a job through the TEC and he's had success in that way and it had only taken a few weeks.' She reflected on the fact that, after a year of mentoring Lisa, she had still not achieved this result: 'It shows you that they've got some problem that's not going to go away within six weeks, it's not just going to disappear like that, it's probably going to stay with them for the rest of their life, but you've got to find a way of making them get over it, so that they can work and they can continue in spite of and with that problem.' These were their dreams of mentoring. How, over eighteen months, did the practice of mentoring work out?

The mentor's tale: going round in circles, getting stuck, and sticking with it

Already, after a year, Yvonne was having serious doubts about her mentor relationship and about Lisa's engagement with the New Beginnings scheme. At the very start of our first interview I asked her how she thought the mentoring was going. 'It has been a long time,' she replied. Like Karen, Yvonne was now disillusioned and frustrated with her experience: 'At first I went through a stage when I thought we were getting somewhere. Lisa had a really good placement and she really enjoyed it, and then that was it. One day, she just decided that she'd had enough. You know, she was sort of saying things, and I managed to drag it out of her in the end that she didn't want to go back. And ever since, it's been sort of stopping and starting. But she's been changing her mind a lot, so at the moment, myself, I'm going through a real period of doubting whether she's actually serious about wanting a job or not. And whether I'm. . . . ' Instead of the neat progression whereby mentors helped young people to offload their problems, clear their heads and concentrate on work as the happy ending, Yvonne was finding tensions and resistance in trying to move Lisa along the problems–work axis. 'She's got the skills,' Yvonne said, 'but whether she wants to use them, I don't know. She's sort of going downhill a bit at the moment, to be honest.'

Throughout their time together, the pattern of placements repeated itself several times. Lisa tried hairdressing, care of the elderly, catering, accountancy (Elaine Peters must have had to work very hard to find such a high-status placement, beyond the normal range of occupations offered by New Beginnings) and administration. All failed. Lisa would start a work placement, receive good reports and declare that she was enjoying it. Yvonne would begin to meet with her only fortnightly, with a view to winding down the relationship. After a few weeks (although, in one case, after just one day), Lisa would tell Elaine Peters at her weekly review that the work was boring, or that she did not like it, and ask for a different placement to be found. Her attendance at Cotswold House would become sporadic, occasionally she would disappear for a week or two, and Elaine would anxiously ask Yvonne to revert to weekly mentoring sessions. There was no ending in sight, and Yvonne was not happy. She understood that Lisa had some deep-seated problems due to her bereavement and the ensuing trauma for her family. She also felt angry about the school's failure to reintegrate Lisa after her mother's death. However, she was becoming impatient with the apparent perversity of Lisa's behaviour.

I asked Yvonne how she dealt with this in her mentoring sessions. She found it very difficult to find things to talk about when Lisa was not on a placement, referring back constantly to New Beginnings' official definitions of the mentor's role: 'I've still got to get back to this thing that we're there to encourage them to work, so we've got to keep talking about work and different jobs or whatever, or what they might want to do, or what's holding them back in the job.' She would try to get the sessions going by talking about anything that might interest Lisa

– pop groups, family, leisure activities, 'girlie things'. But often this had to be 'dragged out of her', 'like getting blood out of a stone'.

Like Karen and Rachel, Yvonne found that her mentee was quite skilful in getting the mentor to do most of the talking. However difficult this felt, though, Yvonne acknowledged the need for some kind of reciprocity within the relationship: 'She's quite happy to sit and listen to you, you know, she'll just let me talk for ages and ages . . . but you have to give something. You can't just say, "Well, tell me about yourself. . . . " If you don't give anything of yourself, how can you get anything back?' Yvonne told stories about her own life that she hoped could offer Lisa a model of how to develop into a coping adult. 'You have to make that clear: "I used to be like you. You're not going to be stuck like this little person forever. Everybody grows and changes and does different things, and that's just the way life is." You know, someone like Lisa, you've got to give her something to grab on to, really.'

As well as trying to role-model in this way, urging Lisa not to fall into the slough of 'getting stuck', Yvonne also promoted her fundamental values of persistence and endurance, 'sticking with it': 'It's strange that there's no one pulling Lisa personally into line and saying, "Hang on a minute, you've got to stick at something".' Yvonne felt that she had to take on this role, as her mother had done with her. By her own account, she did this in a very forthright and directive manner. She recalled sessions where Lisa had come in complaining about her work placement: 'I've said, "You've got to start pulling your socks up". And there is someone to say, "Stop whinging and get on with it!" sometime. There has to come a point where you say, "Well, everybody has got those sort of problems, but you've just got to get on with it". I think that's as far as I get with what is a mentor.'

Alongside all these exhortations, at the same time Yvonne struggled with the contradictions and dilemmas posed by a different kind of explanation of Lisa's lack of progress at New Beginnings. Yvonne did not want to appear like a 'stooge' (as she put it) of WellTEC, promoting only their interests. She felt angry about the way in which Lisa's school had failed to respond to her difficulties. She realized that the options offered by New Beginnings had, so far, provided little formal training or development for Lisa, and were not going to stimulate her interests or potential. She worried that Lisa might have mental health problems that were not being addressed in any way. In the interviews, she often shuttled around a whole series of reflections on Lisa's situation in a confused way.

At the same time, Yvonne's talk had a directive tone, full of imperatives: 'stop this', 'do that', 'you've got to . . . ', and her questioning had an inquisitorial edge, as she 'dragged things out of' Lisa. I wondered how much of Yvonne's 'no-nonsense' approach derived from her experience of caring for her brother and other disabled children, and from the wider culture that such care engendered. None the less, the effect seemed to be counterproductive with Lisa.

'She sort of sits there,' Yvonne complained, 'and she's like [*meek tone*] "Right . . . OK. . . . Right". And sometimes you can just sit there and think: "She's not going to." She'll say she will. She'll say, "Yeah, I will", and in the back of your mind, you know she won't.'

Her directive stance clashed with Lisa's oblique resistance, and Yvonne conveyed a fraught sense of the frustration that resulted: 'What is a mentor? Sometimes I think I'm just a verbal punchbag. And that's what I'm there for. She can come in and say, "The whole world's shite and I don't want to do it." And just get it off her chest.' As a result, she felt Lisa was 'going round in circles', on a 'downward spiral'.

A turning point arrived in the relationship which set the seal on Yvonne's pessimism. She recognized how academically able Lisa was, and how boring the training at New Beginnings and her work placements must have been. Lisa had also talked to her about her ambition of going to college to resit her GCSEs. So one day, Yvonne had broken the New Beginnings rules about meeting only in Cotswold House, and she took Lisa over to Wellshire College to find out about courses. They had gone into the foyer, a large and rather coldly imposing structure, with streams of students milling about. They had picked up a prospectus, which Yvonne proceeded to go through with Lisa in their following sessions, hoping finally to make progress.

However, Lisa never applied to the college, and this taxed Yvonne's patience severely. She felt that Lisa's objections to every option, including that of college, were just a series of 'excuses' for her lack of commitment. 'I've been getting more and more cynical, I think, as time's gone on,' she declared at the start of our second interview. 'We still get on quite well,' she explained, 'but there are times when I sort of sometimes look at her and I'm thinking, you know, is she taking me for a ride here or what? Is she, is she just stringing me along? Is she just wanting to come 'cos it's a bit of attention?' She wondered, as other mentors had done, if she herself, the TEC staff and New Beginnings scheme, or anyone at all could really do much to help young people such as Lisa.

The overall lack of support from WellTEC or UoW had been compounded by the changes that had taken place since the government's announcement that TECs were to be abolished in the restructure of post-16 provision. New Beginnings had been formally wound up, staff changes had taken place, and at UoW, Renée Jones had officially retired. Lisa had been moved on to the *Learning Gateway*, and Yvonne had lost the regular, though brief, contact she had had with Elaine Peters. 'I'd been left in the lurch', she protested. She was also indignant at being mistaken for a trainee as she went in for a mentoring session. The sense of drifting in the relationship connected with a sense of being cut adrift within the institution. Yvonne's only source of support for mentoring now was her mother. She would 'let off steam' to her at home, and was encouraged to persist.

By then, Yvonne seemed to recognize that not only was Lisa 'getting stuck'; her own efforts at mentoring were getting stuck too. 'She's still basically drifting, and we're still doing that circular thing,' she admitted. 'The purpose of mentoring still baffles me.' Nevertheless, her response to getting stuck was to 'stick with it'. This had brought Yvonne some sense of personal satisfaction, 'that Lisa's not run away from me, and that I have persevered with it, and it's sort of brought that back to me again, that you've got to stick with things and not quit, and, you know, you've got to see things through'. It had also brought her 'a lot of stress'. The rewards, such as they were, were not what she had bargained for when she volunteered for New Beginnings. 'I can't remember half the promises that they [*UoW*] made,' she reflected, 'and I just sit there and I think, "Why did I do this?" I put it on my CV, and then I dread anybody asking me about it in an interview. I really dread it, because I think, well, what do I say, you know?' Yvonne felt that her failure to support Lisa into stable employment would mean that she would be seen as a 'time-waster', 'just one of these do-gooders who does airy-fairy things and doesn't get anywhere'. She judged herself, as well as Lisa, by the expected employment outcomes of engagement mentoring, and felt that others would judge her by this criterion too.

By this time readers may well be asking themselves the questions that occurred to me. How could this relationship continue? Perhaps, more to the point, how could it end? It had apparently reached, in Rachel's words, not a new beginning but a dead ending. The only movement seemed to be this circling within a cul-de-sac. Before looking at their dilemma of how to resolve the mentor relationship, let us first hear Lisa's account of her experience at New Beginnings.

The mentee's tale: going round in circles, getting stuck, and not sticking with it

Lisa's account of her experiences had a logic to it. She explained to me that the purpose of work placements at New Beginnings was for her to discover what job she liked. Weekly reviews with Elaine were to find out if trainees liked their current placement. If they were unhappy, Elaine's job was to find them a different one. Lisa chuckled: 'I keep changing my mind!' At our first meeting she was already on her fourth placement. Each time she asked Elaine to move her, the reason she gave was that 'I just didn't like it'. When I asked Lisa how she chose the placements, however, my question was met with silence.

The first time we met, Lisa was quite enthusiastic about her placement as an accountancy trainee, where she had been for four weeks. Six months later, however, this had fallen through, and Elaine had referred Lisa yet again for an interview with the careers adviser. 'She just helped me to decide that I wanted to admin, that was it', Lisa said.

I queried whether this was what Lisa had really wanted to do, or whether the careers adviser had 'twisted her arm'.

Lisa laughed nervously, hiding her face. 'Yeah,' she replied, 'she said I had to make a decision, what I wanted to do.' I probed further, and she told me: 'I was saying something because I had to.'

I asked how someone could have helped her more, and Lisa began to speak more stridently. 'They could have asked me what I'm interested in, and then seen which jobs had them in. I mean, I'm interested in, like, arts and stuff, I could have done something different. They just wanted to know what sort of thing I wanted to do.' Lisa had been asked to choose only from the work-based training options that New Beginnings had to offer. Given that she really wanted to go to college and study academic subjects again, it did not seem surprising that she 'kept changing her mind'. But she was also prevaricating about going back into education. 'I want to go to college next year,' she told me, 'but I still don't know whether I want to go!' She laughed out loud. 'It's really hard for me to make my mind up', she said.

At first I found it hard to understand why Lisa, timid as she appeared, had not pushed for the option of going to college. There are a number of plausible explanations, though. Perhaps she was still traumatized by the idea of going back into an environment with a lot of other young people, and feared that she might be bullied again. Perhaps, having an even greater gap in her education since her mother had died, she feared being unable to catch up with her classmates again. Yvonne had told me that sometimes Lisa 'hung around' at Cotswold House later than she was required to stay. Perhaps she found it a safe and companionable environment, and felt that neither college nor work placements could offer her that. She told me she had found the visit to Wellshire College with Yvonne overwhelming and 'daunting'. Moreover, Yvonne had explained that to go to college would mean losing the £45 a week training allowance she got at New Beginnings, and that it might also be difficult for them to continue mentoring together. Nevertheless, Lisa explained how her mentor was dealing with the college option: 'She's trying to talk me into it! If I don't go, she'll tell me that I'm silly!'

At our final interview Lisa's situation had changed considerably. New Beginnings had come to an end, and she had been enrolled in the laxer and less individualized régime of the *Learning Gateway*. Freed from the pressure to take up placements she did not want, Lisa had not applied for any job vacancies. She told me, almost triumphantly, that she had changed her career goal yet again. She wanted to become a police officer, because it seemed like a job with lots of variety and it did not require examination passes. Yvonne had helped her obtain the necessary application forms. There was only one snag with this plan, though: the Wellshire Police Force did not recruit anyone under the age of 21. There seemed to be no danger, then, of being forced to take up this option, and no danger either of finding out that she did not like it. Lisa liked the *Learning Gateway*, especially the group-based activities that it offered. She had made new friends of her own age there, and developed more confidence in group situations. Looking back on her time at New Beginnings, she had found her work placements tedious. 'New Beginnings is really for girls who are pregnant', she explained. She was not at all sure why she had been on the scheme.

Things at home were improving, too. Her father had a new girlfriend, with small children of her own. Lisa got on really well with her, and liked looking after the young ones when they came to stay. Relations with her father had improved, as had her brother's behaviour. She had also re-established contact with her older brother. She felt she had a lot in common with him, and that he was playing a supportive role in her life. Above all, Lisa thought that she had matured as a person. These developments had affected her relationship with Yvonne. Beyond the framework of New Beginnings, employment outcomes were now less pressing. There was much less need to offload emotional problems or family traumas. This brings us to consider how both of them confronted the stage that their mentor relationship had reached.

Not a happy ending, but an unhappy not-ending

We have already seen how mentoring had become an unhappy experience for Yvonne. She felt stressed about it, 'dreaded' being asked about it at a job interview, and worried about her failure to encourage Lisa to engage with training and employment. The dream of mentoring had not come true, even after eighteen long months. In fact, if anything, it seemed to have got hazier. 'If Lisa had gone off and got herself a job,' she conjectured, 'yes, I can put it on my CV. "Oh yes, I got somebody a job." But it wouldn't really have been down to me, so I don't know what it's done for me really. I'm still trying to figure that one out, along with everything else.'

Not only was it unhappy, it was also not ending. I asked Yvonne how she thought the relationship might conclude. 'I think that's going to be the difficult thing,' she replied, ''cos I've said by the time she's 18, I've got to finish my degree, she's got to get a job, and the closer it gets, you sort of start realizing that that's. . . . How on earth are you going to end it? I'm still . . . I still don't know how to end it.' She wanted a 'softer' way of bringing the relationship to an end, but could not envisage this unless Lisa settled into a job.

Yvonne felt trapped. Letting Lisa offload about her problems, and the frustrations surrounding her repeated failures on the scheme, had become an almost intolerable strain. 'At the end of the day,' she said, 'I've just had to sort of cope with it myself . . . I just have to switch off, otherwise I'd just crack up, you know.' She wanted it to end, but she was afraid of the consequences of saying this to Lisa. 'I don't want to be the one that says, you know, "You're doing my head in, you're not getting anywhere, go away,"' she said. 'I think in some ways I'm scared of bringing it up in case she thinks I'm pushing her away.' Like other mentors, Yvonne felt unable to demonstrate genuineness with her mentee, to be honest with her about her authentic feelings. She waited in the hope that Lisa would suggest herself that they finish mentoring, although she doubted this would happen: 'I'll sort of, every couple of months I'll say to Lisa, "Do you want to still see me?" But I don't think she'll ever tell me the truth face to face if she did decide.'

The dissimulation seemed to be happening on both sides. Lisa was struggling with the same issues, although from a different perspective. The fact that she had fewer personal problems to talk over made it hard to see the point of carrying on with the mentoring. 'It's really awkward,' she said, 'I mean, I don't know whether to tell Yvonne, "Oh, there's no point in doing this any more," or "It's OK, something might happen next week," so I don't know what to do.' Lisa's dream was not of a happy ending, but of a happy not-ending. She kept telling Yvonne that she did want to carry on seeing her. 'How would you like it to go?' I asked. She replied, 'To be friends with Yvonne, really. We could go out together.'

Friendship could become a more reciprocal relationship, especially within Lisa's framework of values, where caring for others had been about allowing them to offload their problems. This view had been reinforced by the way that Yvonne had cared for her. If they stopped mentoring and became friends, Lisa explained, 'I could get to know about her problems more than her just wanting to know about mine. If you just talk about yourself all the time, it's a bit selfish, I think.' She did ask Yvonne questions about herself, especially as she had some idea that Yvonne was finding her studies very difficult, and wished that she could help her to 'get through the boring bits'. As things stood, though, that friendship was not developing, so Lisa was also trapped in an unhappy not-ending.

Unable to move forward, the relationship was grinding to a halt. It was getting harder and harder for them to talk to each other during the mentoring sessions. Lisa told me that: 'Lately, we haven't got anything to talk about, so we talk about watching TV. . . . So it's quite. . . . There isn't that much to talk about any more.' They had once again made their mentoring sessions fortnightly, rather than weekly, ''cos there'll be more to talk about when Yvonne comes, and there still isn't', Lisa explained.

Yvonne was finding it hard to talk too. Sometimes she felt that Lisa did not want to say anything, and was unco-operative. Sometimes Yvonne herself found it hard to find subjects to discuss. She avoided discussing her own problems with Lisa as far as possible. 'I might say, "Oh yeah, I'm stressed out at uni, and it's getting on my nerves," but then I don't want her to think that she's adding to anything, so I won't really tell her anything too deep about myself, 'cos I don't think that that's what she's there for.' This was a conscious ethical stance on Yvonne's part against exploiting her younger and more vulnerable mentee, which placed a very definite boundary between mentoring and friendship. 'I wouldn't treat her like I would treat some of my close friends,' she explained. 'I wouldn't, you know, go and cry on her shoulder for anything, so that's something you have to be aware of. Plus she's a lot younger anyway, so it wouldn't really be appropriate to do that.'

I asked both of them if I could come along and observe one or two of their mentoring sessions as part of my second round of data generation. Their replies are unsurprising, but reveal how uncomfortable the relationship had become. Lisa said, 'It will be a bit awkward, 'cos there's a big glass window now where we sit by it, and every time someone comes past, we stop talking, and wait till they go out again. So I'm not sure.' Yvonne similarly hesitated: 'Well, I'll talk to Lisa about it tomorrow, and we'll see how we feel about it together, 'cos there are times when we sort of go in and it's, like, ten minutes and we're, like, we've got nothing to say now, but that's just the way it goes.'

An impossible fiction

It would be easy to offer an interpretation of this mentor relationship that fits well with some of the research about dysfunctional mentor relationships reviewed in Chapter 2. We could see it as a tale in which Yvonne bullied Lisa, was unable to reflect sufficiently on her own practice, and therefore produced the cycle of repeated failure for Lisa (in her placements) and for herself (in her role as mentor). It offered evidence of the counterproductive nature of directive approaches to mentoring disaffected youth, and revealed the harsh and unpleasant realities of the engagement mentoring model.

For example, following Scandura's (1998: 454) typology of mentoring behaviour that can result in psychological damage, Yvonne could have been presented as a tyrannical mentor, while Lisa's response could be seen as sabotaging Yvonne's efforts and the employment goals of New Beginnings. Yvonne's positive recognition of the dilemmas Lisa faced, such as her desire to return to an academic rather than a vocational pathway, still led her to place Lisa in an impossible bind, as she confronted Lisa with the ultimatum of applying to college (with all the financial and social costs that would entail) or embracing the options at New Beginnings. Lisa's positive respect and affection for Yvonne, on the other hand, was leading to a spoiling of their relationship, as she felt betrayed by Yvonne's refusal to share her own problems in a reciprocal move towards friendship.

There would undoubtedly be a grain of truth in such psychological explanations. However, their partial and weak character is revealed by the way they construct power dynamics in mentoring. As Scandura (1998) explains, bullying and the use of ultimata both focus on the power differential of the mentor over the mentee, and the mentor's ability to impose his or her own values. Sabotage still places the mentee in the role of victim, albeit a subversive victim, but also reveals the dependency that mentors may develop, particularly on achievement by the mentee of expected outcomes. Spoiling may reflect a mentee's sense of having been treated unequally by the mentor. The problem is that all these explanations reduce the question of power to the micro-level of individual interactions, and present the mentor as an abusive perpetrator and the mentee as a passive or reactive victim. By highlighting the similarities and parallels in their experiences, including the subjection of both to the operation of wider and more covert dynamics of power, we can generate a very different understanding. This draws on a more sociological perspective.

There is, of course, an individual level at which power operated in this story, but it is more complex than the existing literature tends to suggest. Yvonne did engage in overt efforts to control Lisa's attitudes, values and behaviour in line with her own. Disciplinary control was at the heart of her attempts to get Lisa to 'stick with it', and her exhortations to 'pull your socks up'. The mentor did indeed appear as tor-mentor in this process. Yet this instigated a dual dynamic. On the one hand, it provoked resistance and sabotage from Lisa, and reflected the counterproductive nature of directive interventions (Egan, 1994; Miller and Rollnick, 1991; Rogers, 1967), which I will discuss further in Chapter 8. On the other, it also demanded that Yvonne exercise self-control, and discipline herself to persevere and endure. She refused to quit although it was 'doing her head in' and 'stressing her out', and she 'dreaded' being asked about her experience. In her stark image of herself as a 'verbal punchbag', Yvonne no longer appeared as the tor-mentor, but as the tormented mentor.

Lisa's resistance was also far from passive. It is interesting to consider how she related the consequences of her 'failures'. Each time she withdrew from a placement, Lisa was able to return to the safe confines of Cotswold House, while Elaine Peters would set about trying to find another placement. As noted above, Elaine was making ever-greater efforts to generate superior opportunities that might engage Lisa's interest. At the same time, each withdrawal led Elaine to ask Yvonne to reinstate the weekly frequency of mentoring sessions, and to redouble her efforts to travel from Arlington, even during holiday periods. Yvonne felt under severe pressure to maintain the relationship, despite her sense of frustration and failure, for fear of the consequences of 'pushing Lisa away' if she suggested they bring their mentoring to an end. In these respects Lisa's resistance can be seen, in part at least, as an active form of power and control over others.

Beyond this individual level, however, there was also a meso-level at which power operated. This requires us to consider how the institutional context impacted on *both* members of the dyad. Yvonne oscillated constantly between her understanding of the institutional imperatives and structural obstacles that had shaped Lisa's trajectory since her mother's death, and an interpretation of Lisa's repeated failures at New Beginnings as deficient or deviant. She debated this fiercely with herself in the course of our interviews, and even attempted to break the cycle by transgressing the strict New Beginnings rules and taking Lisa to visit the college. However, she was drawn inevitably to promote the perspective of the scheme and its employment-related goals, not only because of the role ascribed to mentors through their training course, but also because she was aware that her efficacy as a mentor would be judged according to employment outcomes for her mentee, in part because of the mythology surrounding some of the mentors who had succeeded in these terms.

Lisa in her turn was pressurized to accept pathways and occupations that she did not want to pursue. Staff, including the linked careers adviser, were unable to recognize and therefore break the cycle, because their vision was limited to the options on offer within the scheme. The design of the scheme constructed vocational training as the only suitable route for disaffected youth, and it was difficult for them to revise this view, particularly when a young person was as non-disruptive as Lisa. Like Sharon, her difficulties were interpreted overwhelmingly as deficits, and this blocked the possibility of perceiving the problem as one of institutional errors.

In these respects, the New Beginnings scheme operated to socialize both mentor and mentee into the behaviour required for their respective positions in the workforce. For Lisa, the emphasis was upon compliance, the acceptance of boring and unchallenging work, and the discipline of sustaining this as her long-term future while abandoning higher ambitions. For Yvonne, the emphasis was upon her ability to mobilize reserves of patience in the face of frustration, to demonstrate commitment and caring even when she perceived no rewards, and to survive all this with little or no support. One suspects this might be regarded as useful training for a professional career caring for others, in a climate of diminishing resources for health and social services.

Yvonne's story often reminded me of the young 'care girls' training in homes for the elderly described by Bates (1994a), whose experiences within their families enabled them to adjust to the often traumatic exigencies of care work. Just as 'class-gendered cultural preparation' (Bates, 1994a: 29) served as a criterion to enter youth training, so it also marked Yvonne as someone suitable for volunteer mentoring and a future profession in caring. The experience of mentoring at New Beginnings, which aimed to supplement her future graduate employability, represented (as vocational training did for the 'care girls') a process of 'sifting, screening and further socialisation [which is] not an independent source of pressure, but simply mediates the gravitational pull from labour market segment to class-gendered fraction' (Bates, 1994a: 29). Perhaps this 'gravitational pull' underlay Yvonne's concerns about how her mentoring would be seen by future employers. Even if she could not achieve the dream outcomes of mentoring, and dreaded being challenged about this 'failure', in 'sticking with it' she could at least show her ability to endure in the face of resistance and frustration, and to persist in selfless and unrewarded caring. In this scenario, it is not surprising that she was unable to reflect on her practice in a way that might have allowed her to change it in order to break the cycle. The virtues of endurance and repression of one's own feelings were fundamental to Yvonne's lifelong identity as a carer.

This gendered concept of care was a central aspect of both Yvonne's and Lisa's dispositions, and points to close parallels in their experiences. As I have indicated in Chapter 2, and will discuss more fully in Chapter 7, feminine stereotypes of care serve to oppress women through deeply internalized roles which serve the interests of dominant groupings (Gaskell, 1992; Gilligan, 1995; Walkerdine, 1992). They obstruct rather than enhance the possibility of communication and relationship between individuals through their demand for self-sacrifice and the repression of powerful emotions. This profoundly ideological construction of care was produced and reproduced in both Lisa and Yvonne through the process of mentoring, as each learned more thoroughly from her partner that caring involved the attempt to absorb and neutralize the other's difficulties and pain.

Yet the longer their mentoring went on, the less able they were to escape the idealized images each brought to the process, or to admit that truth to each other. Mentoring had become (to borrow Walkerdine's (1992) phrase) an impossible fiction. No wonder, then, that the relationship descended into immobility and silence. In this respect, the course and outcome of this particular mentor relationship was inextricably bound up with power dynamics that have defined patriarchal class society for millennia. This aspect of the operation of power in Lisa and Yvonne's relationship reveals another layer of complexity in their experiences of mentoring, going beyond the individualized explanations offered by purely psychological theories. It highlights the contradiction in feminist models of mentoring which advocate a basis of nurture rather than control. For Yvonne and for Lisa, nurture through engagement mentoring inevitably involved control: over others, and over oneself. Both mentor and mentee thus became positioned as twin objects of engagement mentoring and its project of transforming dispositions. Their experiences reveal how these employable dispositions may also be deeply gendered.

The stories from this research allow us to revisit the meanings of mentoring in a new light. We can test out theoretical concepts against the mentor relationships experienced at New Beginnings, and identify ideas that help us best make sense of them. In turn, we can construct a new theoretical framework for understanding engagement mentoring, offer a practical critique of this model, and suggest alternative ways forward for policy and practice. In Chapter 7, I focus once more on the power dynamics of mentor relationships first considered in Chapter 2, and I do so through a critical question. Can mentoring represent a form of empowerment, or is it a process of control?

Part III

A new analysis of mentoring

Mentoring for social inclusion

Empowerment or control?

Introduction

After the stories of the mentor relationships at New Beginnings, set in their wider context, we return with the insights they provide to the issues raised in Chapters 1 and 2. What makes mentoring different from other interventions? How does the element of relationship transform the helping process? In short, how does mentoring work? We saw in those opening chapters that engagement mentoring aspires to empower young people, and that critical studies of mentoring have likewise argued for empowering models of good practice. At the same time, policies on mentoring for social inclusion have advanced a rhetoric of empowerment, but often anticipate a high degree of control over its process and outcomes. The case stories from the research at New Beginnings illustrate this tension well, showing how mentors and mentees experienced both empowerment and control in practice.

This reminds us that discussions of power have been the focus of attempts to gain a deeper understanding of mentoring, but have not yet achieved sufficient conceptual and theoretical clarity. In other fields, such as teaching or vocational guidance, there are clear theoretical frameworks, offering various models of practice, and allowing debate and enquiry at a level that can enhance these interventions. The lack of such a clear analytical basis is a serious weakness in the mentoring movement. It hinders the development of sound theory, it undermines the quality of research, and it restricts the available models.

Neither the theoretical basis of mentoring nor its application in practice can advance without a clear understanding of the nature of power and its functioning in mentor relationships. A number of theories of power have been developed from different perspectives. Rather than review them in an abstract way, let us see how each is related to the practice of mentoring, and test their usefulness against the research evidence presented in the four chapters in Part II.

Power and empowerment in mentoring

Until now, most models of mentoring have been based on a fairly crude and simplistic concept of empowerment. The mentor is seen as the powerful member of the dyad, thanks to his or her greater age or experience, and the mentee is seen as relatively powerless, awaiting empowerment by the benign actions of the mentor. The only negative critiques of power focus on its abuse by the mentor. However, this view has been reflected in slightly different ways in the models we considered in Chapter 2.

Levinson *et al.* (1978) advance the classical model of mentoring, based on developmental psychology, which represents power as something that is handed on from the senior to the junior member of the dyad. This view reifies power as a commodity possessed by individuals. It also assumes a zero-sum equation, in which the balance of power swings from the mentor to the protégé over time. For this reason, it identifies the potential for problems in the mentor relationship at the stage of separation. The mentor may perceive the protégé's success as a threat to his or her own status, heralding a personal decline from leadership towards retirement. Thus the protégé's empowerment signals a loss of power on the part of the mentor.

More critical models, such as those advanced within teacher and nurse education (e.g. Gay and Stephenson, 1998; Standing, 1999), present a different view. Here, power is not seen as a commodity, but as a characteristic of individuals. The ideal mentoring practice is portrayed as a reciprocal process in which power is reproduced in the mentee and also enhanced in the mentor. As an attribute, power can be generated, and there is no fixed sum to be apportioned. The balance does not therefore swing from one to the other as in the classical model, but gradually becomes equalized, and the central concern is one of social justice. This view allows meso-level institutional intrusion into the mentor relationship to become visible, showing that such intrusion inhibits the potential for empowerment. However, it offers limited help in accounting for macro-structural influences and their impact upon mentors, and it still fails to account adequately for the agency of mentees.

Other interpretations see the term *empowerment* as a kind of 'social aerosol' (Ward and Mullender, 1991: 21), covering up conflict between disadvantaged people and the professional classes who dominate them, in part, through welfare practices. According to such a view, one-to-one helping interventions such as mentoring have an in-built inequality. Structural and expert professional power over socially excluded individuals can simply be too great. According to this view, mentors should abdicate or at least minimize the authority vested in them by institutions and political legitimation, and seek instead to facilitate collective, youth-led group activities which can challenge oppression and exploitation. This is a perspective on mentoring that has been adopted by many youth workers in the past, particularly those doing detached outreach work (Philip, 1997).

However, the individual mentor relationships formed at New Beginnings reveal an interconnected set of processes for which none of these theories of power can fully account. Young mentees exercised power proactively as they shaped the agendas of their mentoring sessions, sought support for their self-determined goals from their mentors, and resisted the institutional goals of the New Beginnings scheme when these were unwelcome. It would be wrong to represent them as initially disempowered, awaiting empowerment from their mentors. Moreover, as they exercised agency, young people were able to obtain valued and valuable benefits from their mentor relationships, even where these conflicted with the expectations of New Beginnings and produced some negative practical consequences as well.

At the same time, mentors did not have the power to determine the relationship. This was due not only to the young people's role, but also to the parameters of their relationships imposed by the design of the scheme. These parameters were influenced by European policy, expounded in the mentors' training, and reinforced by the social and physical climate at New Beginnings. As a result, some mentors clearly perceived themselves to be subordinate to the power of others in ways that affected their feelings and identities profoundly. The New Beginnings scheme and its staff were also subject to extraneous pressures and constraints that both shaped the design of the scheme and brought about its untimely demise.

While the third, collective model described above offers more help in acknowledging the agency of young people, and the second, critical model acknowledges that the power of institutions can impede the mentoring process, none of these three approaches takes account of the subordination of mentors, and of the mentoring process as a whole, to other forces. What alternative theories of power and empowerment can help us understand this combination of dynamics better? We must turn to more complex analyses that avoid reducing the evident tensions and contradictions in the mentoring process. I begin with post-structural analyses, which are particularly helpful in understanding the processes of subordination that are absent from previous concepts of mentoring.

Empowerment as an 'impossible fiction': a post-structural analysis

Post-structural theories, particularly the work of Michel Foucault, have become highly influential in educational research over the past two decades (Sawicki, 1991). They resist the notion of power as property that can simply be shared or equalized. Power is seen as decentred and relational, operating at an infinite number of points, exercised through action at the same time as being undergone. It is above all disciplinary, and 'individuals . . . are not only its inert or consenting target. They are always also the elements of its articulation. In other words, individuals are the vehicles of power, not its points of application' (Foucault, 1980: 98). It is 'wielded through "normalization" . . . concerned with the bringing about of a certain kind of individual with certain kinds of characteristics' (Quicke, 2000: 307). Already, we can connect such theories with aspects of the mentor relationships at New Beginnings. Staff and managers at New Beginnings regarded mentors as vehicles for their own authority. This authority in turn conveyed the policies that determined the design of the scheme. As an engagement mentoring scheme, New Beginnings imposed normative values on the young people whom it recruited, above all in its goal of ensuring that they developed the characteristics of employability.

This hints at a contradiction or tension within the concept of empowerment itself. In Chapter 1 we saw how empowerment has become a 'guilty obligation' and risk has become moralized (Ecclestone, 1999). Engagement mentoring schemes may actually undermine any potential for genuine empowerment, as mentors and staff encourage young people outside the labour market to reform themselves with a better 'fit' to employer expectations.

> By encouraging the individual to adapt to adverse conditions, to be a 'survivor', such initiatives reinforce the belief that any form of social action is unlikely to succeed, that one should simply accept one's alienation. . . . This 'colonization' of an individual's mental life represents the ultimate in *dis*-empowerment; those whose mental competence is dependent upon the active intervention of others are hardly likely to be competent social actors capable of bringing about progressive change.
>
> (Wainwright, 1996: 78–9)

The road to salvation is dependent upon the acknowledgement of one's own inadequacies, and the compliant surrender of the assessment of one's own needs to others, followed by acceptance of the diagnosis and curative prescription (Baistow, 1994/95). Engaging with the supposedly liberating power of mentoring to 'free . . . young people from disaffection' (Ford, 1999a: 10) simultaneously establishes the legitimacy of *regulation* through surveillance and control. But what happens to those who are irresponsible enough to reject the 'empowerment' offered by engagement mentoring, or who fail to engage with the objectives of mentoring for other reasons? They may be easily re-excluded, and social inclusion may become even harder to effect.

In addition to this moralization of risk, I suggest that we are also witnessing a parallel *moralization of care*, typified by the romanticized evocations of Mentor discussed in Chapter 2. Mentoring is defined not so much by the functions which the mentor performs, but by the emotional commitment the mentor is exhorted to display towards his or her mentee. Care can slip easily into control over the mentee, but it also exerts control over mentors through the tacit oppression of gendered social roles. In this regard, the benefits which are often claimed as empowering for mentors – the development of skills, the broadening of experience, greater understanding of social exclusion and programmes addressing it, or contributing to 'the community' – also exist alongside negative outcomes. Post-structuralism helps us to understand such contradictions, because it offers a way of seeing that power can be *both* productive *and* repressive at the same time. This in turn helps us to understand that planned efforts to create empowerment have no guaranteed or consistent outcomes.

The case stories in this book illustrate the value of this perspective. Hayley's participation in New Beginnings enabled her to construct important peer friendships in an area to which she had recently moved. Her experience on the scheme, and even her dismissal from it, only strengthened her resolve to pursue her ambition of working in childcare. It also allowed her two years' 'space' to begin to overcome her family problems and emotional difficulties, before embarking on a college course that might lead to her chosen career. Her mentor relationship provided welcome support for the progress she made. At the same time, clear constraints were imposed on Hayley. She was not allowed to pursue her career choice while at New Beginnings, nor was she given any effective career guidance. A less determined young person might have been deflected from their ambition by the limited number of work options on offer, and by the stance of the New Beginnings staff. The manner of Hayley's dismissal was something she had to 'get over', and it affected her family through the harsh financial penalties that ensued.

Keith's successful experience as a mentor offers a very different example of the same tensions. He found his mentor relationship with Neil very rewarding on a personal level. His participation in New Beginnings also enabled him to obtain employment at WellTEC once his degree was finished. On the other hand, his participation constrained his ability to express deeply held personal beliefs and important life experiences as a political and trade union activist. When Neil was accused of theft in his work placement, Keith's response (trying to get his mentee to admit to the crime) reinforced the employer's view of Neil as a 'likely suspect'. Although Keith did not believe his mentee was guilty, he followed the advice of New Beginnings staff, rather than discuss issues of trade union representation for a worker who stands accused. Hayley and Keith's stories are only two examples of the contradictory effects of participating in engagement mentoring for both mentees and mentors. The case stories in Chapter 5 showed how other mentors felt compelled to monitor and censor their interactions with mentees. Rachel in particular expresses a sense of forceful taboo, although nothing in the mentors' training or handbook indicated that any topics were forbidden in discussions with mentees.

Foucault's notion of the panopticon may be particularly useful in exploring these processes of self-surveillance, for it helps to explain how power relations are imposed by means other than direct coercion. The original panopticon was devised by Jeremy Bentham, an English philosopher of the eighteenth and nineteenth centuries. It was a circular design for a prison around a central watch-tower, where the inmates are visible to the warders at all times although the warders are invisible to the inmates, ensuring that the dominant power operates through the subordinate inmates themselves. Surveillance does not have to be permanent since it is invisible, but the prisoners discipline themselves for fear of being seen at any time. It operates on the principle that power relations become internalized and reproduced – even amplified – by the individual without the need for overt coercion.

Foucault argues that panopticism may be found in a wide range of social institutions including education, since it facilitates any function (such as engagement mentoring) which seeks to transform individuals' behaviour.

[The panopticon] arranges things in such a way that the exercise of power is not added on from the outside, like a rigid, heavy constraint, to the functions it invests, but is so subtly present in them as to increase their efficiency by itself increasing its own points of contact. The panoptic mechanism is not simply a hinge, a point of exchange between a mechanism of power and a function; it is a way of making power relations function in a function, and of making a function function through these power relations.

(Foucault, 1991: 206–207)

The panopticon is therefore a 'discipline-mechanism: a functional mechanism that must improve the exercise of power by making it lighter, more rapid, more effective, a design of subtle coercion for a society to come' (Foucault, 1991: 209).

The power of unverifiable visibility – or, in this case, audibility – was expressed explicitly by the mentors Karen, Rachel and Yvonne at New Beginnings. They were acutely aware that their mentor sessions might be overheard from neighbouring offices or the corridor at any time. They felt that the physical arrangement of the mentoring room, with its posters about drug use and pregnancy, reflected expectations of their own talk and behaviour, and indicated how they should shape their mentees' behaviour to make them more employable. Fear became associated with its physical ambience, expressed in metaphors of the room as a police cell (in Karen's words) or an examination hall (according to Rachel). As time went on, mentors saw increasingly less of the staff at New Beginnings, yet their sense of being observed and judged grew sharper. As I noted in the commentary on Rachel's story, the pressures came not only from the values of the staff or the goals of the New Beginnings scheme. They also reflected mentors' perceptions of wider social prescriptions about issues such as sexuality and political activism.

To conceive of power as relational and self-disciplinary helps us, then, to understand the subtle pressure on mentors to adapt their own beliefs, values and behaviour, and to develop the requisite personal attitudes and dispositions for engagement mentoring. In addition, the story of Lisa and Yvonne revealed how the operation of disciplinary power connected deeply with gender roles. Mentoring both drew on and reinforced stereotypical feminine attributes for both mentor and mentee. The insights from their story allow us to revisit the link between power and gender in mentoring that we identified in Chapter 2.

Revisiting power and gender in mentoring

In Chapter 2 we saw that a great deal of literature on mentoring uses myths to represent it as a feminine, nurturing, parental/maternal relationship. Such myths portray the goddess Athene as a mentor who displays both 'in-depth care' and 'high standards of professional practice' (Ford, 1999a: 9–10), who is both 'warm' and 'dispassionate' (Ford, 1999a: 13). Such images produce expectations that mentors will act out simultaneously the 'two leading roles of Womanhood': maternal caring for the needs of others, along with professional distance and control (Hochschild,

1983: 175). Although these images are also likely to affect men in the same roles, only a small minority of mentors for socially excluded young people are male. Moreover, the demand for nurture impacts disproportionately on women, given their social conditioning to meet the needs of others before their own, and their lower social status in patriarchal society.

Ford argues that nurturing mentor relationships can help 'to free . . . young people from disaffection' (1999a: 10). However, a combination of feminist and post-structural theory offers two fundamental objections to such a view, and I draw here upon Walkerdine's argument about women primary teachers and their caring role, which can be applied equally well to the experience of mentors. First, this claim of freeing young people assumes that freedom is the opposite of *overt* control. However, as we saw in the previous argument about panopticism, control is more usually exerted by *covert* means. Since this is the case, 'a notion of freedom as freedom from overt control . . . is a sham' (Walkerdine, 1992: 16). Empowering young people to become employable is a contradiction in terms, if employability means compliance with the interests of employers and other dominant groupings.

Second, this myth of liberation obscures its own implications for mentors (I substitute the word 'mentor' for Walkerdine's original 'teacher' here to reinforce the relevance of the argument):

> the position of women as [mentors] . . . is vital to the notion of freeing and liberation implied in such a [model]. *It is love which will win the day*, and it is the benevolent gaze of the [mentor] which will secure freedom from cruel authority in the family as well as [at work]. Through the figure of the maternal [mentor], the harsh power of the authoritarian father will be converted into the soft benevolence of the bourgeois mother. . . . Women [mentors] become caught, trapped inside a concept of nurturance which held them responsible for the freeing of each little individual, and therefore for the management of an idealist dream, *an impossible fiction.*
>
> (Walkerdine, 1992: 16, emphases added)

It is precisely the notion that 'love will win the day' which lies at the heart of Ford's (1999a) notion of selfless love conveyed by *agapé*, his portrayal of Athene, and his comparison of mentoring with good parenting. But it rests on a *denial* of power which exposes the fragility of the liberal feminist arguments discussed in Chapter 2, and of any model of mentoring which treats power as internal to the mentor relationships. If the equation is read as:

$$\text{dyad} + \text{power} = \text{repressive control}$$

with the opposite being read as:

$$\text{dyad} + \text{reciprocity/solidarity/absence of power} = \text{empowerment}$$

we find ourselves denying the invisible and normative operation of more subtle forms of power which work not only against the mentee, but also against the mentor expected to 'free' individual young people.

In practice, Walkerdine (1992) argues that the opposite result is achieved. In denying power, subordination is also denied, and oppression becomes pathologized, *both for the mentor and the mentee*. Within the maternal dyad, the mentor bears a cost as she tries to create the 'ideal' young person out of the 'disaffected' young person, presenting an idealized version of herself as the embodiment of normative behaviour – the role model. Mentoring becomes a 'technology of the self' (Foucault, 1988), promoting selfless dedication to the client without any critical understanding of the social relations in which the relationship is located. The dyad is assumed to inhabit a 'universe outside time and space' (Walkerdine, 1992: 21), supposedly free of structural inequalities and the intense personal stresses they create.

No wonder some mentors felt such discomfort in the room allocated for the mentoring sessions at Cotswold House. Perceived as a barren space enforcing purely verbal interactions, it represents just such a disembodied location. Such insights may also help us to understand, for example, how Karen's initial altruism and dedication turned to pain and frustration, as Sharon failed to make rapid improvement through mentoring. Jane also suffered as she silently absorbed her shock at her mentee's lifestyle and struggled to repress her own outrage at Annette's 'benefit dependency'. This had to be endured in order to present herself as the ideal role model of non-judgemental counsellor, mother, worker, and self-improving returner to education.

Another way of understanding these pressures is through the distinction between *feminine* and *feminist* ethics of care, which may be most apposite in rethinking Ford's (1999a) perspective of *agapé*:

> Care as a feminine ethic is an ethic of *special obligations and interpersonal relationships. Selflessness or self-sacrifice* is built into the very definition if care when caring is premised on an opposition between relationships and self-development. A feminine ethic of care is an ethic of the relational world as that world appears within a patriarchal social order: that is, as a world apart, separated politically and psychologically from a realm of individual autonomy and freedom which is the realm of justice and contractual obligation.
>
> (Gilligan, 1995: 122, emphasis added)

Gilligan argues that such selflessness in fact represents *disconnection from* rather than connection with others, and inhibits the capacity to form healthy bonds. The way in which Yvonne's relationship with Lisa was slowly freezing into silence epitomizes such a stalemate.

This paradox is at the heart of the modern myths of Mentor, including liberal feminist critiques that draw on the dominant discourse as they appeal to the image of Athene. By arguing that a feminist approach to mentoring should embrace nurture in order to be empowering, they become trapped within the régime of truth, since essentialist notions of feminine nurture are socially constructed and regulatory. If *agapé* undermines the very possibility of individual relationship (the Coke-style 'Real Thing') to which mentoring aspires, a *feminist* (rather than feminine) notion of care might have to be framed within a more collective approach. Freedman (1999) reflects this broad challenge in relation to mentoring socially excluded young people. He challenges the current fad for individualized mentoring interventions based on artificial relationships, and argues that resources might be better used to help communities become 'mentor-rich' for their own young people. Such mentor relationships might at least have the virtue of being social and voluntary rather than artificial and legal (according to Almond's (1991) typology discussed in Chapter 2). There would, of course, be far less possibility for their processes and outcomes to be prescribed and controlled by dominant groupings.

The application of post-structural analyses shows us that the power dynamics of mentoring are far more complex than has been recognized in the literature thus far. However, there are a number of contradictions and ambiguities in post-structuralist theories of power (Quicke, 2000). While post-structuralists hold that wherever there is power there is also resistance, it is difficult to discern from their writings how this resistance might coalesce, or to what purpose, given their rejection of 'grand narratives' represented by movements such as socialism or feminism. They expose sharply the often imperceptible workings of power, but offer little hope of challenging dominant groupings and discourses by seeking alternative strategies. These limitations of post-structural theorizing have therefore been seen as disempowering for movements working for social justice (Haber, 1994; Humphries, 1998), since they imply that '[t]he only prospect is the transformation of one "régime of truth" into another' (Quicke, 2000: 312). Foucault's analysis of power as 'bottom up' – whereby dominant groupings expropriate and use for their own benefit mechanisms of power that have already been developed at individual levels – directs analytical attention inevitably to micro-level contexts. It is this lack of account for structural contexts that has proved the Achilles' heel of post-structuralist theorizing, and has invited its most trenchant critiques (see Humphries (1996), Sawicki (1991) and Smart (1988) for in-depth discussions of this point).

By contrast, I have argued strongly that the micro-level interactions between mentors and mentees at New Beginnings cannot be fully understood without also considering both the macro- and meso-level contexts in which they took place. Without such contextualization, the finger of blame points once again at the mentors for their misunderstanding of empowerment and their own abuse of power towards their mentees. The New Beginnings staff would stand similarly accused. This would result in an impoverished understanding of the power dynamics of engagement mentoring relationships, and their complexity would once again be over-simplified. At the same time, the case stories reveal subjective factors that deeply influenced the mentor relationships I studied. The most important of these factors are identity, personal disposition, class culture, gender and life history. I move on, then, to explore another theory of power which provides an even better fit for this evidence. It is drawn from the work of Pierre Bourdieu, and it focuses on the relationship between structure and agency. Bourdieu's work is extensive, and I do not pretend to do justice to its full sweep within the remit of this book, but readers can find an accessible introduction and overview in Bourdieu and Wacquant (1992), and detailed commentaries and debate in, for example, Grenfell and James (1998), Jenkins (1992), and Swartz (1997).

Bourdieu's work overlaps in important ways with post-structural analyses. He, like Foucault, believes that power is relational, rather than a commodity or a characteristic of persons (individual or collective). Power therefore operates through dynamics that may be both enabling and constraining, often at one and the same time. Both thinkers are concerned profoundly with the covert and unrecognized ways in which individuals internalize and reproduce existing relations of power, thus perpetuating domination by hegemonic groups. But Bourdieu's theoretical approach is also constructed partly in opposition to post-structuralism, since it insists on the dialectical interplay of agency and structure in the analysis of specific practices (Swartz, 1997). Particularly relevant to the subject of this book, his work has been applied to young people's school-to-work transitions (Ball *et al.*, 2000; Hodkinson, 1995, 1996, 1997, 1998; Hodkinson *et al.*, 1996; Okano, 1993), and more recently to mentoring (Philip and Hendry, 2000; Smith, 2001). In addition, Reay (1998) has developed a feminist reading of Bourdieu to explain the inadequacy of liberal feminist theories for understanding how class and gender operate in tandem. These reasons alone suggest the value of Bourdieu's concepts as tools for thinking about engagement mentoring.

In the final part of this chapter, then, I draw on his view of power to show how structure and agency interact together in the case stories, to offer a new theorization of engagement mentoring, and to return to the thorny question of how mentoring can be defined. I begin by explaining Bourdieu's most important concepts related to the analysis of power: his notions of 'habitus' and 'field'. We can then go on to consider how these concepts may be used to interpret the case stories from New Beginnings, and to define engagement mentoring more clearly. In the final chapter, they will also help us to consider alternative strategies of mentoring for social inclusion.

Bourdieu's concepts of 'habitus' and 'field': power as a set of relations

Bourdieu uses the term 'habitus' to refer to personal dispositions and predispositions. 'Field' represents any particular context in which individuals are assigned a position, but also seek to position themselves strategically. The two concepts are closely interrelated, and we must avoid the mistake of regarding field as a representation of structure, and habitus as that of individual agency.

For Bourdieu, field and habitus *both* express the dialectical relationship between structure and agency at different levels (Wacquant, 1992). As Hodkinson *et al.* (1996) note, Bourdieu's most frequent metaphor for field is that of a game. It thus comprises context in two ways. It is constituted by the terrain or playing field, and by the rules that regulate play. In this respect it expresses the influence of structure. However, the game is also constructed by those participating in it. They lend the game legitimacy by the very fact of taking part and playing according to its rules, incorporating the influence of structure into their own actions. At the same time, they influence the game by the specific strategies and tactical choices they employ to achieve their own interests or goals. In this regard, the field enables the expression of individual agency, and does not impose an absolute determinism.

It does not imply complete freedom, however, nor equality within the field of play. Players in the game occupy different positions within the field, and these positions represent power relations of domination or subordination (Bourdieu and Wacquant, 1992: 97). Players also enter the game with differing amounts of resources – economic, social or cultural. One of the mediating effects of the field is to determine which resources are ruled out of play and which *count as capital*. Only the latter may be brought into play, circulated, exchanged or accumulated further (Hodkinson *et al.*, 1996; Reay, 1998). Neither power nor capital are conceived of as forms of property, nor as characteristics of individuals or groupings. Akin to Marxist understandings, they are regarded as forms of social relations. In short, 'the field is a critical mediation between the practices of those who partake of it and the surrounding social and economic conditions' (Bourdieu and Wacquant, 1992: 105).

Habitus entails a similar dialectic, since it is both

> a *structuring* structure, which organizes practices and the perception of practices, but also a *structured* structure: the principle of division into logical classes which organizes the perception of the social world is itself the product of internalization of the division into social classes.
>
> (Bourdieu, 1986: 170, emphases added)

In less abstract terms, habitus may be understood as the combination in each person of previous biography, their sense of identity/identities, lifestyle, personality, class, gender and cultural background, and the beliefs, attitudes and values to which I have hitherto referred as 'disposition'. At the same time, habitus is used to express the fact that such dispositions are not purely subjective and unique to each individual in certain respects, but also embody an important collective aspect, *even in those personal respects*: 'To speak of habitus is to assert that the individual, and even the personal, the subjective, is *social, collective*. Habitus is a *socialized subjectivity*' (Bourdieu and Wacquant, 1992: 126, emphases added).

Bourdieu refutes any suggestion that this is an overly deterministic view:

> Habitus is not the fate that some people read into it. Being the product of history, it is an *open system of dispositions* that is constantly subjected to experiences, and therefore constantly affected by them in a way that either reinforces or modifies its structures. It is durable but not eternal!
>
> (Bourdieu and Wacquant, 1992: 133, original emphasis)

Nevertheless, there is a 'relative' degree of closure in habitus, given the weight of prior experiences and class conditioning. Choices and agency are possible, although bounded, and they can bring about transformations of habitus. Thus habitus and field represent mediating factors that both enable and constrain the exercise of power.

How can we apply these notions to the analysis and interpretation of the research data in this study? We can begin by thinking about engagement mentoring as a field. Bourdieu argues that there are three moves to make in understanding any phenomenon (Bourdieu and Wacquant, 1992: 104–105). First, we must analyse how a particular field, such as engagement mentoring, is located within the global 'field of power' in which dominant groupings vie for position (Bourdieu, 1989a, cited in Bourdieu and Wacquant, 1992: 76). In Chapter 1 we saw how engagement mentoring has emerged in the UK as a response to these struggles in the field of power, particularly the drive by Britain's government and employers to compete in global markets.

Second, at the level of the field itself, we must also map out the objective relations between actors within the field. The description of New Beginnings in Chapter 3 and the case stories in Chapters 4 to 6 have shown the different positions occupied by various individuals, social groupings and institutions within engagement mentoring. These positions reveal specific objective relations between the various players at New Beginnings. The scheme tried to cater for the needs of local employers and young people, but the needs of employers quickly became dominant. Some young people tried to assert their own aspirations, but these were sometimes derailed, or led them back into vulnerable situations. Discourses of disaffection placed the young people in a subordinate relationship to the scheme itself, partly through a referral system which compelled them to attend, partly through the imposition of other class and cultural values. Mentors were treated as a vehicle for the authority of the scheme and its staff. For all the valued support that they offered, mentors such as Jane and Karen saw their own value-systems as superior to those of their mentees, and interpreted working-class culture as deviant. Both the young people and the student volunteers were subject to the selection and disciplinary processes applied by the WellTEC and UoW staff, exemplified in the dismissal of the mentees Adrian and Hayley and the mentor Rachel from the scheme.

This list could go on, since the case stories offer a great deal of evidence about the relative positions of individuals in relation to each other, to the scheme, and to broader institutional and structural factors. At the institutional rather than personal level, however, the fate of WellTEC and its impact on New Beginnings offers a further example. Despite the enthusiasm that marked the early partnership between WellTEC and the University of Wellshire, a series of events – internal restructures, official inspection and national policies that abolished TECs altogether – shifted the focus of the scheme and the balance of forces within it. They undermined the partnership with UoW, whose staff felt excluded from decision-making. They caused severe stress among WellTEC employees, leading in turn to staff shortages at periods when large numbers of young people were joining New Beginnings. As a result, mentors were left feeling unsupported, while staff perceived them as unreliable and uncommunicative. This example reveals how the best of individual intentions, and the most positive agency exerted by any of the players, could all be undermined by the actions of more dominant forces in the engagement mentoring field.

Bourdieu advocates a third level of analysis that shifts our attention from the concept of field to the habitus of participants within it. What are the individual and collective aspects of their dispositions? And what are their trajectories within the field? In the case stories, I offered commentaries which often point to the influence of 'disposition', of biography, gender and class background. In the story of Annette and Jane, aspects of their biographies played an important part in their responses to the scheme and to each other. Jane's identification with the ethos of Rogerian counselling was generated by a transformation of her own habitus when she left her secretarial job and became a mother. This led her to resolve the conflict of agendas in the relationship – Annette's desire for support for her pregnancy versus the employment outcomes required by the scheme – in favour of Annette rather than the ordinances of New Beginnings. Annette's ambiguous engagement with New Beginnings seemed linked to two aspects of her habitus. She wanted to achieve some measure of success to prove her father's negative attitudes towards her wrong. On the other hand, her experience of bereavement of her mother, and of being placed into care by her father, meant that she valued very highly the opportunity of starting her own family. She rejected the employment goals of New Beginnings at least in the medium term, as she would not contemplate leaving her daughter in the care of others. Both women expressed typical female gender roles through their identities and choices of action.

These aspects of their habitus brought them together, and took the relationship on to a close and trusting footing. However, other aspects drove them apart. Once Annette had left New Beginnings, she prioritized a support network of other young working-class women and relatives in her neighbourhood. She felt justified in living on benefits until her child was old enough to go to school. However, Jane's bourgeois sense of moral propriety, bound up with her own commitment to the work ethic, and her investment in returning to education to improve herself, created painful difficulties for her. She experienced resentment towards Annette as part of a seemingly hopeless class of benefit dependants, but still she tried to mentor her in a non-judgemental fashion. Annette loosened the ties with Jane, missing appointments and failing to contact her in response to her messages. In turn, Jane's deep need to be needed, her identification of herself first and foremost as a carer for others, was thwarted, resulting in a sense of loss and anger. This is an example of the threat to mentor relationships posed by social distance and cultural misunderstandings between mentors and mentees (Freedman, 1999; Philip and Hendry, 2000).

However, there is a danger in such interpretations of misunderstanding habitus in a weak and incorrect way, that simply explains how individual choices of action can be shaped by more collective predispositions. Such a version of habitus would tend to reproduce, rather than challenge, the weaknesses identified in previous theorizations of mentoring: their tendency to focus on the superior power of the mentor, and to obscure the subjection of the mentor, the dyad and the institutional setting to wider relations of power.

It is perhaps the story of Lisa and Yvonne that is most illuminating in this respect. Far from showing a mentor and mentee set in embattled opposition (though this might be the most facile interpretation), their experiences reflect a profound symmetry when we place them in the context of the engagement mentoring field. The story of their relationship is then transformed from one of powerful mentor versus disempowered mentee, to become a story of the subordination of *both* members of the dyad to a gendered régime of truth: the feminine denial of self in caring for others. Reading this back in hermeneutic fashion to the rest of the data and to the analysis of mentoring literature, we can apply the concept of habitus to engagement mentoring in a much richer and more revealing way.

Redefining engagement mentoring: the dual transformation of habitus through emotional labour

So far, I have made two arguments central to this book. The first is that engagement mentoring seeks to reform young mentees' dispositions in line with employers' demands for 'employability'. The second is that engagement mentoring seeks to engender devotion and self-sacrificing dispositions in mentors through its discourse of feminine nurture. Mentor dispositions are supposed to present an ideal role model of employability, combining warmth and caring with rational action. Both processes represent a form of docility (cf. Foucault, 1991), by which mentors and mentees alike internalize and reproduce existing capitalist and patriarchal power relations.

Such an analysis suggests a very radical new definition of engagement mentoring. Its distinctive function is to transform the habitus of those on both sides of the dyad, to produce and reproduce habitus in a form determined by the needs of dominant groupings, rather than by the needs or desires of mentees or mentors. Habitus is therefore treated as a *raw material*, while mentoring is construed as a *labour process* to reform habitus as a saleable commodity within the labour market – for graduates as well as for socially excluded young people.

What is this commodity? It is the special commodity, labour power, which is essential to capitalists' ability to derive surplus value from any production process (Marx, 1975; Rikowski, 2000). As I argued in Chapter 1, the current economic context has greatly expanded employers' demands of labour power; employers require us increasingly to place our very dispositions at their disposition. Selling our labour power entails also selling our personality and commitment to the employer. In the globalized economy at the turn of the millennium, the repro-duction of labour has become a matter of enlisting not only bodies, but also hearts and minds. Our very selves become dehumanized as human capital. In mentoring, the greatest contradiction is that this brutal commodification of the self is cloaked in the guise of human relationships based on warmth and compassion.

The role of mentors, whether volunteers or professional, situates them within the framework of capitalist labour processes as workers, in spite of their middle-class social status (cf. Ozga, 1988). Volunteer mentors, such as those at New Beginnings, are still subject to the force of exploitation, not only because they are being used increasingly to replace professional, paid workers, but also because their voluntary work represents part of their own pre-employment training and development. What kind of labour process is involved in mentoring with *agapé*, however? How can we understand a labour process that demands, on the part of its workers, loving devotion and self-sacrifice?

Marxist feminist theories are again helpful here. Hochschild (1983) argues that such work represents a labour process that is distinct from the simple dualism of manual and mental labour, and that a further category of labour has to be recognized: that of *emotional* labour. In emotional labour, the emotional style of providing a service or product is part of that service or product itself, since 'in processing people, the product is a state of mind [in the client]' (Hochschild, 1983: 6). Emotional labour is defined as:

> the management of feeling to create a publicly observable facial and bodily display; emotional labor is sold for a wage and therefore has *exchange value* . . . the synonymous terms *emotion work* or *emotion management* [are used] to refer to these same acts done in a private context where they have *use value*. . . . [Emotional] labor requires one to induce or suppress feeling in order to sustain the outward countenance that produces the proper state of mind in others.
>
> (Hochschild, 1983: 7, original emphases)

As it is bought in the labour market, and is therefore controlled and prescribed in its manner of deployment by others, it results in emotional costs to the worker, and can produce intense alienation or 'estrangement' from the self. This is not only because we have to sell our personality as part of our labour power, but because we work upon our own feelings as part of the labour process itself.

This new definition may be applied not only to the images of mentoring critiqued in Chapter 2. Direct examples of emotional labour may be found in the case stories from the research. As we saw in Chapter 3, the mentor training encouraged students to be cheerful, optimistic and encouraging about labour market prospects. It also encouraged them to listen to the young people in non-judgemental ways. However, the experiences of several of the mentors indicate how difficult it was to manage their own feelings. Jane had to suppress her feelings of shock at hearing about her mentee's lifestyle, as well as her indignation at what she perceived to be Annette's benefit dependency and lack of a work ethic, and eventually her annoyance and distress as Annette distanced herself from the relationship. Karen's second interview revealed an intense emotional burden of disgust and frustration with her mentee, and guilt at her feelings, which she had to repress. She and Rachel both described how they also had to suppress feelings of intimidation and fear when in the mentoring room at Cotswold House. Similarly,

Yvonne struggled with frustration, disappointment and anger in a way that 'stressed her out' and 'did her head in', yet she was unable to discuss with Lisa her desire to end the relationship.

Hochschild (1983) is concerned with the inequalities and costs of emotional labour, in the context of the more widely unequal distribution of power and authority in patriarchal capitalist society. The costs of emotional labour tend to manifest themselves in three ways. If the worker continues to try to put her 'heart and soul' into the job, she risks stress and 'burn-out'. If she tries to protect herself by distancing her 'real' self from her work identity, and trying to 'act the part', she risks detachment from her own emotions and low self-esteem for her insincerity. If she tries to separate her 'real' and 'work' selves without succumbing to self-blame, she risks cynicism and guilt. This helps us to understand that habitus comprises not only mental dispositions, but is deeply embodied too. These costs are allocated differentially according to gender and social class, and are increased as institutional mechanisms seek to intensify and regulate the management of emotion. They can be recognized most easily when individuals sense a clash between what they feel and what they sense they ought to feel, and among the mentors at New Beginnings, Karen demonstrates a particularly keen awareness of this breach.

Reay explains how the concept of gendered habitus can help us to understand how structure and agency come together for working women to drive them along stereotyped career trajectories into caring occupations. Although it appears as a choice, undertaking roles that demand emotional labour is often a 'choice of the necessary' (Bourdieu, 1986; see also Bates, 1994a), that explains why women make up the vast majority of both professional and voluntary mentors:

> As well as incorporating challenges and subversions to the prevailing gender order, the concept of gendered habitus holds powerful structural influences within its frame. Gendered habitus includes a set of complex, diverse predispositions. It involves understandings of identity premised on familial legacy and early childhood socialization. As such it is primarily a dynamic concept, a rich interfacing of past and present, interiorized and permeating both body and psyche.
>
> (Reay, in Grenfell and James, 1998: 141)

Hochschild (1983) argues that predisposition to emotional labour is reinforced in four crucial ways by the adaptive nature of women's gendered habitus. First, women have learned to exchange emotion as a resource, because they have limited and unequal access to economic and material resources. Second, women are expected to specialize in one aspect of the gendered division of labour: caring. Nurture is based on the adaptation of women to the needs of others. This is neither 'natural' nor an innately female instinct, but is socially constructed and enacted. Third, the subordinate status of women as a gender renders individual women more vulnerable to the displacement of feelings by others. (Yvonne and Lisa's stories in Chapter 6 both demonstrate the burden of absorbing the pain of others through their own caring.) Fourth, the power difference between men and women means that such 'women's work' is more likely to be invisible or unrecognized. Emotional labour and its costs go entirely unaddressed in accounts of mentoring, as they were in the New Beginnings training and support for mentors.

The stories of the female mentors at New Beginnings allow us to apply such a notion of gendered habitus. In Jane's story we considered the paradox, in Rogerian counselling terms, of trying to display both empathy and authenticity, and the way in which Jane privileged empathy and abandoned efforts towards authenticity. This paradox is inseparable from Ford's (1999a) image of Athene. While used to *invoke* the process of emotional (and therefore managed) labour, it *evokes* our nostalgia for unmanaged feeling through celebrating a Romantic vision of spontaneity and warmth, 'The Real Thing'. This evocation, in turn, makes mentors' emotions more susceptible to being managed and shaped in dominant groupings' interests. According to Hochschild (1983), the filtering of candidates for jobs involving emotional labour – and we can note here most New Beginnings mentors' aspirations to become teachers, social workers, personal advisers and professional mentors – begins well before their actual recruitment and formal training in those jobs. It begins with the marketing of the role itself, and modern references to mentoring in the *Odyssey* may be seen as just such a marketing method.

However, the exploitation of habitus as a raw material in a process of emotional labour brings some problems with it. How realistic were expectations that young people's habitus could be transformed in a few months from disaffection to employability? The evidence from these case stories confirms the theoretical supposition that such transformations are extremely difficult to effect. For Bourdieu, as we have seen, habitus is adaptive and can be transformed, but not easily. It is 'enduring' and 'durable', and as Hodkinson *et al.* (1996) have shown, transformations may often be the result of unpredictable serendipity.

Adrian is perhaps the best example of a young person who clearly perceived that his 'life had been turned round' by his experience of mentoring. Over the few months before he was dismissed from the scheme, his relationship with Pat had a radical effect on his identity. The serendipitous reappearance of his long-absent father at the same time no doubt contributed to this 'turning point', and widened substantially his previously bleak 'horizons for action' (Hodkinson *et al.*, 1996). Nevertheless, Adrian's disposition changed only partially in line with that demanded by New Beginnings. He believed he could gain employment, and had tried repeatedly to access other routes into the labour market after leaving New Beginnings. However, his newly broadened horizons for action meant that he aspired to higher-status opportunities than New Beginnings could offer. He was not prepared to accept and adapt to work he perceived as boring in a placement where he believed he was being treated unjustly. He found himself unable to turn up on time or even attend regularly, and was therefore deemed incapable of demonstrating proper levels of employability.

Sharon's habitus, on the other hand, appeared to have been unaffected by the mentoring she received at New Beginnings, although it was interesting to see how she deployed an entirely different persona when attending the scheme, in contrast to the one I witnessed when I visited her at home. Annette actively controlled her mentoring sessions with Jane to develop her evolving habitus as a young mother. Like Adrian, this strengthening of habitus led her away from the direction in which New Beginnings hoped to lead young people. Lisa's habitus as 'caring', and the way she shouldered the burden of others' problems, seemed to have been reinforced by the mentoring which Yvonne provided. The provision at New Beginnings, and Yvonne's efforts to promote the aims of the scheme, were all to no avail, however, in their attempts to adapt Lisa's habitus to the work opportunities on offer. The aspect of her habitus which she designated as 'clever', and which expressed itself in her abiding desire to return to college to study academic subjects, endured. Yet we can see how Lisa's habitus also shifted once she had left New Beginnings. The group activities at the *Learning Gateway* allowed her to mature and socialize with her peers, while improvements in her family situation made her more optimistic about the future.

However, the evidence from the case stories suggests that it may be easier to work on the habitus of mentors than of mentees. Using the notion of gendered habitus and its adaptive nature for women, it is not surprising that there was much less to do in transforming the dispositions of mentors. Most who volunteered to mentor were women. They had usually already engaged in processes of emotional labour, and had dispositions which led them to do so. Karen, for example, had lived through the disruption of her family and their attempts to support her brother during his period of drug dependency. She was training as a primary teacher. Yvonne had long experience of caring for her disabled brother and working in a respite home with other disabled children. She aimed to become a social worker. Jane had worked in the self-help group she founded for new mothers, and had trained as a counsellor for over a year. She hoped to become a professional mentor.

It is interesting to note here that Rachel did not come to mentoring through a similar process. Although she tried to comply with the expectations of mentoring at New Beginnings, she had no experience of caring for or supporting others, and her career aspiration was to pursue her creative art. She was not used to engaging with emotional labour in a way that might have enabled her to adapt and 'fit in', and consequently, from the start, she felt marginalized. This leads us to consider a final set of issues in understanding mentoring for social inclusion: the claim that it can enhance participants' social and cultural capital.

Can engagement mentoring enhance social and cultural capital?

The terms 'social capital' and 'cultural capital' have become very fashionable in educational policy and research of late, including in the field of mentoring. Bourdieu (e.g. 1986) advances a radical interpretation of these notions, linked closely to class distinction, race and gender. Cultural capital therefore includes not only the possession of formal qualifications, but also other cultural markers such as styles of speech, dress and physical appearance, and the ability to function with confidence in particular social milieux. Social capital comprises the networks and contacts that enable access to employment and other systems of social support.

One view of mentoring is that it can empower disadvantaged young people by increasing their social and cultural capital, and thereby reduce inequalities in the labour market (Aldridge *et al.*, 2002; Philip, 1997; Raffo, 2000; Raffo and Hall, 1999). Parallel arguments have also been advanced with regard to mentors. Mentoring can supposedly increase mentors' cultural capital by helping them to make sense of challenges and dilemmas they face as adults, and by developing their psychosocial skills for supporting others (Philip and Hendry, 2000). Forrest (2002) makes similar claims for the closely related practice of befriending socially excluded young people.

However, we need to investigate more closely claims that mentoring can increase cultural and social capital. My intention here is not to question the empirical evidence these authors use to support their case, or to cast doubt upon the benefits of mentoring identified by participants in their research. It is to point once again to the need for more clarity in the use of these concepts to analyse and interpret such evidence.

As I noted earlier in this chapter, Bourdieu's concept of cultural and other forms of capital is related intimately to his primary concept of field. Different forms of capital constitute a secondary concept, since all players bring resources to a particular field, but it is the field that determines to what extent these resources may be accumulated, circulated and exchanged. In short, the field defines which resources count as capital, and which do not. Therefore the resources that count in one field may not count in another. How does this apply to the evidence presented here about engagement mentoring in general, and about the mentor relationships at New Beginnings in particular?

The stories of the young people throw these issues into sharp relief, and again, Adrian is a prime example. He was able to add considerably to his very limited cultural and social resources through his experience of mentoring. He developed better communication skills, gained confidence in both personal and work situations, and raised his aspirations. He also gained important social resources: the support of his father to obtain independent housing, the skill to identify and bond with mentors in other situations, the ability to establish relationships with his peer group. However, although his resources increased dramatically compared with his previous situation, they did not count as capital within the narrow limitations imposed by the engagement mentoring field. His aspirations were deemed to be too high, and his new-found confidence was taken to imply he no longer needed support. Consequently, they came to appear not as cultural and social capital but as deficit and deviance, leading to Adrian's re-exclusion.

Sharon provides an extreme example of a different kind. Throughout her time at New Beginnings, she was seen by staff, and eventually by her mentor Karen, as an 'empty shell', as having 'no communication skills', no realistic career ambitions, and no work experience. She was also seen as a completely isolated individual.

At New Beginnings, her work placements kept failing, staff could not see any way forward for her, and they even suspected that she was manipulating them. Karen eventually railed against her as someone who just 'did not care' about bettering herself. Yet in her own community, it was possible to see the resources that Sharon possessed, however limited. She had a strong social network of neighbours, family and friends. She appeared confident within her community. She worked regularly, although in the grey economy, looking after children, which suggested that she was seen there as someone trustworthy and reliable. In the field of engagement mentoring, however, her cultural and social resources were not transformed into capital, but became invisible. Sharon became regarded as an 'empty' person, at best an embodiment of deficit, at worst a symbol of poor working-class deviance.

But what of mentors? Given that they are likely to start out with greater cultural and social capital than the young people, are they also likely to accumulate disproportionately more? This is not a simple equation. As the mentoring of socially excluded young people has expanded to unprecedented proportions, large numbers of volunteers are being drawn in, as at New Beginnings. Most receive far less training than the New Beginnings mentors (cf. Skinner and Fleming, 1999), and this contrasts sharply with the lengthy higher education courses, probationary work experience and professional qualifications traditionally demanded of practitioners working with socially excluded young people. Even many of those employed to undertake mentor roles, such as learning mentors and personal advisers in schools and *Connexions* services, are no longer given the opportunity to obtain professional-level qualifications, but are restricted to associate professional/technical qualifications such as the NVQ Level 3 in Advice and Guidance (Colley, 2001b). This is one of the ways in which mentoring serves to limit the cultural capital of those working in this field, and it is legitimated by the myths of Mentor. If mentoring is assumed to be an activity that comes 'naturally' to anyone, and if women are assumed to be 'naturally' caring, the skills involved become devalued. The predispositions and experiences which enable women to adapt to nurturing roles are indeed a form of resource, but they cannot be transformed into capital in the engagement mentoring field.

At New Beginnings, individual mentors were encouraged to volunteer with promises of enhanced cultural capital: the development of transferable skills useful in the labour market, a valuable addition to their CV and so on. Some mentors clearly gained resources that counted through their participation. Keith not only developed his ability to communicate and work with young people, but also made the social contacts with scheme staff that landed him a job at Cotswold House as a personal adviser in the *Learning Gateway*. Jane looked likely to find work as a professional mentor, although she preferred to pursue her contacts at the Probation Service. Their resources counted in the engagement mentoring field.

However, other mentors did not appear to have enhanced their cultural or social capital, and may even have lost out in this regard. Karen, Rachel and Yvonne all felt that they had lost confidence through their experiences at New Beginnings. For all their efforts, both Rachel and Yvonne felt that they could not declare their experience on their CV or job applications. Rachel feared that a bad reference might result. Yvonne 'dreaded' being asked about an experience she perceived as failure. She felt that her inability to reform Lisa as employable would make her appear less employable too. These perceptions arose from the tension between the goals of the scheme and the agency exercised by young people.

These examples show that care is needed in investigating the potential of mentoring to generate social and cultural capital for mentors or mentees. As with other outcomes of mentoring, individual experiences will differ and may often be contradictory. Most importantly, however, we have to understand how context affects these outcomes. It is not enough to hear (or worse still to assume) that participants have brought cultural and social resources to mentoring, or increased these resources through mentoring. We also need to ask whether the specific context – the field in which mentor relationships are located – allows these resources to count as capital, dismisses them as absent or lacking in worth, or constructs them negatively in terms of deficit and deviance.

The Bourdieuian framework, then, allows us to redefine engagement mentoring as a process of emotional labour that seeks to work upon and reform the habitus of both mentor and mentee. However, an understanding of habitus raises questions about the feasibility and the ethics of such a project. Combined with an understanding of the contextual field, it allows us to see how social inequalities may also be covertly produced and reproduced. This theoretical analysis suggests major flaws in policies to develop engagement mentoring as a key intervention for social inclusion, and calls into question the practices these policies promote. It also suggests that the evidence of the case stories is not simply idiosyncratic, but provides lessons that may be generalized more broadly. They are stories which demonstrate that engagement mentoring is indeed an impossible fiction.

There are many stories that still remain untold, many analyses and interpretations that could be offered:

> It is difficult to know where to end, when to stop reflecting on the clues uncovered in the last story, when to stop pointing out one more contradictory juxtaposition in the situation and the selves portrayed, and when to stop writing.
>
> (Ellis, 1995: 162, cited in Hodkinson *et al.*, 1996: 157)

However, I move on now to a final set of issues for the concluding chapter: in the light of this critical analysis and redefinition of engagement mentoring, what are the implications for policy, for practice and for future research? How can we reconceptualize mentoring for social inclusion in terms of possibility rather than fiction, in terms of empowerment rather than control?

Chapter 8

Mentoring for social inclusion
Issues for policy, practice and research

The relationship between research, policy and practice

> [R]esearch communities need researchers who try to make sense of the world by being close to it and who can disrupt assumptions about, for example, the motivations and actions of disadvantaged groups.
>
> (Edwards, 2002a: 165)

Throughout this book, my analysis has revealed many negative aspects of the engagement mentoring model. At times I have doubted the value of formal mentoring altogether, finding it difficult to envisage more progressive ways forward for such an individualized intervention. My own experiences, values and beliefs favour more collective ways of helping young people to become active citizens, which might help them to understand their position in the social and economic structures of the world, and then endeavour to change it. However, it is not within the scope of this book to elaborate a more radical approach to the problems of social exclusion and inequality. To do such alternative visions justice, I refer readers to educators such as Paula Allman (1999), Paolo Freire (1972), Glenn Rikowski (2001a) and Chris Searle (1997) (to name but a few), whose work has focused on the development of emancipatory educational practices.

The purpose of this final chapter is to present some cutting-edge issues for policy, practice and research, raising debates that will help the mentoring movement advance beyond its current limitations. The first set of issues relate to broad principles and effective approaches in mentoring for social inclusion. I then suggest recommendations for those directly involved in the practice of mentoring for social inclusion – including young people. Finally, I present an agenda for further research.

All of these conclusions raise at least as many questions as answers, as good research should. But it goes somewhat against the grain in today's climate, where the emphasis is on 'evidence-based practice' and the search for firm answers. Evidence-based practice privileges control-and-predict research, such as large-scale surveys and experimental trials, which claim to be objective and value-free. The hope is that they can tell policy-makers what works, and therefore also tell practitioners what they should do, with a high degree of certainty.

One problem with this approach is that it can silence the voices of those who are neither policy-makers, practitioners nor researchers: in this case, the young people who are treated as the raw material of the engagement mentoring experiment. Another problem is one that is rife in the field of mentoring as a whole: it is awash with guidelines for good practice, but these have done little to overcome the fundamental weaknesses of mentoring. Issuing more would only add to the problems of a movement which cannot see the wood for the trees. What the mentoring movement needs is clearer conceptualization and a sounder theoretical base.

This in turn requires a different perspective on research, one which rejects a laboratory-style approach, and challenges policy-makers' desire for certainty and simple prescriptions. Such a perspective does not aspire to evidence-based practice, but rather to theory-based policy and practice, and practice-based evidence. It suggests that more effective progress can be made by disrupting the assumptions on which policy is based, encouraging critical reflective practice in the field, and learning to live with uncertainty as an element of creative knowledge production (Atkinson, 2003; Edwards, 2002b; Warmington, 2003).

Responsible research is an engaged social science that grounds itself in the experiences of the field (Edwards, 2002a). It works with practitioners and other participants in the field to do justice to the meanings *they* make in practice, and to interpret those experiences in value-laden ways. In this way, research can focus productively on the future by asking 'big questions like "what kinds of learners for what kind of society?"' (Edwards, 2002a: 158). Not only does such an approach acknowledge the agency of all participants in mentoring for social inclusion, but it supports their agency as the driver for transformation. It advances a notion of reflective practice that seeks to challenge the deep-rooted power relations that impact on mentor relationships (cf. Issitt, 2000). So while I do not offer here a list of standards for mentoring practice, I will propose some fundamental recommendations for policy, for practice, and for future research.

These recommendations are driven by twin concerns. The first is that mentoring for social inclusion is here, and it appears to be here to stay for some time. Policy-makers are promoting mentoring; entire professions devoted to youth support – especially youth services and former careers services – are being drawn into mentoring; and many thousands of volunteers concerned about social exclusion are becoming involved. This simple fact means that researchers, however critical, have an obligation to go beyond exposing 'misrecognitions' and 'régimes of truth', important as this task may be. We cannot simply dismiss mentoring. We have a responsibility to raise issues and questions that can engage policy-makers and practitioners in dialogue and debate to advance our thinking about mentoring.

My second concern emerges from the voices of the young people who took part in this research. Although many of those around them – WellTEC and UoW managers, New Beginnings staff, mentors, and myself as the researcher – were losing faith in the mentoring process, the young people involved expressed far more positive views. They directed their efforts to making the most of mentoring for social inclusion, while setting their own terms within their mentor relationships. So I begin by reviewing this most important finding of my research: that young people value mentor relationships which they choose and negotiate themselves.

Making the most of mentoring for social inclusion

The stories from New Beginnings show that the young people almost always enjoyed their experience of mentoring, and placed a high value on their mentor relationships. They compared them favourably with other interventions they had encountered, especially with social workers and psychologists. They tried to use mentoring in constructive ways to pursue their own aspirations and agendas, and some of them perceived dramatic benefits as a result.

The nature of the sample inevitably reflects the minority of young people who decided to take up the option of mentoring at New Beginnings. Freedman (1999) notes that mentoring is not appropriate for all young people. Those whom we have met in this book were individuals who were disposed and able to establish ongoing relationships with the student volunteers. Most also wanted to enter the labour market, although not necessarily on the restricted terms offered at that scheme. However, all the young people identified some benefits from mentoring, and some of them – such as Adrian, Annette and Hayley – received crucial support from their mentors at difficult moments of transition. The benefits of one-to-one mentoring appeared to be realized most fully as the young people went on to more collective encounters with family, peers and community networks. This often led them to feel more socially included, though not in terms of the employment-related definition of social inclusion espoused by the present government. Mentoring made a difference, and in some cases that difference was profound.

This evidence reinforces the findings of previous research that has investigated the views of young people on mentor relationships, using qualitative methods to generate in-depth data. Ford (1999a), Freedman (1999) and Philip (1997, 2000a; Philip and Hendry, 1996) all concur: when young people are allowed to negotiate mentor relationships on the basis of their own needs and concerns, they usually perceive mentoring in a highly positive way, and can identify important benefits they have gained from the experience. Moreover, this individual work is not necessarily counterposed to group-based educational practices (Ford, 1999b), including those that have an emancipatory purpose. Evidence from a long tradition of informal community education (e.g. Foley, 1999; Fordham et al., 1979; Merton and Parrott, 1999) suggests that an initial period of one-to-one support may be a vital precursor for some members of marginalized and disadvantaged communities to be able to participate in collective learning that can lead to action for change. Mentoring can make a difference in this way too.

But there is a contradiction here. Some of the most successful mentor relationships at New Beginnings were ended abruptly by the young person's re-exclusion from the scheme. For some of these young people, their dismissal reinforced broader aspects of social exclusion. Adrian felt his chances of entering the labour market were growing slimmer as he lost access to youth support services after the age of 18. Hayley's future at college was uncertain: even if she was accepted for a course in childcare, she will have faced financial difficulties trying to study full-time beyond the age of 18. Similar problems also confronted Lisa. Although not dismissed from the New Beginnings scheme, Annette felt very strongly that she faced prejudice due to the influence of official discourses about teenage pregnancy and parenthood, and unfairness in the labour market due to welfare-to-work policies. The very benefits that young people had gained from mentoring – confidence, raised aspirations, support to pursue their own values – once again placed them beyond the narrow, employment-defined pale of social inclusion.

At the same time, UoW students who had made a substantial commitment as volunteer mentors at New Beginnings generally felt that the experience had been an anxious and demoralizing one. With the exceptions of Keith and Jane, rather than enhance their cultural capital with increased confidence to enter the labour market, mentoring had had the opposite effect for most of them, and we have seen the sharpest expressions of this loss of confidence from Rachel and Yvonne. Some mentors felt guilty because they could not achieve the outcomes expected by the scheme and some developed hostility towards their mentees as a result. Despite their best intentions to promote social inclusion in a broad sense, New Beginnings staff also suffered stress as they tried to ensure employment-related outcomes. As a consequence, the scheme degenerated in an atmosphere of denigration and blame.

The paradox is evident. The focus on 'hard' outcomes – the development of employability and progression into a limited range of youth training – undermined the benefits of 'soft' outcomes such as increased confidence, better health and higher aspirations. To all appearances, these young people had been offered intensive personal support, yet some had still refused to engage with the labour market. We can see how a discourse of blame against these individuals, and against the volunteer mentors, arose at New Beginnings. Thanks to the unrealistic goals of the engagement mentoring model, embedded in the design of the scheme, failure was often snatched from the jaws of success. How can this paradox be overcome? How can mentoring policies avoid such counterproductive results?

Mentoring is a 'soft' intervention

We saw in Chapter 2 that recent policies on youth support and guidance have begun to re-acknowledge the importance of soft outcomes. Nevertheless, hard, employment-related outcomes dominate mentoring for social inclusion, and determine the funding of services such as *Connexions*. The audit culture that prevails in our education system reinforces hard outcomes as the definitive measure of success. Policy-makers therefore insist that interventions are designed increasingly around outcomes that are easily measurable, sometimes irrespective of their feasibility in practice. In this climate, practitioners' objections to such targets are deflected by the difficulty of measuring soft outcomes at all. They are also silenced by the need to secure funding and to show that targets have been met, however creative the accounting for these targets may sometimes be. At the same time, researchers' evaluations of mentoring programmes reinforce these self-fulfilling prophecies, and perpetuate assumptions that mentoring *per se* is inherently beneficial. This makes it difficult to find points of engagement with constructive policy critique and with reflective practice. How can we break out of this vicious cycle?

Watts (2000) suggests that it is useful to apply the hard/soft distinction not only to the outcomes, but also to the *processes* of social interventions. His argument, advanced in relation to career development practice, can be applied equally well to mentoring. Dyadic helping interventions, based on personal interactions and relationships, should be seen as 'soft' instruments of policy. That is to say, they are processes that:

> work *through* individuals, rather than *on* them. At their heart is the notion of the 'active individual': that individuals should be encouraged to participate in determining their role in, and their contribution to, the society of which they are a part. They thus link individual needs to societal needs on a voluntaristic basis.
>
> (Watts, 2000: 303, original emphases)

This person-centred, voluntaristic principle has underpinned soft interventions such as guidance, counselling and youth work for decades, and, as Jane's approach to her relationship with Annette shows, could also inform mentoring. This would require, however, a recognition that engagement mentoring is not the only model. A range of models for mentoring exist, and alternatives might be both more equitable and more effective. The findings and analysis presented in this book can be linked with evidence from black and Asian models designed to challenge institutional racism (Forbes, 2000; Majors *et al.*, 2000), community and youth work models (Philip and Hendry, 1996; Philip, 1997; Smith, 2002), volunteer befriending (Forrest, 2002; Philip and Shucksmith, 2000), and professional mentoring interventions with vulnerable young people (Philip and Shucksmith, 2000). Taken as a whole, this body of research reveals that there is a broad spectrum of mentoring styles, ranging from highly informal, unplanned relationships to the formal, planned and prescribed approach that typifies engagement mentoring. The extremes of these styles are summarized in Table 8.1 (see Colley (2002), for a fuller discussion). They reinforce Gay and Stephenson's (1998) conclusion that more prescriptive approaches allow external interests to influence mentoring interventions, produce relationships that are essentially triadic rather than dyadic, and are therefore less empowering.

We could add another factor – that of funding – to those outlined in Table 8.1. Informal mentoring is either unfunded or, where it forms the basis of a looser planned model such as youth work or befriending, it is often difficult for

Table 8.1 Mentoring styles: informal and formal

Informal	Formal
Unplanned	Planned
Voluntary participation	Degree of compulsion
Individual goals	Policy and institutional goals
High level of negotiation	Low level of negotiation
Shared background and experiences	Social distance
High social intensity	Low to medium social intensity
Self-sought friendship	Relationship mediated by matching process
Indefinite time-span	Limited time-span
Less directive	More directive
Difficult to track	Intensely monitored on specific criteria
Located in familiar surroundings	Located in institutional settings
Relates to wider social ties and peer group	Focuses on individual
Rooted in the local community	Separate from local community

programmes to obtain funding. Engagement mentoring, on the other hand, now attracts central and long-term funding. This highlights policy-makers' preference for mentoring processes which appear to be more easily measured and controlled. Yet the overwhelming evidence from this and other studies is that informal approaches are the most effective. Models of mentoring for social inclusion should therefore demonstrate the following aspects as far as possible:

- low external control;
- high intentionality and voluntarism on the part of both mentor and mentee;
- person-centred goals rather than organizational goals;
- locus of decisions about goals should be internal to the dyad;
- open-ended (or less tightly limited) time frames;
- artificial relationships allowed to deepen into social and voluntary relationships;
- evaluation on the basis of participants' judgement and perceptions;
- awareness of and responsiveness to the 'field' or setting in which mentoring is located.

But what of the outcomes? Not only policy-makers, but those who run mentoring schemes, professionals who liaise with them, and mentors and mentees themselves, all have an interest in practical outcomes of mentoring that might promote social inclusion. Here there are two sets of contrasts that can be drawn from the available evidence. The first, summarized in Table 8.2, distinguishes between the ideal outcomes to which informal mentoring and formal mentoring aspire. The second, summarized in Table 8.3, distinguishes between the ideal outcomes of engagement mentoring and the actual outcomes that this model risks producing.

Table 8.2 Ideal outcomes of mentoring: informal and formal

Informal	Formal
Young people identify own needs	Expert diagnosis of young people's needs
Young people find ways to meet needs	Rectifying young people's skill deficits
Education for social and political awareness	Education for economic competitiveness
Active citizenship	Labour market entry
Allowing young people to experiment with and create new identities	Developing dispositions for employability in young people
Reducing alienation	Reducing crime and antisocial behaviour
Fostering solidarity within communities	Fostering solidarity between classes
Enhancing young people's existing social ties	Enhancing young people's social capital
Enhancing mentors' cultural capital	Enhancing mentors' cultural capital

Table 8.3 Ideal vs. potential outcomes of engagement mentoring

Ideal outcomes	Potential outcomes
Expert diagnosis of young people's needs	Young people's own needs ignored
Rectifying young people's skill deficits	Young people are pathologized
Education for economic competitiveness and interests	Pressure to comply with dominant norms
Labour market entry	Entry into low-paid and low-status opportunities; re-exclusion from the labour market; deflection from academic aspirations
Developing dispositions for employability in young people	Alienation
Reducing crime and antisocial behaviour	Increasing social prejudice against young people
Fostering solidarity between classes	Increased hostility of middle classes towards disadvantaged youth
Enhancing young people's social capital	Pathologizing existing social networks
Enhancing mentors' cultural capital	Limiting mentors' cultural capital

These contrasting outcomes, illustrated so well by the case stories at New Beginnings, suggest that the following should also be considered carefully when designing and implementing mentoring for social inclusion:

- the underlying political purposes for which mentoring is used;
- the underlying economic purposes for which mentoring is used;
- the association of mentoring with different types of knowledge and learning;
- the degree to which mentoring encourages individual passivity or collective citizenship and action;
- the degree to which mentoring reproduces or redresses social inequalities.

Today's policy-makers evidently – and understandably – wish to assert more formal control over mentoring in the hope of ensuring their targets for social inclusion are met. They therefore maintain mentoring on an individual basis, determine its goals, and prescribe the nature of the mentors' role in a 'hard' interventionist way. However, the contrast between the rhetoric of mentoring and the stories of mentoring at New Beginnings reveals how current policies for youth transition misunderstand social reality. Like previous policies before them, they are based on technical rationality (Hodkinson and Sparkes, 1995) and 'a fallacious view that a wide range of different interests and purposes can be combined in an unproblematic way' (Hodkinson *et al.*, 1996: 135).

As Watts (2001b) suggests, what is needed on the part of policy-makers is a self-denying ordinance. The 'soft' nature of mentoring interventions means that policy can only achieve its desired goals if, at the same time, it relinquishes these goals as the operating principle on which practice should be based. Such a stance would allow greater consonance with holistic practice:

> [An] issue here is the relationship between public objectives and private objectives, and how far public objectives are expected to impinge on . . . practice at the point of intervention. In particular, do policy-makers expect practitioners to pursue the public objectives in their dealing with an individual client; or are they willing to allow practitioners to address the individual's interests, in the confidence that, when aggregated, this will meet the public objectives too?
>
> (Watts, 2001b: 2)

The evidence from this study suggests that the control policy-makers exercise makes it difficult, in actual practice, to obtain the results they desire. While representing mentoring as a close *natural* bond, policies promote a model of *legal and artificial* mentor relationships designed to work *on* the habitus of mentors and mentees, rather than a model of *social and voluntary* relationships that work *through* individual's active participation and negotiation. This approach appears thoroughly contradictory. But why is it also so counterproductive?

Practical and ethical rationales for less directive mentoring

Soft interventions, often described as 'person-centred' or 'non-directive' (following Rogers, 1951, 1967), have a serious practical rationale. Egan's seminal work on skilled helping (1994) draws on a wealth of evidence that more directive styles of intervention simply do not work. They do not work because they evoke resistance, which blocks the client from solving problems and moving forward. To be effective, Egan argues, helping must have goals that are consistent with the client's own values, and the client must feel ownership of those goals. The helper therefore has a crucial responsibility to ensure that any targets set are genuinely determined by the client rather than by the helper or any other third party. Miller and Rollnick (1991) argue that this is true even for clients who demonstrate harmful behaviour, such as substance abuse, and that motivation for change has to be developed through a non-directive approach. The findings from this study of New Beginnings and from other research on mentor relationships (e.g. Freedman, 1999; Ford, 1999a; Ford *et al.*, 2003; Gay and Stephenson, 1998; Millwater and Yarrow, 1997; Philip, 1997, 2000a) support this view, demonstrating that externally imposed goals serve only to disempower mentees or to provoke their active resistance.

There is also an important ethical rationale for soft interventions, already suggested above: the principle that individuals have a right to self-determination, and that their participation in society should be a voluntary one. This means acknowledging diverse values, rather than imposing one normative value-system. The insistence on a unitary set of values in engagement mentoring represents a clash of values between policy-makers, professional practitioners or volunteer mentors, and young people involved in mentoring, that is likely to undermine success at best, and result in injustices at worst.

Law (2000) discusses the problem of 'system orientation' (see also Law, 1977, 1978, 1979), a term used to describe the pressures on practitioners to abandon ethical codes of practice, comply with official systems and targets, and promote the interests of dominant groupings over those of individual clients. When policy becomes overprescriptive, practitioners who maintain a person-centred stance may find their situation becomes untenable, or even face punitive legal sanctions. He cites the highly publicized case of two youth workers at a Cambridge hostel for socially excluded youth, who were prosecuted and imprisoned for keeping residents' drug use confidential from the police. Their intention had been to build trusting relationships as a basis to help these young people, rather than enforcing rules in a way that might alienate them altogether, but they paid a heavy personal price for practising their professional ethics.

Law suggests a range of similar instances in which *Connexions* personal advisers might similarly fall foul of legislation, in supporting clients whose values and aspirations do not fit the policy mould. We have also seen how mentors at New Beginnings felt under pressure to promote the employment-related goals of the scheme. As we can see from their different responses to this pressure and to their mentees' resistance, some were more likely to comply with official expectations than others. However, the majority – including even the most radical-minded individuals such as Keith and Rachel – experienced painful pressures of self-surveillance, and curbed expression of their own identities and beliefs as they internalized the values of the scheme. This suggests that the design of mentoring programmes should try to minimize the pressures of system orientation, and allow mentors and mentees a greater degree of autonomy in developing their relationships.

Engagement mentoring thus finds itself in an unethical and impractical paradox – an impossible fiction – because despite the centrality of the human bond to mentoring, this model is centred on 'delivery rather than relationship' (Smith, 2002: 8). A more ethically and practically tenable paradox in mentoring for social inclusion might therefore be that a 'hands-off' approach to policy proves more likely to achieve the outcomes they desire for larger numbers of young people. But other outcomes might also be beneficial. What shifts might encourage less prescriptive approaches to policy in mentoring for social inclusion, and maximize the benefits to young people?

Policy shifts for social inclusion

As we have seen, engagement mentoring focuses on the need to alter the beliefs and attitudes of socially excluded young people. Here, I argue that two shifts are required in the beliefs and attitudes of others towards socially excluded youth. Furthermore, young people's beliefs and attitudes towards employment could indeed be altered, but this may require some 'hard' interventions on the part of government. However, such interventions would need to be of a very different character than that of engagement mentoring.

Thinking differently about social exclusion

The first policy shift I propose relates to the meanings we ascribe to the term 'social exclusion' (and similar terms such as 'at risk', 'disaffected' or 'hardest to help'). Watts (1999) argues that current UK policy interprets social exclusion as a combination of deficit and deviance in those who are socially excluded. This is then expressed, as we saw in Chapter 1, in lists of personal characteristics attributed to disadvantaged youth, which focus on their presumed shortcomings, ranging from disability and lack of qualifications to fecklessness and criminality.

These lists pervade official documents and impact powerfully on mentors, because they are used (as in the Youthstart Initiative and *Connexions*) to define target groups for intervention. They figure in initial training and induction programmes, in policy guidelines for service delivery, and in team meetings discussing the day-to-day implementation of mentoring. Practitioners are forced to characterize young people according to these categories, and mentoring for social inclusion becomes centred on fixing deficits and reforming deviance (Colley, 2001a). But if mentoring is seen as a means to 'top up' the social and cultural capital of young people and to work on their habitus, this approach makes it hard to recognize the existing resources they possess, and easy to dismiss the social networks in which they are included. Making the most of mentoring for social inclusion also means making the most of resources that young people bring to the process.

A more productive way to understand social exclusion is to see it as a process that society inflicts on disadvantaged young people, rather than as a characteristic of young people themselves. In this light, it is no longer young people who appear as a threat to society: society and its unequal structures constitute a threat to young people. Their disengagement from formal education, training and employment may therefore be seen as a rational form of disaffection, in some cases at least (Ford, 1999a; Williamson and Middlemiss, 1999). Such a view rejects the way that current policies on youth transitions are:

> so commonly expressed now in the reductionist terms of the requirements of international economic competitiveness, [and] are almost exclusively concerned with the production of future workers with particular skills or dispositions. . . . [T]he work ethic and human capital theory generate between them a very utilitarian version of what it is to be a young person in contemporary society.
>
> (Maguire *et al.*, 2001: 199)

Altering the policy discourse from social *exclusion* back to social *inequality* would mean that, rather than looking for ways to 'improve' young people, we could start by acknowledging the positive resources they possess. Using the framework based on Bourdieu's ideas outlined in Chapter 7, instead of trying to reform individuals' habitus, attention could be turned to the 'field', and those aspects of education, training and employment fields which render so many young people's resources worthless. How can policy-makers and practitioners start to address the problems posed by institutional settings and systems, rather than focusing on individuals? How can the nature of the field be changed to allow their resources to function as social and cultural capital? How can we avoid the impossible fiction in which policies reverse the roles of structure and agency, by expecting individuals – socially excluded young people and their mentors – to create solutions to problems that are rooted in social structures (Colley and Hodkinson, 2001)?

Changing attitudes towards socially excluded youth

To alter the field means engaging in ongoing advocacy and systems change (cf. Hopson and Scally, 1979), challenging deeply entrenched cultures in education and training systems and among employers. In 1996, Hodkinson *et al.* claimed that 'the evidence of deep-seated inequalities in the youth labour market in the UK, linked to structural divisions of class, gender, and ethnicity, is overwhelming' (1996: 154). As I write seven years later, this claim is no less true. The Equal Opportunities Commission have just released their annual statistics (Equal Opportunities Commission, 2003). Their report shows that government-supported youth training, like the labour market as a whole, remains heavily gender stereotyped, with the vast majority of young women entering work in personal services, and the vast majority of young men entering craft-related trades. These young women will go on to earn just 75 per cent of their male counterparts' rates of pay. Those from ethnic minority groups are two and a half times as likely to be unemployed as whites, and the disabled have only half the chance of finding work as the able-bodied. These trends are clearly reflected in young people's trajectories in Wellshire and in the opportunities on offer at New Beginnings, as we saw in Chapter 3.

Young people experiencing these inequalities do need support and advocacy at an individual level, as well as through careers education, to expand their own horizons for action. But this does not in itself address the structural obstacles and discrimination they face from others. Disappointingly, discussion of these issues is entirely absent from policy documents analysing social exclusion, such as *Bridging the Gap*. Structural problems require structural solutions, and these require political advocacy with those who control the training and employment markets. Unfortunately, the youth support and guidance services that should provide such advocacy have a poor track record in challenging gender and racial stereotyping or discrimination (Rolfe, 1999; Wrench and Hassan, 1996; Wrench and Qureshi, 1996).

Mentoring for social inclusion should aim to transform others' attitudes, values, behaviours, beliefs that discriminate against disadvantaged youth, as well as institutional discrimination and other barriers. A small number of black and Asian mentoring projects have tried to take this approach, as we saw in Chapter 1. However, the difficulties they encountered suggest that this is a difficult and long-term process that is unlikely to produce the swift results politicians need to achieve. It is also deeply challenging for individual mentors to confront institutional racism in this way. Altering the field also requires government-led policies to promote some 'hard' interventions in relation to social and economic structures.

'Hard' interventions for social inclusion

The policy analysis I have undertaken here, along with the evidence of the mentor training and staff attitudes at New Beginnings, show that socially excluded young people often stand accused of failing to value the benefits of youth training and of paid employment. Mentors such as Jane, Karen and Yvonne came to feel frustration, as they encountered their mentees' resistance to the placements on offer. This reinforced official explanations that young people exclude themselves, because they do not value the opportunities open to them. Once again, there is something of a reversal of the social and economic realities here. We could pose the issue very differently, by asking the question: What signs do others, in positions of power and authority, give about the value of these opportunities?

Just one example, which is particularly relevant to the situation of young people at New Beginnings, is the level of the minimum training allowance paid to 16- and 17-year-olds. At only £40 per week, it is less than half the income officially regarded as the 'poverty line' (£103 per week), and has fallen dramatically in real terms since it was first introduced twenty years ago (Chatrik and Convery, 1999). As Williamson and Middlemiss (1999) point out, deciding that youth training is a 'mug's game', and turning to the 'grey' economy instead, is a conclusion that is far from irrational for many disadvantaged young people. Access to financial independence and the ability to consume cultural and leisure goods are important signifiers of the transition to adulthood – and of personal success – in the globalized world. So there is a serious contradiction here too. Policies expect socially excluded young people to value youth training as a transition route to adulthood and the labour market, and demand that they accept the discipline imposed on adult workers in order to become employable. Yet the low level of the training allowance seems to treat young people as children, assuming they will remain dependent on their families. The signal this is likely to give out is that powerful stakeholders do not themselves value these opportunities. Hard intervention by government to increase the allowance, or greater willingness on the part of employers to add to the allowance, might therefore be far more effective mechanisms than mentoring to dispose young people more favourably towards training opportunities. Of course, Lisa's and Hayley's stories also show that work-based training is not the automatic solution to disengagement.

Many similar hard interventions could be suggested: tackling low pay in employment; introducing positive discrimination to regulate against inequalities in the labour market; imposing a legal obligation on employers to be proactive in providing quality education and training for young people, rather than the current situation which places the burden of demanding this right on young people themselves. Such issues are not only for policy-makers. They are also issues for those involved in mentoring at the level of practice, who should advocate with policy-makers for systems change, rather than seeking only to change young people to fit existing systems.

This leads to a number of recommendations for those involved in mentoring at the level of practice: mentors, programme staff, managers *and* the young people who become mentees are all part of my intended audience here. These recommendations are premised on a fundamental belief that practice can be improved by gaining a deeper understanding of mentoring and the issues that surround it. A series of questions at the end of each recommendation also suggests criteria by which mentors (volunteers and professionals alike) and mentees (and their families or support workers) might judge the quality of mentor programmes and make decisions about becoming involved.

Recommendations for practice

Critical reflection involves awareness of and commitment to anti-oppressive practice, that seeks to understand and change the social and political context of practice, as well as actions of practitioners. While technical expertise is necessary we need to beware of seeking formulae to deal with difficult situations, which may require spontaneity and complex judgements. This involves building 'a cycle of critical reflection to maximise the capacity for critical thought, and produces a sense of professional freedom and a connection with rather than a distance from clients' (Pietroni, 1995: 43).

(Issitt, 2002: 75)

Engage in critical reflective practice

This recommendation underpins all those that follow. Reflective practice has become a well-worn phrase in the education and welfare professions, but I use it here with the specific meaning outlined by Issitt in the above quotation. This definition of reflective practice is particularly appropriate in the field of mentoring, where we have seen that 'connection with' mentees is of the essence, but all too often degenerates into 'distance from' them, as habitus resists reform and the alienating effects of emotional labour come into operation. Those involved in mentoring need to set aside time to reflect on what is happening in mentor relationships and in the settings which create them. Such reflection may be more effective if it is undertaken as a collective process within support networks, be they for mentors or for young people being mentored, rather than as 'a private affair that is about survival' (Issitt, 2000: 131).

- To what extent does the mentoring programme create space for critical reflection and welcome the challenges from mentors and mentees that might ensue?
- Why have you become involved in mentoring?
- What aims do you hope to achieve through mentor relationships, and what are the aims of others?

Overcome the atomizing effects of individual mentoring

As I have argued above, individual mentoring may be a necessary precursor to involving some socially excluded young people in more inclusive group activities. However, the danger is that the experience of mentoring remains atomized, as it did for the mentors and mentees at New Beginnings. This made it difficult for most of them to resist the official version of mentoring, which marginalized the needs and desires of young people as well as the advocacy that some of their mentors undertook. Programmes should provide mentors with opportunities to come together to engage in collective reflection on their practice, and, where such opportunities are not made available by scheme managers, mentors should try to create them. They should also negotiate with the young person the benefits of engaging in collective activity with their peers.

- How can mentors and mentees find ways to come together, even where explicit opportunities may not be provided by the scheme, or where these opportunities are dominated by other agendas?
- How can young people's interests be placed at the centre of mentoring?

Understand mentoring more clearly

Those involved in mentoring – not only implementing it, but also planning and designing it – need to read the available in-depth research on mentor relationships with young people in order to develop a clearer understanding of the mentoring process. Awareness of a range of models beyond engagement mentoring allows informed choices about the most appropriate form of mentoring to adopt, and the spectra of mentoring styles and outcomes already outlined in this chapter (summarized in Tables 8.1, 8.2 and 8.3) will be of help. They focus attention on the power dynamics of mentor relationships, and how different institutional arrangements can facilitate more empowering or more directive practice.

- How do the institutional arrangements for mentoring shape the power dynamics of mentor relationships?
- Do they preserve these relationships as dyadic rather than triadic?
- Do they encourage the voluntary and intentional participation of mentees, or does compulsion – overt or subtle – influence their involvement?
- Where are the goals of mentoring decided, and by whom?

Question myths of Mentor

Practitioners need to unravel the stories that are told about mentoring – including much of the available research – and to examine whether they are based on appropriate evidence. They also need to question the rhetoric and myth that surround mentoring, and to use the discussion in Chapter 2 to help them make judgements about research reports. By thinking about the stories of mentoring that are told and those that are left untold, it is possible to tease out assumptions about the mentor's role. These assumptions may be informed by dominant power relations, especially gender relations that maintain the oppression of women and involve them in emotional labour. These can result in subtle but intense exploitation of women's stereotyped role as carers and nurturers.

- What is the purpose of each research report?
- Whose voices are heard in research?
- How is the mentor's role constructed?
- What emotional demands does this role place upon mentors?
- What mentor support is provided by the mentoring programme?
- Does it offer both personal and collective opportunities for support?
- How far does it acknowledge the emotional demands of mentoring?
- How can mentors protect themselves against overburdening expectations?
- How can they avoid self-sacrifice that may lead to feelings of alienation and resentment towards their mentee?

Reflect on theories of power in mentoring

In Chapter 7, I showed that a theory of power underpins each particular framework for mentoring. Participants in mentoring should reflect on these theories of power, test them out against their own experiences and personal or professional values, and consider how their own practice can be shaped by this understanding. Some responses might be to alter one's practice, or alternatively to challenge other stakeholders' approaches, or aspects of institutional arrangements.

- What understanding of power underpins mentoring in each particular situation?
- How does this affect the mentoring process?

Analyse the role of the 'field'

Using Bourdieu's concept of 'field' can help us to think about the relative positioning of different players in mentoring. We can use it to ask who dominates the field and who is subordinate within it. This moves away from criticism of young people for self-exclusion, and it moves away from criticism of individual mentors and staff when things go wrong. It helps all involved to think about the context in which mentoring takes place. It reveals constraints upon agency, as well as the spaces in which less powerful players – mentees and mentors – can exercise agency and advance their own aspirations and values.

- Who are the players in the mentoring field, and what power relations exist between them?
- What are the underlying social, political and/or economic purposes for which mentoring is being used?
- Does mentoring encourage individual passivity and acquiescence, or promote active citizenship that might challenge inequalities in the status quo?

Understand the implications of 'habitus'

Bourdieu's other main concept, habitus, is a theoretical tool that can be enormously helpful when applied in practice. Here, it can help us respect the being of persons involved in mentor relationships. Thinking about habitus is a way of acknowledging others in a genuinely holistic way, and understanding how their horizons for action have evolved. They are delineated both by individual dispositions and choices that are susceptible to change (although this is rarely predictable), as well as by collective and social structures of class, gender and race that are deeply internalized, and which are therefore very difficult to change. Such a perspective helps avoid a deficit model of mentoring.

- What are the life histories and background experiences of partners in mentor relationships?
- How do these shape their participation in mentoring?
- How are their horizons for action and career trajectories affected by structures and structural inequalities?
- What sort of change in habitus is anticipated by each mentoring programme?

- Does mentoring seek to work *on* or *through* the persons involved?
- How feasible are expectations of change?

Think differently about social exclusion

It may be more effective and less stressful for those involved in mentoring to think of social exclusion as a process that society imposes on its most disadvantaged members, rather than as a set of characteristics attributed to them. Mentors and programme staff should avoid pathologizing socially excluded young people, and this can be done partly by focusing on social inequalities and institutional discrimination, and the ways in which these affect young people's futures. They should be aware of potentially punitive consequences of re-exclusion that can unintentionally be built into scheme designs, especially if mentor relationships are tied to 'hard' outcomes that are inappropriate or unachievable for some young people.

- What are the meanings that are given to 'social exclusion'?
- How do they impact on the mentoring process?
- How does the scheme propose to address discrimination, stereotyping and structural obstacles faced by young people?
- What are the risks of re-exclusion in this scheme?
- How can these risks be minimized?

Think differently about social inclusion

Rather than adopting an approach that seeks to fix young people's deficits and deviance, and fit them into narrowly drawn boundaries of social inclusion defined primarily by paid employment, we can think about the challenge quite differently. The social, economic and legal boundaries of social inclusion could be expanded, so that fewer young people are made to experience exclusion, and so that it is easier to escape marginalization. This means sustained advocacy with those who are more powerful in the field (in Bourdieu's sense), to change attitudes towards socially excluded youth, and to encourage 'hard' interventions and structural changes on the part of policy-makers.

- How and where are the boundaries of social inclusion drawn?
- What conditions are imposed on young people when they seek routes out of marginalization?
- What advocacy (including self-advocacy on the part of young people) is needed to challenge narrow definitions of social inclusion?

Allow young people's resources to act as social and cultural capital

Those involved in mentoring should acknowledge and promote the acceptance of multiple cultures and value-systems, rather than assuming unitary values. They should be aware of the potential for dominant groupings to impose their values and interests at the expense of both mentors and mentees. In particular, those involved in mentoring should pay positive attention to the resources that young people bring with them, including social networks and streetwise skills. Mentoring offers a potential space to explore how the 'field' might be changed to allow young people's resources to circulate, accumulate and exchange as social and cultural capital, instead of ruling them out as invalid currency.

- How can we interpret young people's knowledge, skills, experiences and values in the most positive way?
- What changes do we need to make to the rules and conditions of the 'field', so that young people's resources can count as capital?

These recommendations do not address the day-to-day detail of how to do mentoring, but propose ways to overcome the basic flaws of the mentoring movement: its lack of conceptual clarity and its weak theoretical base. My belief and hope is that such understanding will be a great deal more empowering for all of those partners than a list of 'action points', because it allows them to locate their individual interactions in the wider context. I move on finally to consider some issues for future research.

Further research is needed on emotional labour

Whitehead *et al.* (2002) describe the experiences of a small sample of *Connexions* personal advisers devoting themselves to 'going the extra mile' on behalf of young socially excluded clients. Their findings echo aspects of mentors' experiences at New Beginnings:

> External influences on the personal adviser's role come through the frame of reference through which they work. And it was through these external influences that the interviewees chose to express a mixture of feelings. Some seemed to have a balanced mix of feelings where their anger at 'the system' and sadness for their clients' situations was balanced by their sense of reward when clients were able to overcome their difficulties. Others, however, felt almost overwhelmed by their feelings of frustration and helplessness, and by the seemingly relentless nature of the job.
>
> (Whitehead *et al.*, 2002: 31)

They question the adequacy of supervision arrangements to help personal advisers cope with the emotional stress of such work, but also highlight the way this stress was created by structural problems that they, as individuals, could not resolve:

The interviewees who had experience of placing young people in bed and breakfast accommodation were universal in their condemnation of the practice. Not only were they filled with anger at having to place young people in 'horrendous' conditions, but they also suffered feelings of guilt about doing so. There was a sense that this act alone confirmed that they were failing in their role 'to ensure the best start in life for every young person' [the slogan of *Connexions*]. . . . The severity and diversity of the difficulties faced by homeless young people can have a significant emotional impact on personal advisers working with them. Personal adviser training seems to be inadequate to equip those who take on the role with coping strategies to help them maintain their own equilibrium. . . . This situation is far from ideal.

(Whitehead *et al.*, 2002: 31)

Such problems are unlikely to be resolved, however, without policy-makers and practitioners acknowledging and understanding the nature and effects of emotional labour. As I showed in Chapter 7, the highly gendered allocation of emotion work is linked to the subordinate and oppressed status of women in our society. This means that it usually goes unrecognized within caring roles. It tends to be undervalued, making it difficult to provide adequate training and support mechanisms, since complex skills are interpreted merely as dispositions that are supposed to 'come naturally' to women. Of course, men in such roles are also affected in their day-to-day practice by these assumptions.

It is difficult to suggest how the emotional burden on mentors and others in similar roles can be overcome without further research. Since the 1980s, there has been little research on emotional labour that goes beyond descriptions of caring and customer service work. With the notable exception of Bates' work on the training of care assistants (1990, 1991, 1994a), there is little that explores the role of education and training in preparing people for this aspect of caring roles. Recent reports on *Connexions* by the education inspectorate (OFSTED, 2002) and the ICG (2003) indicate that arrangements to support personal advisers through supervision are still unclear, and have not yet been implemented across the service. The analysis I have offered here of emotional labour in the work of mentors should be tested out more broadly among other groups of mentors and personal advisers. More theoretical work also needs to be done to understand emotion from a critical perspective, particularly its function in education and training and employment at all levels. The work of James (1989) and Heller (1979) on the social regulation of feeling, and that of Bates (1990, 1991, 1994a) and Colley *et al.* (2002) on the reproduction of class and gender through vocational education and training, indicate the potential for both empirical work and theory-building, and offer a small but valuable knowledge base from which to pursue research in this area.

For independent qualitative research on mentoring

I end by reiterating the assertions made by Merriam (1983) twenty years ago. We need more research into mentor relationships, and we need research that is qualitative and interpretive. We need to be open to evidence that surprises us, and we need to value less certain but possibly deeper truths, 'seeking to understand traces, influences and meanings' (Edwards, 2002a: 166). Research should investigate the experience of mentoring in relation to the participants' life histories and habitus. It should also locate mentoring within its specific context or field, revealing the power relations between stakeholders, and analysing those dimensions of the field that influence the style of mentoring and its outcomes. While quantitative surveys have their part to play in providing a background picture of the mentoring movement, they cannot provide insights into mentoring processes, and we need to understand these far better. In-depth, qualitative methods allow participants to tell their own stories and express more fully their experiences, sentiments and beliefs. This is particularly important if young mentees' voices are to be heard.

No research is entirely without bias, and is always influenced by the values of the researcher. However, I have argued that research into mentoring has been unacceptably biased until now, in ways that have been harmful to both mentees and mentors. It has been flawed by assumptions that mentoring is inherently beneficial, irrespective of its design and context, and by the conformative pressures on evaluation research that is linked to funding. Researchers investigating mentoring must make their own perspective and values thoroughly clear, so that others can judge their findings appropriately. From my own standpoint, I argue that more needs to be done to investigate mentoring through the lens of social inequalities: class, gender, race, sexuality and disability are all issues that arose, some more centrally than others, in this one, small-scale study.

In turn, practitioners and policy-makers should take critical research seriously, and engage with its findings. Smith's (2002) recent critique of *Connexions* raised many of the problems that I have analysed in engagement mentoring here: its 'limited and limiting view of young people' (p. 6), its surveillance and control over young people and those working with them, and its narrow employment-related goals. Tom Wylie, chief executive of the National Youth Agency (NYA), responded in defence of government policy, describing Smith's case as 'a rather tired '70s argument about social control' (NYA, 2003). But if we are genuinely to tackle the injustice of social exclusion, critical analyses should not be dismissed in this way. Wylie's response tends to suggest that the discourse of social *inclusion* may be silencing debate about social *inequality*. Rather than producing simplistic statements of 'what works', research on mentoring should be used to develop our thinking about what *happens*, in all its diversity. Only this can help us to understand how mentoring works, and how it works differently for different people in different situations. This sort of knowledge is likely to be more empowering for mentors, and for managers of mentoring initiatives, than good practice guidelines which ignore the complex realities they actually face.

There are many stories that remain untold in this book, and, as I complete it, there are already new angles and themes that I wish to pursue in the future. I hope that readers will have gained new insights of their own into mentoring from the stories I have told here. They are a few among many threads that could have been followed, but I believe my tales of mentoring are better than many. They tell a deeper truth, and that truth is worth telling in the name of social justice. Whether others agree or disagree, if this book creates space for critical discussion and debate about mentoring, it will have been a success.

References

Ahier, J. (1996) 'Explaining economic decline and teaching children about industry: some unintended continuities?', in J. Ahier, B. Cosin and M. Hales (eds) *Diversity and Change: Education, Policy and Selection*, London: Routledge.

Aldridge, S., Halpern, D. and Fitzpatrick, S. (2002) *Social capital: a discussion paper*. Online. Available HTTP: <http://www.cabinet-office.gov.uk/innovation/2001/futures/social capital.pdf> (accessed 10 July 2002).

Alleman, E. (1986) 'Measuring mentoring – frequency, quality, impact', in W.A. Gray and M.M. Gray (eds) *Mentoring: Aid to Excellence in Career Development, Business and the Professions Vol. II*, Vancouver: International Association for Mentoring.

Allman, P. (1999) *Revolutionary Social Transformation: Democratic Hopes, Political Possibilities and Critical Education*, Westport, CT: Bergin and Garvey.

Almond, B. (1991) 'Human bonds', in B. Almond and D. Hill (eds) *Applied Philosophy: Morals and Metaphysics in Contemporary Debate*, London: Routledge.

Anderson, E.M. and Lucasse Shannon, A. (1995) 'Toward a conceptualisation of mentoring', in T. Kerry and A.S. Shelton Mayes (eds) *Issues in Mentoring*, London: Routledge.

Anderson, G. (1989) Critical ethnography in education: origins, current status and new directions, *Review of Educational Research*, 59, 3: 249–270.

Armstrong, P. and Zukas, M. (1997) Power, peers and professional development: the diversity of mutual learning, *SCUTREA 1996 Conference Proceedings*, Leeds: University of Leeds.

Atkinson, E. (2003) '"Producing different knowledge and producing knowledge differently": postmodernism and the possibilities for educational research', paper presented at the Annual Conference of the American Educational Research Association, New Orleans, April 2000, under the title: 'What can postmodern thinking do for educational research?'

Avis, J., Bloomer, M., Esland, G., Gleeson, D. and Hodkinson, P. (1996) *Knowledge and Nationhood: Education, Politics and Work*, London: Cassell.

Baistow, K. (1994/95) Liberation and regulation? Some paradoxes of empowerment, *Critical Social Policy*, 42: 34–46.

Ball, S.J., Maguire, M. and Macrae, S. (2000) *Choices, Pathways and Transitions Post-16: New Youth, New Economies in the Global City*, London: RoutledgeFalmer.

Barthes, R. (1972) *Mythologies*, London: Cape.

Bates, I. (1990) No bleeding, whining Minnies: the role of YTS in class and gender reproduction, *British Journal of Education and Work*, 3, 2: 91–110.

—— (1991) Closely observed training: an exploration of links between social structures, training and identity, *International Studies in Sociology of Education*, 1: 225–243.

—— (1994a) 'A job which is "right for me"? Social class, gender and individualization', in I. Bates and G. Riseborough (eds) *Youth and Inequality*, Buckingham: Open University Press.

—— (1994b) ' "When I have my own studio . . . ": the making and shaping of "designer" careers', in I. Bates and G. Riseborough (eds) *Youth and Inequality*, Buckingham: Open University Press.

Bayliss, V. (1998) Redefining work: careers guidance tomorrow, *Careers Guidance Today*, 6, 4: 16–17.

Beck, U. (1992) *Risk Society: Towards a New Modernity*, London: Sage.

Benioff, S. (1997) *A Second Chance: Developing Mentoring and Education Projects for Young People*, London: Commission for Racial Equality/Crime Concern.

Blair, T. (1999) Foreword, in Social Exclusion Unit, *Bridging the Gap: New Opportunities for 16–18 Year Olds*, London: The Stationery Office.

Blechman, E.A. (1992) Mentors for high risk minority youth: from effective communication to bicultural competence, *Journal of Clinical Psychology*, 21, 2: 160–169.

Bourdieu, P. (1986) *Distinction: A Social Critique of the Judgement of Taste*, London: Routledge.

—— (1989a) *The Field of Power*, unpublished lecture, University of Wisconsin at Madison, April.

—— (1989b) The corporatism of the universal: the role of intellectuals in the modern world, *Telos*, 81, Fall: 99–110.

Bourdieu, P. and Wacquant, L.J.D. (1992) *An Invitation to Reflexive Sociology*, Cambridge: Polity Press.

Bridges, W. (1998) Career development in a new key, *Careers Guidance Today*, 6, 3: 9–14.

Brine, J. (1998) The European Union's discourse of 'equality' and its education and training policy within the post-compulsory sector, *Journal of Education Policy*, 13, 1: 137–152.

Casson, M. (1979) *Youth Unemployment*, London: Macmillan.

Chatrik, B. and Convery, P. (1999) *A third of TECs pay only minimum training allowances*, *Working Brief*, 102. Online. Available HTTP: <http://www.cesi.org.uk/_newsite2002/publications/wb/w102/trnallow.htm> (accessed 23 January 2003).

Cochran-Smith, M. and Paris, C.L. (1995) 'Mentor and mentoring: did Homer have it right?', in J. Smyth (ed.) *Critical Discourses on Teacher Development*, London: Cassell.

Cohen, P. (1986) *Rethinking the Youth Question*, London: Post-16 Education Centre/Youth and Policy.

Colley, H. (2000a) 'Deconstructing "realism" in career planning: how globalisation impacts on vocational guidance', in K. Roberts (ed.) *Careers Guidance Constructing the Future: A Global Perspective*, Richmond: Trotman/Institute of Careers Guidance.

—— (2000b) 'Mind the Gap: policy goals and young people's resistance in a mentoring scheme', paper presented at British Educational Research Association Annual Conference, Cardiff University, September 2000.

—— (2001a) An ABC of mentors' talk about disaffected youth: Alternative lifestyles, Benefit dependency, or Complete dunces? *Youth and Policy*, 72: 1–15.

—— (2001b) Righting re-writings of the myth of Mentor: a critical perspective on career guidance mentoring, *British Journal of Guidance and Counselling*, 29, 2: 177–198.

—— (2001c) 'Understanding experiences of engagement mentoring for "disaffected" young people and their student mentors: problems of data analysis in qualitative research', paper presented at British Educational Research Association Annual Conference, University of Leeds, September 2001.

—— (2001d) 'Unravelling myths of Mentor: power dynamics of mentoring relationships with "disaffected" young people', unpublished Ph.D. thesis, Manchester Metropolitan University.

—— (2002) 'Mentoring – a case study of informal learning becoming formalised', working paper for the Learning and Skills Development Agency project 'Non-formal Learning: Mapping the Conceptual Terrain', University of Leeds.

—— (2003) Engagement mentoring for socially excluded youth: problematising an 'holistic' approach to creating employability through the transformation of habitus, *British Journal of Guidance and Counselling*, 31, 1: 77–98.

Colley, H. and Hodkinson, P. (2001) Problems with 'Bridging the Gap': the reversal of structure and agency in addressing social exclusion, *Critical Social Policy*, 21, 3: 337–361.

Colley, H., James, D. and Tedder, M. (2002) 'Becoming the "right person for the job": vocational habitus, gender and learning cultures in Further Education', paper presented at Learning and Skills Research Network Annual Conference, University of Warwick, December 2002.

Conkey, M.W. (1991) 'Original narratives: the political economy of gender in archaeology', in M. diLeonardo (ed.) *Gender at the Crossroads of Knowledge: Feminist Anthropology in the Postmodern Era*, Berkeley: UCL.

Delamont, S. (1999) 'Confessions of a ragpicker', in H. Hodkinson (ed.) *Feminism and Educational Research Methodologies*, Manchester: Manchester Metropolitan University.

DeMarco, R. (1993) Mentorship: a feminist critique of current research, *Journal of Advanced Nursing*, 18, 8: 1242–1250.

Department for Education and Employment (DfEE) (1996) *Equipping Young People for Working Life: A Consultative Document on Improving Employability through the 14–16 Curriculum*, Rotherham: Cambertown (Ref. CD1).

—— (1997) *Labour Market Quarterly Report, November 1997*, Sheffield: DfEE Skills and Enterprise Network.

—— (1998a) *The Learning Age: A Renaissance for a New Britain*, London: HMSO.

—— (1998b) *Moving On 1997: Pathways Taken by Young People Beyond 16*, Sudbury: DfEE Publications.

—— (1999a) *Attack on youth dropout goes nationwide*. Online. Available HTTP: <http://www.dfee.gov.uk/news/96.htm> (accessed 3 November 1999).

—— (1999b) *Ethnic minority pupils must have the opportunity to fulfil their potential*. Online. Available HTTP: <http://www.dfee.gov.uk/news/90.htm> (accessed 3 November 1999).

—— (1999c) *Prime Minister and David Blunkett launch action plan – inner city education*. Online. Available HTTP: <http://www.dfee.gov.uk/news/126.htm> (accessed 3 November 1999).

—— (1999d) *Learning to Succeed: A New Framework for Post-16 Learning*, London: The Stationery Office.

—— (1999e) *A Guide to Relevant Practice in The Learning Gateway for 16 & 17 Year Olds*, Nottingham: DfEE Publications.

—— (2000a) *The Connexions Strategy Document*, Nottingham: DfEE Publications (Ref. CX2).

—— (2000b) *Labour Market and Skill Trends 2000*, Nottingham: Skills and Enterprise Network/DfEE Publications (Ref. SEN 373).

—— (2000c) *Skills for All: Proposals for a National Skills Agenda – Final Report of the National Skills Task Force*, Sudbury: DfEE Publications (Ref. SK728).

Dishion, T.J., McCord, J. and Poulin, F. (1999) When interventions harm: peer groups and problem behaviour, *American Psychologist*, 54, 9: 755–764.

Dondero, G.M. (1997) Mentors: beacons of hope, *Adolescence*, 32, 128: 881–886.

DuBois, D.L. and Neville, H.A. (1997) Youth mentoring: investigation of relationship characteristics and perceived benefits, *Journal of Community Psychology*, 24, 3: 227–234.

Ecclestone, K. (1999) Care or control? Defining learners' needs for lifelong learning, *British Journal of Educational Studies*, 47, 4: 332–347.

Edwards, A. (2002a) 'Responsible research: ways of being a researcher', presidential address to the British Educational Research Conference, *British Educational Research Journal*, 28, 2: 157–168.

—— (2002b) 'Seeking uncertainty: educational research as an engaged social science', paper presented at the Australian Association for Educational Research, Brisbane, December 2002.

Egan, G. (1994) *The Skilled Helper: A Problem Management Approach to Helping* (5th edn), Pacific Grove: Brooks/Cole.

Ellis, C. (1995) On the other side of the fence: seeing black and white in a small town, *Qualitative Inquiry*, 1, 2: 147–167.

Employment Support Unit (ESU) (1999a) *Youthstart: En Route to Success*, Birmingham: ESU.

—— (1999b) *Innovation and Inclusion: Report of the Conference and Exhibition, September 1999*, Birmingham: ESU.

—— (1999c) *Youthstart: Learning from Experience, Report of the National Conference and Exhibition, December 1999*, Birmingham: ESU.

—— (2000a) *Mentoring Young People: Lessons from Youthstart*, Birmingham: ESU.

—— (2000b) *Young People and the Labour Market: Lessons from Youthstart*, Birmingham: ESU.

Equal Opportunities Commission (2003) *Facts about women and men in Great Britain*, Manchester: Equal Opportunities Commission. Online. Available HTTP: <http://www.eoc.org.uk/cseng/research/factsgreatbritain2003.pdf> (accessed 23 January 2003).

European Commission (EC) (1998) *Unlocking Young People's Potential*, Luxembourg: Office for Official Publications of the European Communities.

Fagenson, E.A. (1988) The power of a mentor: protégés' and nonprotégés' perceptions of their own power in organisations, *Group and Organization Studies*, 13, 2: 182–194.

Ferguson, R., Pye, D., Esland, G., McLaughlin, E. and Muncie, J. (2000) Normalized dislocation and new subjectivities in post-16 markets for education and work, *Critical Social Policy*, 20, 3: 283–305.

Fitz-Gibbon, C. (2000) 'Cross-age tutoring: should it be required in order to reduce social exclusion?', in G. Walraven, C. Parsons, D. van Veen and C. Day (eds) *Combating Social Exclusion Through Education: Laissez-faire, Authoritarianism or Third Way?*, Louvain/Apeldoorn: Garant.

Foley, G. (1999) *Learning in Social Action: A Contribution to Understanding Informal Education*, Leicester: NIACE.

Forbes, A. (2000) *Concepts of Mentoring*, lecture at the Manchester Metropolitan University, February 2000.

Ford, G. (1999a) *Youthstart Mentoring Action Project: Project Evaluation and Report Part II*, Stourbridge: Institute of Careers Guidance.

—— (1999b) *Career Guidance and Socially Excluded Young People: Working with Groups*, Stourbridge: Institute of Careers Guidance.

Ford, G., Bosley, S., Gratton, P., Hawthorn, R., McGowan, B. and Watkins, C. (2003) *Challenging Age: Information, Advice and Guidance for Older Age Groups*, Sheffield: DfES Publications.

Fordham, P., Poulton, G. and Randle, L. (1979) *Learning Networks in Adult Education: Non-Formal Education on a Housing Estate*, London: Routledge & Kegan Paul.

Forrest, K. (2002) 'Befriending young people: the fostering or loaning of friendship? A qualitative study exploring befrienders' experiences', unpublished M.Litt. thesis, University of Aberdeen.

Foucault, M. (1980) *Power–Knowledge: Selected Interviews and Other Writings 1972–1977*, Brighton: Harvester Press.

—— (1988) 'The political technology of individuals', in L.H. Martin, H. Gutman and P.H. Hutton (eds) *Technologies of the Self: A Seminar with Michel Foucault*, Amherst: University of Massachusetts Press.

—— (1991) *Discipline and Punish: The Birth of the Prison*, trans. A. Sheridan, London: Penguin.

Freedman, M. (1995) 'From friendly visiting to mentoring: a tale of two movements', in S. Goodlad (ed.) *Students as Tutors and Mentors*, London: Kogan Page.

—— (1999) *The Kindness of Strangers: Adult Mentors, Urban Youth and the New Voluntarism*, Cambridge: Cambridge University Press.

Freire, P. (1972) *Pedagogy of the Oppressed*, Harmondsworth: Penguin.

Furlong, A. and Cartmel, F. (1997) *Young People and Social Change: Individualisation and Risk in Late Modernity*, Buckingham: Open University Press.

Gardiner, C. (1995) 'The "Beat" Project for young offenders in Birmingham', in D. Megginson and D. Clutterbuck (eds) *Mentoring in Action: A Practical Guide for Managers*, London: Kogan Page.

Garmezy, N. (1982) 'Foreword', in E.E. Werner and R.S. Smith (1982) *Vulnerable But Invincible: A Study of Resilient Children*, New York: McGraw-Hill.

Gaskell, J. (1992) *Gender Matters from School to Work*, Milton Keynes: Open University Press.

Gay, B. and Stephenson, J. (1998) The mentoring dilemma: guidance and/or direction?, *Mentoring and Tutoring*, 6, 1: 43–54.

GHK Economics and Management (2000) *The Early Implementation of the Learning Gateway by the Careers Service*, Nottingham: DfEE Publications (Ref. RR203).

Giddens, A. (1990) *The Consequences of Modernity*, Cambridge: Polity Press.

Gilligan, C. (1995) Hearing the difference: theorizing connection, *Hypatia*, 10, 2: 120–127.

Gleeson, D. (1996) 'Post-compulsory education in a post-industrial and post-modern age', in J. Avis, M. Bloomer, G. Esland, D. Gleeson and P. Hodkinson, *Knowledge and Nationhood: Education, Politics and Work*, London: Cassell.

Glynn, C. and Nairne, B. (2000) *Young People's Attitudes to Work, Careers and Learning*, Horsham: Roffey Park.

Golden, S. and Sims, D. (1997) *Review of Industrial Mentoring in Schools*, Slough: NFER.

Green, A. (1997) 'Core skills, general education and unification in post-16 education', in A. Hodgson and K. Spours (eds) *Dearing and Beyond: 14–19 Qualifications, Frameworks and Systems*, London: Kogan Page.

Grenfell, M. and James, D. (eds) (1998) *Bourdieu and Education: Acts of Practical Theory*, London: Falmer Press.

Grossman, J.B. and Tierney, J.P. (1998) Does mentoring work? An impact study of the Big Brothers Big Sisters Program, *Evaluation Review*, 22, 3: 403–426.

Gulam, W. and Zulfiqar, M. (1998) Mentoring – Dr. Plum's elixir and the alchemist's stone, *Mentoring and Tutoring*, 5, 3: 46–56.

Haber, H.F. (1994) *Beyond Postmodern Politics: Lyotard, Rorty, Foucault*, New York: Routledge.

Haensley, P.A. and Parsons, J.L. (1993) Creative, intellectual and psychosocial development through mentorship: relationships and stages, *Youth and Society*, 25, 2: 202–221.

Haggerty, B. (1986) A second look at mentors, *Nursing Outlook*, 34, 1: 16–24.

Harrison, J. and Klopf, G.J. (1986) 'Dual perspectives of a mentoring relationship', in W.A. Gray and M.M. Gray (eds) *Mentoring: Aid to Excellence in Career Development, Business and the Professions*, Vancouver: International Association for Mentoring.

Harvey, D. (1997) *The Condition of Post-Modernity*, Boston, MA: Blackwell.

Hasluck, C. (1999) *Employers, Young People and the Unemployed: A Review of Research*, Sheffield: Employment Service (Ref. ESR12).

Heller, A. (1979) *A Theory of Feelings*, Assen: Van Gorcum.

Hochschild, A.R. (1983) *The Managed Heart: Commercialization of Human Feeling*, Berkeley and Los Angeles: University of California Press.

Hodkinson, P. (1995) 'Careership and markets: structure and agency in the transition to work', unpublished Ph.D. thesis, University of Exeter.

—— (1996) 'Careership: the individual, choices and markets in the transition to work', in J. Avis, M. Bloomer, G. Esland, D. Gleeson and P. Hodkinson, *Knowledge and Nationhood: Education, Politics and Work*, London: Cassell.

—— (1997) 'Contrasting models of young people's career progression', in J. McNeill (ed.) *Careers Guidance: Constructing the Future*, Richmond: Trotman/Institute of Careers Guidance.

—— (1998) 'Career decision making and the transition from school to work', in M. Grenfell and D. James (eds) *Bourdieu and Education: Acts of Practical Theory*, London: Falmer Press.

Hodkinson, P. and Sparkes, A.C. (1995) Markets and vouchers: the inadequacy of individualist policies for vocational education and training in England and Wales, *Journal of Education Policy*, 10, 2: 189–207.

Hodkinson, P., Sparkes, A.C. and Hodkinson, H. (1996) *Triumphs and Tears: Young People, Markets and the Transition from School to Work*, London: David Fulton.

Holden, C. (1999) Globalization, social exclusion and Labour's new work ethic, *Critical Social Policy*, 19, 4: 529–538.

Hollway, W. and Jefferson, T. (2000) *Doing Qualitative Research Differently: Free Association, Narrative and the Interview Method*, London: Sage.

Hopson, B. and Scally, M. (1979) *Strategies for Helping*, Leeds: University of Leeds, Counselling and Career Development Unit.

House of Commons Education and Employment Committee (1998) *Disaffected Children Volume I: Report and Proceedings of the Committee*, London: The Stationery Office.

Humphries, B. (1996) 'Contradictions in the culture of empowerment', in B. Humphries (ed.) *Critical Perspectives on Empowerment*, Birmingham: Venture Press.

—— (1998) *The baby and the bath-water: Hammersley, Cealey Harrison and Hood-Williams and the emancipatory research debate*. Online. Available HTTP: <http://www.socresonline.org.uk/socresonline/3/1/9.html> (accessed 18 February 2001).

Industry in Education (1996) *Towards Employability: Addressing the Gap Between Young People's Qualities and Employers' Recruitment Needs*, London: Industry in Education.

Institute of Career Guidance (ICG) (1999) *Focusing the Work of the Careers Service*, Stourbridge: ICG (Positional Statement No. 38).

—— (2003) *Career Guidance: One Aim, Three Routes*, Stourbridge: ICG.

Issitt, M. (2000) 'Critical professionals and reflective practice: the experience of women practitioners in health, welfare and education', in J. Batsleer and B. Humphries (eds) *Welfare, Exclusion and Political Agency*, London: Routledge.

—— (2002) 'Taking the experience route: accrediting competence through feminism and critical reflective practice', unpublished Ph.D. thesis, Manchester Metropolitan University.

James, N. (1989) Emotional labour: skill and work in the social regulation of feelings, *Sociological Review*, 37, 1: 15–42.

Jameson, F. (1984) Post-modernism or the cultural logic of late capitalism, *New Left Review*, 146: 85–106.

Jeffs, T. and Smith, M.K. (1996) Young people, youth work and a new authoritarianism, *Youth and Policy*, 46: 17–32.

Jeffs, T. and Spence, J. (2000) New Deal for young people: good deal or poor deal?, *Youth and Policy*, 66: 34–61.

Jenkins, R. (1992) *Pierre Bourdieu*, London: Routledge.

Keep, E. (1997) 'There's no such thing as society . . . ': some problems with an individual approach to creating a Learning Society, *Journal of Education Policy*, 12, 6: 457–471.

Kram, K.E. (1988) *Mentoring at Work: Developmental Relationships in Organizational Life*, Lanham, MD: University Press of America.

Law, B. (1977) System orientation: a dilemma for the role conceptualisation of 'counsellors' in schools, *British Journal of Guidance and Counselling*, 6, 1: 129–148.

—— (1978) The concomitants of system orientation in secondary school counsellors, *British Journal of Guidance and Counselling*, 6, 2: 161–174.

—— (1979) The contexts of system orientation in secondary school counselling, *British Journal of Guidance and Counselling*, 7, 2: 199–211.

—— (2000) Fasten your seatbelts: orienteering the ethical landscape, *Careers Guidance Today*, 8, 4: 33–36.

Levinson, D.J., Darrow, C.N., Klein, E.B., Levinson, M.H. and McKee, B. (1978) *The Seasons of a Man's Life*, New York: Ballantine.

Levitas, R. (1996) The concept of social exclusion and the new Durkheimian hegemony, *Critical Social Policy*, 16, 1: 5–20.

Lister, R. (1998) From equality to social inclusion: New Labour and the welfare state, *Critical Social Policy*, 18, 2: 215–225.

Long, J. (1997) The dark side of mentoring, *Australian Educational Researcher*, 24, 2: 115–133.

Lyotard, J-F. (1973) *The Postmodern Condition: A Report on Knowledge*, Manchester: Manchester University Press.

MacDonald, R. (1997) 'Dangerous youth and the dangerous class', in R. MacDonald (ed.) *Youth, the 'Underclass' and Social Exclusion*, London: Routledge.

McIntyre, D., Hagger, H. and Wilkin, M. (eds) (1993) *Mentoring: Perspectives on School-Based Teacher Education*, London: Kogan Page.

Maclagan, I. (1992) *A Broken Promise*, London: Youthaid/The Children's Society.

McPartland, J.M. and Nettles, S.M. (1991) Using community adults as advocates or mentors for at-risk middle school students: a 2-year evaluation of Project RAISE, *American Journal of Education*, 99, 4: 568–586.

Maguire, M., Ball, S.J. and Macrae, S. (1999) Promotion, persuasion and class-taste: marketing (in) the UK post-compulsory sector, *British Journal of Sociology of Education*, 20, 3: 291–308.

Maguire, M., Ball, S.J. and Macrae, S. (2001) Post-adolescence, dependence and the refusal of adulthood, *Discourse*, 22, 2: 197–211.

Majors, R., Wilkinson, V. and Gulam, B. (2000) 'Mentoring black males in Manchester', in K. Owusu (ed.) *Black British Culture and Society: A Text Reader*, London: Routledge.

Marx, K. (1975) *Wages, Price and Profit*, Moscow: Progress Publishers.

Megginson, D. and Clutterbuck, D. (1995) 'Mentoring in action', in D. Megginson and D. Clutterbuck (eds) *Mentoring in Action: A Practical Guide for Managers*, London: Kogan Page.

Merriam, S. (1983) Mentors and protégés: a critical review of the literature, *Adult Education Quarterly*, 33, 3: 161–173.

Merton, B. and Parrott, A. (1999) *Only Connect: Successful Practice in Educational Work with Young Adults*, Leicester: NIACE.

Miller, A. (2002) *Mentoring for Students and Young People: A Handbook of Effective Practice*, London: Kogan Page.

Miller, W.R. and Rollnick, S. (1991) *Motivational Interviewing: Preparing People to Change Addictive Behaviour*, New York: Guilford Press.

Millwater, J. and Yarrow, A. (1997) The mentoring mindset: a constructivist perspective?, *Mentoring and Tutoring*, 5, 1: 14–24.

Moustakas, C. (1990) *Heuristic Research: Design, Methodology, and Applications*, Newbury Park, CA: Sage.

Murray, C. (1990) *The Emerging British Underclass*, London: Institute of Economic Affairs.

National Youth Agency (NYA) (2003) *Wylie defends 'Transforming Youth Work'*. Online. Available HTTP: <http://www.nya.org.uk/news-2.htm> (accessed 24 January 2003).

Noe, R.A. (1988) An investigation of the determinants of successful assigned mentoring relationships, *Personnel Psychology*, 41: 457–479.

O'Donnell, J., Michalak, E.A. and Ames, E.B. (1997) Inner-city youths helping children: after-school programs to promote bonding and reduce risk, *Social Work in Education*, 19, 4: 231–241.

Office for Standards in Education (OFSTED) (2002) *Connexions Partnerships: The First Year 2001–2002*, London: OFSTED (Ref. HMI 521).

Okano, K. (1993) *School to Work Transition in Japan*, Clevedon: Multi-Lingual Matters.

Ozga, J. (ed.) (1988) *Schoolwork: Approaches to the Labour Process of Teaching*, Milton Keynes: Open University Press.

Philip, K. (1997) 'New perspectives on mentoring: young people, youth work and adults', unpublished Ph.D. thesis, University of Aberdeen.

Philip, K. (2000a) Mentoring: pitfalls and potential for young people?, *Youth and Policy*, 67: 1–15.

—— (2000b) *A Literature Review on Mentoring Prepared for the Joseph Rowntree Foundation*, Aberdeen: Centre for Educational Research, University of Aberdeen.

Philip, K. and Hendry, L.B. (1996) Young people and mentoring – towards a typology?, *Journal of Adolescence*, 19, 3: 189–201.

Philip, K. and Hendry, L.B. (2000) Making sense of mentoring or mentoring making sense? Reflections on the mentoring process by adult mentors with young people, *Journal of Community and Applied Social Psychology*, 10: 211–233.

Philip, K. and Shucksmith, J. (2000) *Making a Difference? A Qualitative Study of Mentoring Interventions with Vulnerable Young People*, project proposal to Joseph Rowntree Foundation, University of Aberdeen.

Phillips-Jones, L. (1999) *Skills for Successful Mentoring of Youth: Competencies of Outstanding Mentors and Mentees*, Grass Valley: CCC/The Mentoring Group.

Pietroni, M. (1995) 'The nature and aims of professional education for social workers: a postmodern perspective', in M. Yelloly and M. Henkel (eds) *Learning and Teaching in Social Work: Towards Reflective Practice*, London: Jessica Kingsley.

Piper, H. and Piper, J. (1999) 'Disaffected' young people: problems for mentoring, *Mentoring and Tutoring*, 7, 2: 121–130.

Piper, H. and Piper, J. (2000) Disaffected young people as the problem. Mentoring as the solution. Education and work as the goal, *Journal of Education and Work*, 13, 1: 77–94.

Quicke, J. (2000) A new professionalism for a collaborative culture of organizational learning in contemporary society, *Educational Management and Administration*, 28, 3: 299–315.

Raffo, C. (2000) Mentoring disenfranchised young people, *Education and Industry in Partnership*, 6, 3: 22–42.

Raffo, C. and Hall, D. (1999) Mentoring urban youth in the post-industrial city, *Mentoring and Tutoring*, 6, 3: 61–75.

Raffo, C. and Reeves, M. (2000) Youth transitions and social exclusion: developments in social capital theory, *Journal of Youth Studies*, 3, 2: 147–166.

Reay, D. (1998) 'Cultural reproduction: mothers' involvement in their children's primary schooling', in M. Grenfell and D. James (eds) *Bourdieu and Education: Acts of Practical Theory*, London: Falmer Press.

Reed, E. (1975) *Woman's Evolution*, New York: Pathfinder Press.

Reid, H. (1999) Barriers to inclusion for the disaffected: implications for 'preventive' career guidance work with the under-16 age-group, *British Journal of Guidance and Counselling*, 27, 4: 539–554.

Rhodes, J. (1994) Older and wiser: mentoring relationships in childhood and adolescence, *Journal of Primary Prevention*, 14: 187–196.

Rhodes, J., Ebert, L. and Fischer, K. (1992) Natural mentors: an overlooked resource in the social networks of adolescent mothers, *American Journal of Community Psychology*, 20, 4: 445–461.

Richardson, L. (1990) *Writing Strategies: Reaching Diverse Audiences*, London: Sage.

Rikowski, G. (2000) 'That other great class of commodities: repositioning Marxist educational theory', paper presented to the British Educational Research Association Annual Conference, Cardiff University, September 2000.

—— (2001a) *The Battle for Seattle: Its Significance for Education*, London: Tufnell Press.

—— (2001b) Education for industry: a complex technicism, *Journal of Education and Work*, 14, 1: 29–49.

Ringwalt, C.L., Graham, L.A., Paschall, M.J., Flewelling, R.L. and Browne, D.C. (1996) Supporting Adolescents with Guidance and Employment (SAGE), *American Journal of Preventive Medicine*, 12, 5: 31–38.

Roberts, A. (1998) The androgynous mentor: bridging gender stereotypes in mentoring, *Mentoring and Tutoring*, 6, 1–2: 18–30.

—— (2000a) Mentoring revisited: a phenomenological reading of the literature, *Mentoring and Tutoring*, 8, 2: 145–170.

—— (2000b) 'The androgynous mentor: an examination of mentoring behaviour within an educational context', unpublished Ph.D. thesis, University of Birmingham.

Roche, G.R. (1979) Much ado about mentors, *Harvard Business Review*, 57, 1: 14–28.

Rogers, C.R. (1951) *Client Centred Therapy: Its Current Practice, Implications and Theory*, London: Constable.

—— (1967) *On Becoming a Person: A Therapist's View of Psychotherapy*, London: Constable.

Rolfe, H. (1999) *Gender Equality and the Careers Service*, Manchester: Equal Opportunities Commission.

Samuel, R. (1999) *Island Stories: Unravelling Britain (Theatres of Memory Vol.II)*, London: Verso.

Sassen, S. (2000) *Cities in a World Economy* (2nd edn), London: Pine Forge Press.

Sawicki, J. (1991) *Disciplining Foucault: Feminism, Power and the Body*, New York: Routledge.

Scales, P.C. and Gibbons, J.L. (1996) Extended family members and unrelated adults in the lives of young adolescents: a research agenda, *Journal of Early Adolescence*, 16, 4: 365–389.

Scandura, T.A. (1998) Dysfunctional mentoring relationships and outcomes, *Journal of Management*, 24, 3: 449–467.

Scandura, T.A. and Viator, R.E. (1994) Mentoring in public accounting firms: an analysis of mentor–protégé relationships, mentoring functions and protégé turnover intentions, *Accounting, Organizations and Society*, 19: 717–734.

Searle, C. (1997) *Living Community, Living School*, London: Tufnell Press.

Shea, G.F. (1992) *Mentoring: A Guide to the Basics*, London: Kogan Page.

Skinner, A. and Fleming, J. (1999) *Mentoring Socially Excluded Young People: Lessons from Practice*, Manchester: National Mentoring Network.

Smart, B. (1988) *Michel Foucault*, London: Routledge.

Smith, J. and Spurling, A. (1999) *Lifelong Learning: Riding the Tiger*, London: Cassell.

Smith, J.K. (1993) *After the Demise of Empiricism: The Problem of Judging Social and Educational Enquiry*, New Jersey: Aldex.

Smith, K. (2001) The development of subject knowledge in secondary initial teacher education: a case study of physical education student teachers and their subject mentors, *Mentoring and Tutoring*, 9, 1: 63–76.

Smith, M.K. (2002) *Transforming youth work – resourcing excellent youth services: a critique*. Online. Available HTTP: <http://www.infed.org/youthwork/transforming_youth_work_2.htm> (accessed 24 January 2003).

Social Exclusion Unit (SEU) (1999) *Bridging the Gap: New Opportunities for 16–18 Year Olds*, London: The Stationery Office.

Stammers, P. (1992) The Greeks had a word for it . . . (five millennia of mentoring), *British Journal of In-Service Education*, 18, 2: 76–80.

Standing, M. (1999) Developing a supportive/challenging and reflective/competency education (SCARCE) mentoring model and discussing its relevance to nurse education, *Mentoring and Tutoring*, 6, 3: 3–17.

Stepney, P., Lynch, R. and Jordan, B. (1999) Poverty, exclusion and New Labour, *Critical Social Policy*, 19, 1: 109–127.

Stronach, I. (1989) Education, vocationalism and economic recovery: the case against witchcraft, *British Journal of Education and Work*, 2, 1: 5–31.

Stronach, I. and Morris, B. (1994) Polemical notes on educational evaluation in the age of 'policy hysteria', *Evaluation and Research in Education*, 8, 1–2: 5–18.

Swartz, D. (1997) *Culture and Power: The Sociology of Pierre Bourdieu*, Chicago, IL: University of Chicago Press.

Times Educational Supplement (2000) One to one: why mentoring is a must, *Times Educational Supplement*, 16, 21 January.

Toucan Europe (1999) *Dealing with Disaffection: EASTLINK Investment Corridor SRB Action Research Project*, Manchester: EASTLINK.

Usman, K. (2000) *Concepts of Post-school Mentoring*, lecture at the Manchester Metropolitan University, February 2000.

Vandevelde, H. (1998) Careers education and guidance as a navigational system for employability in the global market, *Careers Guidance Today*, 6, 3: 24–25.

Wacquant, L.J.D. (1992) 'Preface', in P. Bourdieu and L.J.D. Wacquant, *An Invitation to Reflexive Sociology*, Cambridge: Polity Press.

Wainwright, D. (1996) The political transformation of the health inequalities debate, *Critical Social Policy*, 49: 67–82.

Walkerdine, V. (1992) 'Progressive pedagogy and political struggle', in C. Luke and J. Gore (eds) *Feminisms and Critical Pedagogy*, London: Routledge.

Ward, D. and Mullender, A. (1991) Empowerment and oppression: an indissoluble pairing for contemporary social work, *Critical Social Policy*, 32: 21–30.

Warmington, P. (2003) 'Lifelong learning as leverage for change: disrupting research narratives', paper presented at the Lifelong Learning Institute, University of Leeds, February 2003.

Waters, M. (1995) *Globalization*, London: Routledge.

Waters, M-A. (1994) 'What the 1987 stock market crash foretold', in M-A. Waters (ed.) *New International No.10*, New York: 408 Printing and Publishing.

Watts, A.G. (1999) Mind over matter of exclusion, *Careers Guidance Today*, 7, 1: 18–26.

—— (2000) Career development and public policy, *Career Development Quarterly*, 48, 4: 301–312.

—— (2001a) Career guidance and social exclusion: a cautionary tale, *British Journal of Guidance and Counselling*, 29, 2: 157–176.

—— (2001b) 'Introduction', in L. Bezanson and E. O'Reilly (eds) *Making Waves, Volume 2: Connecting Career Development with Public Policy*, Ottawa: Canadian Career Development Foundation.

Werner, E.E. and Smith, R.S. (1982) *Vulnerable But Invincible: A Study of Resilient Children*, New York: McGraw-Hill.

Whitehead, N., Chapman, E. and Ronan, J. (2002) Going the extra mile: emotional impact of supporting homeless youngsters, *Career Guidance Today*, 10, 4: 30–31.

Wijers, G.A. and Meijers, F. (1996) Careers guidance in the knowledge society, *British Journal of Guidance and Counselling*, 24, 2: 185–198.

Williamson, H. and Middlemiss, R. (1999) The Emperor has no clothes: cycles of delusion in community interventions with 'disaffected' young men, *Youth and Policy*, 63: 13–25.

Wolcott, H.F. (1994) *Transforming Qualitative Data: Description, Analysis and Interpretation*, Thousand Oaks, CA: Sage.

Wrench, J. and Hassan, E. (1996) *Ambition and Marginalisation: A Qualitative Study of Underachieving Young Men of Afro-Caribbean Origin*, London: The Stationery Office.

Wrench, J. and Qureshi, T. (1996) *Higher Horizons: A Qualitative Study of Young Men of Bangladeshi Origin*, London: The Stationery Office.

Wright-Mills, C. (1970) *The Sociological Imagination*, Harmondsworth: Penguin.

Zippay, A. (1995) Expanding employment skills and social networks among teen mothers: case study of a mentor program, *Child and Adolescent Social Work Journal*, 12, 1: 51–69.

Index